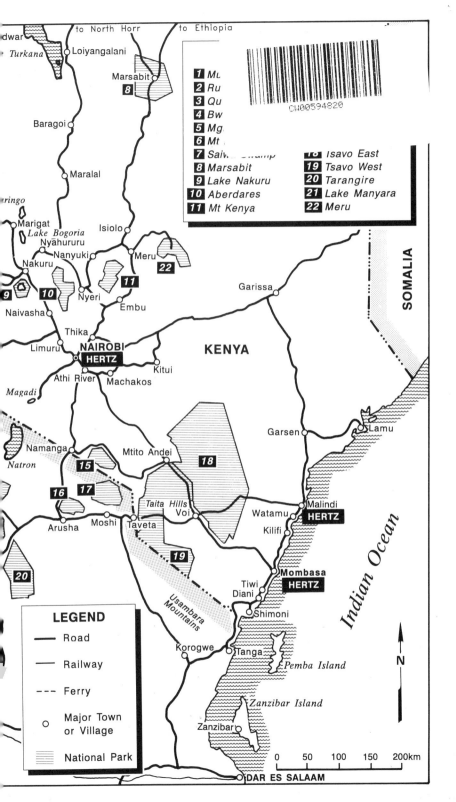

See page 50

VISITORS' GUIDE TO KENYA

VISITORS' GUIDE TO KENYA

HOW TO GET THERE · WHAT TO SEE · WHERE TO STAY

Philip Briggs

SOUTHERN
BOOK PUBLISHERS

ISBN 1 86812 533 5

First edition, first impression 1995

Published by
Southern Book Publishers (Pty) Ltd
PO Box 3103, Halfway House 1685

While the authors and publisher have endeavoured to
verify all facts, they will not be held responsible for any
inconvenience that may result from possible
inaccuracies in this book.

Cover photograph by Anup Shah, ABPL
Cover design by Insight Graphics
Maps by Ingrid Booysen
Set on 10/11.5 pt Palatino
by Kohler Carton & Print, Pinetown
Printed and bound by Kohler Carton & Print, Pinetown

ACKNOWLEDGEMENTS

The successful research for this book is in large part thanks to the help and support of the following companies:

Kenya Airways (South Africa), Third Floor, North State Building, cnr Market and Kruis Streets, Johannesburg; tel: (011) 3378620/4; fax: 3373670.

Hertz-UTC, Fedha Towers, Muindi Mbingu Street, PO Box 42196, Nairobi; tel: (02) 331960; fax: 726931.

Block Hotels, PO Box 40075, Nairobi; tel: (02) 540780; fax: 543810.

On a personal level, I would like to thank Roger Hartley and the staff of Block Hotels, and Mrs Belsoi of Msafiri Inns, for their efficiency and enthusiasm in organising my stays at the various hotels in their groups; Loekie Lavery of Kenya Airways for arranging a comfortable flight from Johannesburg to Nairobi; Zull Dhanji of Hertz-UTC for the use of a reliable vehicle which got me into most of Kenya's game reserves, even when the road ahead looked impassable; Mr Barua, Publications Editor of Kenya Wildlife Services, for his enthusiasm and for allowing me access to Kenya's game reserves; Ms T Masha of Kenya Railways, for my first, and highly enjoyable, taste of first class rail travel in Kenya.

On the home front, my eternal gratitude goes to Laura Grant, for once again joining me on part of my travels, for her support throughout, and her keen sub-editor's eye.

The Nairobi Youth Hostel became my home from home during this trip. So a big thank you to Ben, Ignatius, James, Morris and Reuben for a reliable welcome from friendly faces whenever I came to town.

Finally, thanks to everyone who kept me company along the way: my fellow hostellers Armita, Bob, Charity, Denise, Elizabeth, Jason, Katrin, Kevin Thorne, Kevin of the Milkshakes, and Mary; the managers of Mountain Lodge, Mount Elgon Lodge and Meru Mulika Lodge; the chief warden of Meru National Park; Matthew Moscrop, Kelly-Anne Reed and family, Kim McCarthy, Scott Kearin, Brian from Seattle, Edward the bird-supremo at Samburu Lodge and all the others whose names I was too absent-minded to ask or remember.

CONTENTS

HOW TO USE THIS GUIDE

This guide has been structured to aid tourists in making the best use of their time in East Africa. Chapter one provides an overview of the area including physical details and a historical framework. Chapter two covers general information of use to the visitor, such as public transport, visas and photography. Chapter three includes an overview of the region's main attractions, tips on how to compile a suitable itinerary and organise a safari, and suggestions for visitors with special interests. The next six chapters each cover a logical region, and they are structured, as far as possible, along the sort of routes that tourists are likely to use. The final two chapters cover the prime tourist attractions in neighbouring Tanzania and Uganda.

1 AN INTRODUCTION TO KENYA

Kenya is Africa's leading tourist destination, a land of wild landscapes, exciting contrasts and prolific wildlife. Above all, it is the game reserves that draw tourists to Kenya, and rightly so. There is Masai Mara, where the world's greatest wildlife spectacle unfolds annually as millions of wildebeest cross the Mara river from Tanzania's Serengeti plains; where, even when the wildebeest return south, lions are literally waiting around every corner. There is Lake Nakuru, a small alkaline lake fringed bright pink where up to two million flamingos flock around its shallow waters. Or the desert reserve of Samburu, where typical African plains mammals are replaced by the finely striped Grevy's zebra, the boldly marked reticulated giraffe, the brilliant cobalt vulturine guineafowl, and the impala-meets-giraffe anomaly that is the gerenuk antelope.

There is, of course, more to Kenya than large mammals. Offshore reefs host a dazzling array of colourful fish, while, back on land, well over 1 000 bird species have been recorded. Just one forest, Kakamega, supports more primate species than a country as large as South Africa. The ever-changing scenery ranges from palm-fringed beaches though rocky deserts and montane forests to the snowcapped peaks of Mounts Kenya and Kilimanjaro.

Kenya's people are as diverse as the landscape: a cultural melting pot that includes the frenetically modern denizens of Nairobi, the relaxed old-world Islamic Swahili people of the coast, and such fiercely proud traditional pastoralists as the Masai and Samburu. On the coast, mysterious jungle-bound ruins pay testimony to an ancient trading culture that flourished while Europe was embroiled in the Middle Ages.

Kenya's tourist industry has developed to accommodate everyone; from those seeking five-star luxury to budget travellers looking for somewhere to sleep for a couple of dollars. There is an excellent range of game reserve lodges and coastal resorts to which you can fly from Nairobi, or be escorted in the comfort of a minibus. Service is superlatively friendly, standards are high, and prices are favourable by international standards. Kenya also offers infinite scope for cheap, off-the-beaten-track exploration: relaxed meanderings facilitated by worn but efficient public transport, and a network of lesser-known campsites and self-catering establishments.

The above words are not hyperbole, but an expression of love for a country and region that never fails to enthral me. Since 1986, I have spent almost a year backpacking around the country during four separate visits, and over six months travelling in neighbouring Tanzania and Uganda. If I had six months free tomorrow, I'd go back again.

. . . AND TO EAST AFRICA

To many people Kenya and East Africa are synonymous: it comes as a surprise when they realise that many of the region's best known attractions – Kilimanjaro, Ngorongoro Crater, Serengeti and the mountain gorilla reserves – are in neighbouring Tanzania and Uganda. But the political boundaries that shape modern East Africa are mere hangovers of the colonial carve-up. The Tanzanian towns of Arusha and Moshi (the bases for visits to Serengeti and Kilimanjaro) are only half a day by road from Nairobi. They are as easily visited from Nairobi as anywhere in Kenya.

I believe that the scope of a guide to Kenya should place the possibilities open to tourists above the constraints of arbitrary political boundaries. I have, therefore, devoted a chapter each to northern Tanzania and Uganda. There are already plenty of guide books to Kenya on the market; this book is unique in that it provides a regional overview of options open to fly-in tourists to Nairobi.

THE COUNTRY

Kenya covers an area of 582 646 square km, bisected by the equator and ranging in altitude from sea level to 5 200 m. The country is bordered by the Indian Ocean to the east, Tanzania to the south, Uganda to the west, and Somalia, Ethiopia and Sudan to the north. The capital of Kenya is Nairobi, with a population of over one million. Other major towns are Mombasa, Kisumu and Nakuru.

The section of Kenya south of the equator is characterised by a varied climate and topography. The coast is hot and humid all year round, while the area between the coast and Nairobi is hot, dry and relatively flat. The more temperate and fertile highlands of central and western Kenya are bisected by East Africa's dominant geographical feature, the Great Rift Valley; the valley floor is hot and dry and holds a string of beautiful small lakes. Other important geographical features include Mount Kenya, the second highest mountain in Africa, and Lake Victoria, the largest lake on the continent. Africa's highest mountain, Kilimanjaro, straddles the Kenyan border but its peaks are in Tanzania. The area of Kenya north of the equator is uniformly dry and relatively little visited by tourists.

Kenya supports a large number of different ethnic groups, who between them represent four of Africa's five linguistic groups. The official languages, English and KiSwahili, are both spoken widely in urban centres, though KiSwahili is the lingua franca in rural areas.

A HISTORICAL FRAMEWORK

Human life is thought to have evolved in the East African Rift Valley, as evidenced by fossil finds at places like Olduvai Gorge in Tanzania and Lake Turkana in northern Kenya. Until about 3 000 years ago, East Africa was occupied by Stone Age hunter-gatherers similar in origin to the Khoisan of southern Africa.

Kenya is a melting pot of Africa's various linguistic groups. Apart from a few remaining hunter-gatherers, who live in isolated groups in highland forests, the oldest inhabitants of the region are probably the Somali Cushitic-speakers who live in the northern desert. The Bantu-speaking predecessors of modern ethnic groups such as the Swahili, Kikuyu, Luhya and Akamba arrived in the region from West Africa about 2 000 years ago. More recent arrivals are Nilotic-speakers such as the Luo, who settled the Lake Victoria basin about 500 years ago, and the Masai and Samburu who moved into the Rift Valley from Ethiopia in the 17th century.

The early history of the East African coast is best viewed separately from that of the interior. By about AD 800, ships from Shiraz (Persia) had entered into regular trade with the Bantu-speaking people of the coast, leading to the emergence of the Swahili culture and language. This Shirazi era of trade peaked in the 13th to 15th centuries, when cities such as Mombasa, Malindi and Kilwa traded gold and ivory with ships from as far afield as Persia, China and India, and it ended in the 16th century, when the Portuguese attacked several coastal cities and occupied Mombasa.

The history of the coast and the interior became intertwined in the Omani era. In 1840, the Sultan of Oman moved his capital to Zanzibar. Over the next 40 years, Omani caravans penetrated deep into the interior, disrupting the existing social structures as they captured an estimated million Africans and herded them to the coast for sale as slaves.

The slave trade was abolished in 1873. Shortly after that, East Africa was carved up by Europeans, with Tanganyika going to Germany, and Zanzibar, Kenya and Uganda to Britain. Tanganyika fell under a British mandate after the First World War.

The end of British rule in Kenya was hastened by the Mau-Mau rebellion of the 1950s, which resulted in the deaths of 32 British settlers. It is often forgotten that some thousands of Kenyans were slaughtered by the colonial power in random punitive raids. Kenya was granted independence in 1963. Shortly thereafter the first prime minister, Jomo Kenyatta, made it a one-party state. Kenyatta died in 1978, to be succeeded by Daniel arap Moi, who was returned to power in the country's first multi-party election in 1992.

Since independence, Kenya has pursued a predominantly free market economy, bolstered by Western aid. It is now among the wealthiest and most developed countries in Africa.

2 PRACTICAL INFORMATION

OVERLAND FROM SOUTH AFRICA TO KENYA

You can travel overland between Johannesburg and Nairobi in your own vehicle, on public transport or with an overland truck tour. The direct route via Harare, Lusaka and Dar es Salaam can be done in about 10 days, but three or four weeks is a more realistic minimum if you want to enjoy the trip.

Of the three options, most people would elect to drive. There's no doubt this allows the most freedom to explore, but it also requires the highest level of organisation. Spares are difficult to locate and competent garages may be hundreds of kilometres apart. Don't think about it unless you have a reliable vehicle, a good stock of parts and adequate mechanical skills. Bear in mind, too, that a vehicle requires a high degree of vigilance – you can't just lock your baggage in a room – and that it isolates you from local people.

Overland trucks generally take about four weeks or so for the journey between Harare and Nairobi. Truck trips require less organisation than driving yourself, while still giving access to places that are difficult to reach with public transport. The disadvantage of an overland truck trip is the large group size, which can result in all sorts of tensions, and inevitably isolates you from local cultures. Much of the success of these trips depends on the skills of the driver. Some are knowledgeable about Africa and good at defusing group tensions; just as many are macho cowboys whose knowledge of Africa is confined to the purchase and imbibing of cheap stimulants.

Public transport limits the opportunities for visiting remote reserves, but it is the cheapest way of doing the trip, it forces interaction with local cultures, and there's a lot less to go wrong than if you have your own vehicle. If you are prepared to use your feet and imagination, the opportunities for adventure are just as great as they are for motorised travellers. My feeling, having done this trip several times, is that unless you have the money and skills to finance and organise a motorised trip properly, using public transport is the best option. It beats driving up in a substandard vehicle or using an overland truck on every count.

Public transport connections

Buses cover all the main routes, but they are best avoided over long distances. Reliable rail services connect Johannesburg to Harare and Bulawayo; Bulawayo to Victoria Falls; Kapiri Mposhi to Dar es Salaam and Dar es Salaam to Moshi, Mwanza and Kigoma. Travelling between Livingstone and Kapiri Mposhi is the only instance where I would recommend a bus over a train.

The nicest form of public transport is a lake ferry. Ferries connect all ports on the Malawian shore of Lake Malawi, and Itungi port and Mbamba Bay in Tanzania (where Lake Malawi is known as Lake Nyasa). The weekly Lake Tanganyika ferry leaves Mpulungu (Zambia) on Friday mornings and arrives in Kigoma (Tanzania) on Sunday and Bujumbura (Burundi) on Monday. Ferries connect the main Tanzanian ports on Lake Victoria and there is an international service which leaves Mwanza every Sunday afternoon for Port Bell (Uganda).

Further information

Drivers are referred to Bob Swain's and Paula Snyder's *Through Africa* (Bradt Publications) and the Overland to the Equator series in the February to April 1994 issues of the South African magazine *Getaway*. For travel on public transport, the choice is between *Africa on a shoestring* (Lonely Planet) and *Backpackers' Africa* (Bradt Publications).

Due to their scope, these regional guides are all rather patchy and dated and you are advised to carry a specific guide to any country you plan to explore in depth. Between them, Southern Book Publishers and Bradt Publications have one-country titles to the whole region.

If you are considering an overland truck, Wild Frontiers, PO Box 781329, Sandton; tel: (011) 8834345; fax: (011) 8832556, run Landrover trips for small groups, and their drivers seem to be a cut above the average.

The best map of southern and eastern Africa is Michelin number 995.

FLYING TO KENYA

Nairobi is the focal point of travel within East Africa and Jomo Kenyatta Airport is among the busiest airports on the continent. Most major European and African airlines fly to Nairobi, but there are no direct flights from North America or Australia.

Kenya Airways flies directly between Nairobi and the following destinations: Addis Ababa, Bombay, Bujumbura, Cairo, Copenhagen, Dar es Salaam, Dubai, Entebbe/Kampala, Frankfurt, Harare, Jeddah, Khartoum, Kigali, Lilongwe, London Heathrow, Paris, Seychelles, Stockholm, Zanzibar and Zurich. They have link-up services with other airlines to most European and African capitals. SAA also flies between Johannesburg and Nairobi.

Kenya Airways and American Airlines flights link at London Heathrow between Nairobi and the following cities in the USA: Boston, Chicago, Los Angeles, Miami and New York. Air Canada does a similar link-up to Toronto.

Coming from Europe, London is the best place to get cheap tickets to Nairobi. The Africa Travel Shop, 4 Medway Court, Leigh Street, London, WC1H 9QX, tel: (071) 3871211 is recommended.

An increasing number of international flights stop at Mombasa, including Kenya Airways flights from Johannesburg to Nairobi.

VISAS AND RED TAPE

All visitors to Kenya require a passport valid for six months after the end of their stay. Visas are required by all except citizens of Britain, Denmark, Eire, Ethiopia, Finland, Germany, Sweden, Spain, Turkey and most Commonwealth countries. This sort of thing is subject to change; it is advisable to check current requirements with the nearest Kenyan embassy.

Visas can be issued with a minimum of fuss at any Kenyan embassy or High Commission. South Africans need visas, though this might change now that South Africa is part of the Commonwealth. There is no Kenyan embassy in South Africa at present, but visas can be arranged through most travel agents or the Visa Shop in Johannesburg, tel: (011) 3317811. Alternatively, you can get a visa on arrival at Jomo Kenyatta Airport.

All visitors to Kenya are issued with a free visitor's pass on arrival, valid for up to three months. If your visitor's pass expires, it is imperative you renew it. This is a straightforward procedure and can be done at Nyayo House in Nairobi or any other immigration office.

WHEN TO VISIT

Kenya straddles the equator so there is little seasonal variation in temperature. The hottest months are December to March and the coolest months May to August, but they only differ by a few degrees. Approximately two-thirds of the country's rain falls during what is known as the long rains between March and June. The so-called short rains in October and November are relatively insignificant.

Kenya can be visited at any time of year. There are, however, several factors which might influence when you want to visit. The peak season, December and January, is worth avoiding if possible. The coast in particular gets crowded at this time of year; accommodation prices rocket and the quality of service tends to suffer. The months between June and September offer the best general game viewing, with August through to October the time to see the wildebeest migration in the Masai Mara. Hikers and climbers will want to avoid the long rains.

CLOTHING AND DRESS CODES

If weight is a concern, a pair of cotton trousers or a skirt (preferably one covering the knees), shorts, three or four shirts, and enough underwear and socks to last a week will be adequate. Avoid clothes made of artificial fabrics. Many parts of Kenya cool down at night, so take a sweater. You only need more substantial warm clothing if you plan to hike in mountainous areas. If you expect to hike, decent walking shoes or hiking boots are also essential. Make sure they provide ankle support and have a good grip. Sandals, trainers and flip-flops are fine for everyday use.

In many parts of East Africa, particularly the Islamic coast, it is frowned upon for women to expose their knees or shoulders and for men to bare their chests. There is no law preventing you from dressing skimpily, but it will give offence and may generate hostility. As a rule, you can wear what you like on recognised tourist beaches (as long as you are wearing something!) and in game reserves.

Overly casual attire and designer safari outfits will mark you out as a tourist. Expatriates are sensitive to local dress codes and thus dress more formally: men in jeans or cotton trousers and a proper shirt, women in a skirt covering the knees. The advantages of looking like an expatriate are considerable, particularly in Nairobi where it will divert the attentions of safari touts, con artists and the like.

Some budget travellers think that scruffy clothes will emphasise the difference between them and regular tourists and thus endear them to locals. In fact, the opposite is true. Many Africans have told me that Westerners wouldn't dress like that at home and by doing so in Africa they are demonstrating their disrespect for Africans.

HEALTH

The greatest risk to your health in East Africa is malaria. Otherwise it is a healthy place to visit and very few travellers suffer anything more serious than the odd bout of the runs.

Preparations

Going to Kenya from elsewhere in Africa, you may be required to produce certificates of vaccination against yellow fever and cholera. I would also advise vaccination against meningitis and typhoid, as well as polio and tetanus boosters. The new vaccination against hepatitis is expensive but thought to be highly effective, and worth getting if you expect to be travelling rough or to be in the country for a long time.

Rabies is normally transmitted by a bite or even a scratch from an infected animal. It can be carried by any mammal, but is most commonly passed on to humans by dogs and bats. A vaccination is recommended if you are likely to be handling animals or if you intend to go caving. Note that symptoms can appear anywhere between 10 days and a year after transmission. It is incurable once symptoms appear; if you are bitten you should get to a doctor as soon as possible.

Do not visit East Africa without a medical policy that will enable you to fly home for treatment if necessary. These can be bought through any travel agency.

Malaria

Malaria is a killer, responsible for the deaths of a million Africans every year. The disease is transmitted to humans by the female anopheles mosquito, which is widespread in East Africa at altitudes below 1 800 m. It is essential that you take every reasonable precaution against contracting malaria, by taking prophylactic drugs and doing your best to avoid being bitten by mosquitoes.

Until recently, the recommended prophylactic for East Africa was the combination of Chloroquine (taken weekly) and Paludrine (taken daily). Most doctors now favour the mefloquin-based drug Lariam, which surveys show to be more effective and to have fewer side effects. There is no question of Lariam's relative effectiveness, but I've heard several anecdotal reports from reliable sources that suggest it can have serious psychological side effects. If you have a history of depression or any other psychological illness, it might be wise to avoid Lariam or, if you use it, to be alert to the potential side effects and change med ication if necessary.

Prophylactics reduce the risk of contracting malaria but they do no provide immunity. Resistant strains are widespread and if you suspec you have malaria, get to a doctor as quickly as possible. Malaria i usually curable when it is treated in time. If you expect to travel in areas where medical help will be unavailable, you may want to carry medication for treatment with you. Halfan is regarded as the mos effective at present, and is available over the counter from pharmacist in Nairobi.

Resistance patterns in East Africa are forever changing. A drug tha is effective now may not be in a year or two. Seek current advice from your doctor.

The normal incubation period for malaria is between two and fou weeks. You are advised to continue taking your pills for four week after you leave a malarial zone. Although it is highly unusual, incu bation can take longer. If you display symptoms associated with malaria even a few months after returning home, alert your doctor to the fac that you may have been exposed to it.

Many tourists take their pills and assume that is all that is required but even the most effective pills offer no more than 90 per cent pro tection. You should also make every possible effort to avoid being bitten. Anopheles mosquitoes emerge towards dusk and bite at any time through the night. They hunt at ground level, which is why such a high proportion of bites are around the ankle. Towards dusk you should change into long trousers, put on thick socks, and rub insec repellent onto exposed parts of your body. When you retire, the bes protection is a mosquito net. Mosquito coils are reasonably effective and widely available in East Africa. A fan will inhibit mosquito activity

Diarrhoea

This is the most frequent complaint experienced by travellers to Eas Africa. Normally it will clear up if you stop eating solid foods for 2 to 36 hours. Diarrhoea commonly results in dehydration, so you should drink as much as possible. You can make your own rehydration fluid by mixing a couple of teaspoons of glucose or sugar and a pinch of sal into any liquid – at a push, a bit of salt mixed into a flattened cola wil do the trick. Don't take blockers such as Imodium or Lomotil unless i is absolutely unavoidable.

Diarrhoea is most often caused by contaminated food or drinking water. The most effective way to purify water is by boiling it for two to five minutes. Water purification tablets are reasonably effective. You are unlikely to pick up bugs from freshly-cooked food.

If diarrhoea persists beyond a couple of days, or you notice blood in your stools, it's possible you have a more serious infection. There's no reason to panic, but it's advisable to get a stool test just in case.

Bilharzia

This disease is endemic in many East African rivers and lakes. It is caused by worms which live in freshwater snails and is most likely to be contracted in well-vegetated, stagnant water. Bilharzia is normally curable, but there is a growing amount of resistance to treatment. Try not to swim unless you are sure the water is bilharzia free. If you do swim in dubious water, it's worth knowing that the parasite is unlikely to infect you if you spend less than ten minutes swimming and dry off immediately.

AIDS

The HIV virus is widespread throughout East Africa. Uganda is thought to have the highest incidence in the world and Kenya and Tanzania are not far behind. Despite the social devastation this is causing locally, there is no reason why it should affect tourists. AIDS awareness in East Africa is high and the chance of being confronted with an unsterilised needle is small, but it might be wise, nevertheless, to carry a couple of sealed hypodermic needles in your medical kit. The risks associated with unprotected sex, particularly with a prostitute, barely need stating. Condoms are widely available.

Mountain health

Visitors who intend to climb any of East Africa's large mountains should be aware of the potential effects of high altitude. Nobody with a known heart or respiratory condition should contemplate climbing these mountains; even if you have a slight cold it is unwise to climb until you have recovered.

It is normal for climbers to experience physical discomfort at high altitudes: typically a combination of headaches, nausea, fatigue, loss of appetite and sleeplessness. These are not in themselves a cause for concern, but they should be monitored. If symptoms become severe or are accompanied by coughing up blood, shortness of breath when at rest, gurgling in the chest, disorientation, lack of co-ordination or hallucinations, you may be dealing with cerebral or pulmonary oedema. The afflicted person should descend immediately. A common symptom of cerebral oedema is loss of judgement: the affected person is unlikely to recognise how sick he or she is. It's up to other members of the party to persuade the sufferer down.

Altitude-related problems generally manifest themselves above 4 000 m and the risk increases with altitude. Symptoms are rarely severe on Mount Meru and the Ruwenzoris; they are most likely to become life-threatening on Kilimanjaro. The risk is linked to speed of ascent. People who climb Kilimanjaro over six days are at less risk that those who climb in five days. It helps to walk at a gentle pace and take frequent stops on the way up.

Climbers will encounter sub-zero temperatures. Bring plenty of warm clothing, gloves, balaclava, windproof jacket and waterproof clothing in the rainy season. A warm sleeping bag and insulation mat are essential. There is a risk of hypothermia above the snow line – symptoms include uncontrollable shivering and in severe cases disorientation, confusion and lethargy. Hypothermia is potentially fatal and you should attempt to raise the body temperature by putting on warm, dry clothes and getting into a sleeping bag. If this doesn't work, ask your guide to fetch the rescue team.

The equatorial sun is particularly fierce at high altitudes. Wear sun glasses and cover exposed parts of your body with sunblock.

MONEY

Currency

The unit of currency is the Kenyan shilling, which is divided into 100 cents. Current rates of exchange are around Ksh 60 to the US dollar, Ksh 90 to the pound sterling and Ksh 15 to the South African rand. Most things in Kenya can be paid for in local currency. The best way to carry your money is in US dollar travellers cheques. Dollars are the recognised tourist currency and no matter what country you come from, you'll find it easiest to budget and think in dollars.

Foreign exchange

There are foreign exchange desks in most banks and upmarket hotels, though the latter offer poor rates, charge a high commission and only offer the service to hotel residents. Changing money can be time-consuming; allow an hour or so. Banking hours are 8h30 to 13h00 on weekdays and 8h30 to 11h00 on the first and last Saturday of the month. The foreign exchange desks in the banks on Kenyatta Avenue in Nairobi are open every Saturday morning and there is a 24-hour foreign exchange desk at Jomo Kenyatta Airport.

There isn't a black market worth speaking about in Kenya. Anyone who approaches you in the street is setting you up.

Credit cards

American Express, Visa and Diners Club cards are accepted by most tourist hotels, safari companies and tourist-orientated shops and hotels.

GETTING AROUND KENYA

Car hire

Hiring a vehicle is the best way to visit the game reserves, allowing you the freedom to explore at will. Most safari companies offer car rental, but their vehicles are not always well maintained. I would advise using a recognised car rental company; Hertz and other international companies are represented in Nairobi, Mombasa, Malindi and Diani Beach.

A 4x4 vehicle is essential if you intend visiting game reserves. Suzuki jeeps are the most popular: compact but reliable, though reputedly a bit wobbly at high speeds. Weekly rates are lower than daily rates. Addresses of car hire companies are given under town details.

Driving tips

Petrol and diesel are available in all Kenyan towns and at most game reserve lodges. Fuel is cheaper than in South Africa but more expensive than in the USA.

Main roads are tarred and generally in reasonable shape. Be wary of potholes, however, especially on the Nairobi-Mombasa road. Unsurfaced roads vary in condition: some are excellent, others appalling. Details of individual roads are given throughout the guide.

The main problem in Kenya is the cavalier attitude of other drivers. Overtaking on blind curves and the like is quite normal – drive defensively.

Finally, watch out for unexpected speed bumps. You can assume there are a few on the approach to every small village. Slow down a a precaution.

Air

Kenya Airways flies between Nairobi, Mombasa, Malindi and Kisumu. Coastal charter companies run daily flights to Lamu from Mombasa and Malindi. Upmarket safari companies do fly-in safaris to most game reserves.

Rail

The overnight train between Nairobi and Mombasa is a popular and pleasant way of getting to the coast. The compartments are in good condition and the food and service are excellent. Trains leave at 19h00 every day in both directions, arriving at around 8h00 the next morning. First class has two-berth sleepers and second class has four-berth sleepers. Compartments are single sex unless booked by a party. Ticket costs are inclusive of meals and bedding.

Daily trains between Nairobi and Kisumu leave in each direction at 18h00 and arrive at around 8h00 the next morning. There are three trains a week between Nairobi, Eldoret and Malaba on the Ugandan border. These leave Nairobi at 15h00 on Tuesday, Friday and Saturday and Malaba at 16h00 on Wednesday, Saturday and Sunday.

There is a weekly train service between Nairobi and Kampala in Uganda.

Boat

The only boat service within Kenya is a ferry between Kisumu and smaller ports on Lake Victoria.

Road transport

There is a good network of public transport on Kenya's roads. Buses cover most routes, and are generally the safest form of road transport. Most buses operate on a fill-up-and-go basis, and they continually stop to pick up passengers until people are literally hanging out of the door. Bus tickets are invariably very cheap.

A number of companies run direct bus services on major routes. These are slightly more expensive than normal buses, but have several advantages: departure times are scheduled, and the trip will be faster and more comfortable because all passengers are seated and there are usually only one or two stops. Akamba is Kenya's leading company, with services connecting Nairobi to Mombasa and most points in western Kenya. The Akamba booking office in Nairobi is on Libya Street. Hood and Coast buses are also recommended between Nairobi and the coast. Seats on these buses should be booked a day ahead.

On minor routes, buses are replaced by a plethora of maniacally-driven light vehicles. These generally operate on a fill-up-and-go basis, though on routes where there are only one or two vehicles a day, there may be a loosely followed departure time. Light vehicles can be divided into three types: minibuses, shared taxis and matatus. Minibuses are the best option: safer than matatus, not too crowded, and generally pretty quick. Shared taxis are also fair, and because they generally fill up with passengers going the whole way, there aren't too many stops. Matatus are best described as sardine tins on wheels, usually covered pick-up trucks with cramped seating along the sides. They are horribly overcrowded, continually stop to pick up more passengers, and accidents are commonplace. Avoid them where there is an alternative.

Matatu and bus stands in larger towns are invariably chaotic, but you'll usually find the vehicle you want in the end. Don't pay for a ticket until the vehicle is full – and watch out for the trick of filling a vehicle with random hangers-on to lure in paying passengers. Matatu conductors sometimes overcharge tourists, especially in western Kenya. Irritating as this is, there's not a lot you can do about it unless you know the fare for the route you're taking. If the fare sounds high, query it.

Getting out of Nairobi and Mombasa can be very confusing. Buses and matatus leave from several different stands, and petty theft is a real problem. I strongly recommend you use a taxi to find your bus or minibus departure point. Most taxi drivers are helpful once you've agreed a fare, they know where different vehicles leave from and they will make sure you get on one that's leaving soon. Also, you can keep your luggage safe in the boot until you've sorted out which vehicle you're leaving on.

Hitching

Hitching is fair on the Mombasa highway and the main road between Mombasa and Kisumu. On little-used routes, the line between hitching and public transport becomes somewhat blurred. Any vehicle driven by a local is likely to give hitchers lifts, but a fare will be charged. Note that the thumbs-up hitching signal used in the West won't mean anything to Kenyans; wave your arms flamboyantly instead.

ACCOMMODATION

Accommodation is rarely a problem. Prices are competitive by international standards and standards are high. Accommodation described in this guide has been divided into two broad categories: tourist class and budget. This reflects a real division in Kenya's tourist industry. There is an excellent infrastructure of hotels and game lodges catering exclusively for tourists while on another level there's a network of hotels, local lodgings and hostels catering to the local market and budget travellers.

Within each of these categories I have used specific terms to indicate relative price and quality. Tourist-class accommodation is referred to in three general price brackets: luxury, upmarket and modest. Luxury consists of exclusive, five-star accommodation, and will generally cost upwards of US $200 for a double room. Upmarket hotels are reliable, package tour-oriented places in the three to four-star bracket, and typically cost between US $80 and US $150 double. Modest hotels are less pretentious and perhaps slightly run-down or employ dithery staff, but they are perfectly adequate for most tourists. Prices range between US $30 and US $80 double.

Tourist-class hotels charge a variety of rates depending on your eating arrangements. You can assume that most game lodge and tented camp rates include meals, while town and beach hotel rates are bed and breakfast only. Bear in mind, too, that there are often seasonal price variations on the coast and in game reserves. High season runs from November or December to Easter, and low season from Easter to June or July. August to October is treated as high season in some game reserves.

The two main types of budget accommodation are cheap hotels and local lodgings. The former are "proper" hotels which don't quite meet tourist-class standards but which still have self-contained rooms, hot running water, and a bar and restaurant. Cheap hotels are popular with local businessmen and tourists on a small budget, and they are often excellent value for money, ranging from about US $10 to US $15 double.

Local lodgings are geared almost entirely to the local market. There are lodgings of this sort in virtually every village and they proliferate in most towns. Typically, they offer cell-like rooms with no furnishing other than a bed. They have communal toilets and showers. Some local lodgings are undeniably dirty and noisy, others are very pleasant. If you look around it's normally possibie to find a clean, secure room. Many budget travellers make extensive use of local lodgings.

Other budget accommodation includes bandas (basic huts), self-catering cottages and hostels (places offering dormitory accommodation). As a rule, self-catering accommodation works out at approximately the same as a cheap hotel, while bandas and dormitories are similar in price to local lodgings.

Throughout the book I refer to self-contained rooms. These are rooms with a private bath/shower and toilet.

Booking

In December and January it is advisable to book hotel rooms and self-catering accommodation in advance, especially along the coast and in game reserves. During the remainder of the year, you're reasonably safe just arriving unannounced, though obviously it makes sense to book if you're heading to an isolated establishment.

At the lower end of the budget range it's not normally necessary to book. Even if your first choice is full, you'll find a room elsewhere. If you're travelling on public transport, it's difficult to plan a precise itinerary anyway.

Many of Kenya's best hotels are part of a chain; if you're making your own arrangements, it's easier to book as much as possible through one chain. Details of the main hotels are given in the main part of this guide, but chain addresses are as follows:

African Tours and Hotels (AT&H), PO Box 30471, Nairobi; tel: (02) 336858; fax: 336961
Buffalo Springs Lodge (Buffalo Springs)
Golden Beach Hotel (Diani Beach)
Kabernet Hotel (Kabernet)
Kilugani Lodge (Tsavo West)

Mombasa Beach Hotel (Mombasa)
Milimani Hotel (Nairobi)
Mountain Lodge (Mount Kenya)
Ngulia Lodge (Tsavo West)
Olkurruk Lodge (Masai Mara)
Sirikwa Hotel (Eldoret)
Sunset Hotel (Kisumu)
Trade Winds Hotel (Diani Beach)
Voi Safari Lodge (Tsavo East)

Alliance Hotels, PO Box 49839, Nairobi; tel: (02) 332825; fax: 219212
Africana Sea Lodge (Diani Beach)
Naro Moru River Lodge (Mount Kenya)
Jadani Beach Hotel (Diani Beach)
Safari Beach Hotel (Diani Beach)

Block Hotels, PO Box 47557, Nairobi; tel: (02) 335807; fax: 340541
Indian Ocean Beach Club (Diani Beach)
Jacaranda Hotel (Nairobi)
Keekorok Lodge (Masai Mara)
Lake Baringo Club (Lake Baringo)
Lake Naivasha Hotel (Lake Naivasha)
Larsen's (Samburu)
Nyali Beach Hotel (Mombasa)
Outspan Hotel (Nyeri)
Samburu Lodge (Samburu)
Shimba Hills Lodge (Shimba Hills)
Treetops (Aberdares)

Kilimanjaro Safari Club, PO Box 30139, Nairobi; tel: (02) 227136; fax: 219982
Amboseli Lodge (Amboseli)
Kilimanjaro Safari Lodge (Amboseli)
Kimana Lodge (near Amboseli)
Tsavo Inn (Mtito Andei)
Tsavo Safari Camp (Tsavo East)

Lonrho Hotels, PO Box 58581, Nairobi; tel: (02) 216940; fax: 216796
Aberdare Country Club (near Nyeri)
The Ark (Aberdares)
Mara Safari Club (Masai Mara)
Mount Kenya Safari Club (near Nanyuki)
Norfolk Hotel (Nairobi)
Ol Pejeta (near Nanyuki)

Rusinga Island Camp (Lake Victoria)
Sweetwaters (near Nanyuki)

Msafiri Inns, PO Box 42013, Nairobi; tel: (02) 330820; fax: 227815
Golf Hotel (Kakamega)
Homa Bay Hotel (Homa Bay)
Izaak Walton Inn (Embu)
Marsabit Lodge (Marsabit)
Meru Mulika Lodge (Meru National Park)
Mount Elgon Lodge (Mount Elgon)
Tea Hotel (Kericho)

Prestige Hotels, PO Box 74888, Nairobi; tel: (02) 338084; fax: 217278
Mara Intrepids Club (Masai Mara)
Samburu Intrepids Club (Samburu)

Sarova Hotels, PO Box 30680, Nairobi; tel: (02) 333248; fax: 211472
Ambassadeur (Nairobi)
Lion Hill Lodge (Lake Nakuru)
New Stanley Hotel (Nairobi)
Panafric (Nairobi)
Sarova Mara Camp (Masai Mara)
Sarova Shaba Lodge (Shaba)
Whitesands Hotel (Mombasa)

Serena Lodges, PO Box 48690, Nairobi; tel: (02) 710511; fax: 718103
Amboseli Serena Lodge (Amboseli)
Mara Serena Lodge (Masai Mara)
Samburu Serena Lodge (Samburu)
Serena Beach Hotel (Mombasa)
Serena Hotel (Nairobi)

Windsor Hotels, PO Box 74957, Nairobi; tel: (02) 219784; fax: 217498
Island Camp (Lake Baringo)
Kichwa Tembo (Masai Mara)
Siani Springs Tented Camp (Masai Mara)
Windsor Golf and Country Club (Nairobi)

Let's Go Travel, Caxton House, Standard Street, PO Box 60342, Nairobi; tel: (02) 340331; fax: 336890, is an exceptionally useful booking agent which can make reservations for hotels in all the above chains, as well as most privately run tourist-class hotels. They also act as agents for several self-catering establishments. If you're travelling around the country independently, their free pamphlet with up-to-date prices of almost all hotels in Kenya is useful.

Camping

Budget travellers should seriously consider carrying a tent. Most towns and reserves in Kenya offer camping facilities of some sort. Although camping is often little cheaper than staying in the most basic guest-houses, it is generally more pleasant. And a tent offers some insurance against getting stuck, particularly if you are travelling off the beaten track. A tent is essential if you intend to hike in undeveloped areas such as the Cheranganis.

Designated campsites are generally secure and in most cases I have few qualms about leaving my rucksack in the tent while I go off for the day. It's a matter of judgement. Camping in undesignated places is also safe in most parts of the country, though you should either camp well away from the road and from human settlements, or else camp close to a settlement with the permission of the headman. In these circumstances, it would be imprudent to leave your tent unguarded. In small villages, ask if there's somewhere you can camp: the school ground or police compound for instance. Camping in undesignated places at the coast is highly inadvisable.

Camping Gaz cylinders can be bought in Nairobi and in most other large towns.

LANGUAGE

English is widely spoken in Kenya, especially in large towns and at tourist-class hotels. The local lingua franca is KiSwahili, a coastal language which was spread through the interior by Omani traders in the 19th century and is spoken as a second language by most Kenyans and Tanzanians.

While it is not strictly necessary to know any KiSwahili in Kenya, it is polite to know at least a few phrases, and it will come in very handy if you travel off the beaten track. Several different phrase books are available from bookshops in Nairobi, but a few key phrases follow.

Phrases

Jambo	Hello
Habari?	How are you?
Mzuri	Fine
Karibu	Welcome
Asante (sana)	Thank you (very much)

Mzungu	European
Mwafrika	African
Iko soda?	Is there a soda?
Iko/Kuna	There is
Haiko/Hakuna	There is not
Nataka soda	I would like a soda
Iko wapi . . .?	Where is . . .?
Hapa	Here
Unakwenda wapi?	Where are you going?
Nakwenda Mwanza	I am going to Mwanza
Unatoka wapi?	Where have you come from?
Natoka Nairobi	I have come from Nairobi
Unaisha wapi?	Where are you from?
Naisha Australia	I am from Australia
Unasema Kiingereza?	Do you speak English?
Nasema KiSwahili kidogo tu	I speak only a little Swahili
Ndiyo	Yes
Hapana	No
Shillingi ngape/Bei gani?	How much does it cost?
Kubwa	Big
Kidogo	Small
Hakuna matata	No problem
Sawa	Fine, OK
(Nataka) kulipa	(I want) to pay
Sasa	Now
Bado	Later
Moto	Hot
Baridi	Cold
Choo (rhymes with go)	Toilet
Polepole	Slowly

Numbers

Moja	1
Mbili	2
Tatu	3
Nne	4
Tano	5
Sita	6
Saba	7
Nane	8

Tisa	9
Kumi	10
Kumi na moja	11
Ishirini	20
Thelathini	30
Arobaini	40
Hamsini	50
Sitini	60
Sabini	70
Themanini	80
Tisini	90
Mia moja	100
Mia moja na kumi na moja	111
Elfu	1 000

SWAHILI TIME

Travellers using public transport should be alert to the fact that Swahili time is different to Western time by six hours, so that saa moja (hour one) is seven o'clock in the morning or in the evening, saa mbili (hour two) is eight o'clock, etc. Morning, afternoon, evening and night are called asubuhi, alasiri, jioni and usiku respectively. Saa tatu asabuhi is 9h00; saa tatu usiku (or jioni) is 21h00.

Western time is widely used in Kenya, but less so in Tanzania where bus departures are often advertised in Swahili time. The simple way to get round this is to ask the time in Swahili – saa ngape? – and make the necessary adjustment.

People with limited English may convert the time to English without making the necessary adjustment: in other words if a bus leaves at saa sita you may be told it leaves at six. There's much less room for ambiguity if you check the time in Swahili: ask whether the person means saa sita or saa kumi na mbili. This sort of confusion is unusual in Kenya but commonplace in Tanzania.

CULTURAL EXPECTATIONS

This rather delicate and difficult area can cause all sorts of misconceptions. Many people arrive in East Africa with romantic expectations about Africans and feel completely let down when they find that in the cities everyone is dressed in Western or Islamic clothing and that all the colourful ethnic people they meet in rural areas want to sell them something.

Disillusionment of this sort is most extreme for tourists on organised trips, who should expect the Masai villages they are ferried through, and the Samburu dancing they witness, to be contrived. With almost a million tourists passing through Kenya every year, most of whom are with organised tours and most of whom want to see traditional Masai, how could such encounters be anything else? To complain, as many tourists do, that Kenyans are commercialised, or to gripe whenever they are asked to pay to take a photograph, is to miss the reality. Semi-professional posers and dancers are meeting a demand, and they have every right to expect payment.

Independent travellers will also experience a certain amount of hustling, but the very nature of independent travel allows for greater intermingling with ordinary citizens, the vast majority of whose livelihoods are not intertwined with tourism. If you want to see something of rural East Africa, if you want to discover that most East Africans, even the poorest, are disarmingly open and hospitable, then I strongly urge you to spend a few days exploring off the beaten track. For obvious reasons it would be counterproductive to recommend individual places, but virtually any small town or village will provide the opportunity to meet local people in uncontrived situations.

It is the 1990s in Kenya as much as it is anywhere else in the world. To go there expecting an entirely traditional society is as unrealistic as going to the USA and expecting to walk onto what seems like the set of a cowboy film. Too many tourists arrive in East Africa with absurd preconceptions. If you believe that the culture of the villager is somehow more valid than that of the urbanite, if you feel betrayed each time you perceive cultural purity to be tainted by westernisation, then you are bound to feel let down and to learn nothing. East Africa has been a cultural melting pot since prehistoric times (the Masai and Samburu, to many visitors the archetypal people of East Africa, only arrived in the Kenyan Rift Valley at around the time the Dutch colonised the Cape of Good Hope). The notion of cultural purity has little historical basis and much of the fascination of modern Africa lies in the vibrant interchange between traditional and exotic cultures. An evening in a small town bar will probably teach you more about Africa today than any number of camera-based exchanges in tourist-orientated villages. The only sensible attitude to any country is to accept it, and to try to understand it, on its own terms.

BARGAINING

This is another delicate subject, one which I feel is often misrepresented in travel guides and misunderstood by tourists. It is often asserted that everything in Africa is negotiable, and to some extent this is true. It can, for instance, be assumed that curio sellers, taxi drivers and matatu conductors will often ask an inflated rate from tourists, but there are many other situations where bargaining is inappropriate.

The problem facing tourists is that they often don't know what a fair price is. If you unquestioningly pay what you are asked for a bus ride, then realise that everyone else is paying less, woe betide the conductor of the next bus you take – even if he is asking you the right price straight away.

A further complicating factor is the very notion of a fixed price. In many instances, there simply isn't one. At most markets, bargaining is normal even among locals. Curio stalls, too, seem pretty whimsical about what they first ask and what they will settle for. It is better to approach bargaining as part and parcel of the East African experience: it can be fun, and there is rarely any need to become aggressive or petulant.

Matatus, however, generally do have fixed fares and overcharging tourists is commonplace, particularly in western Kenya and Uganda. The ideal is to be philosophical about this. Nobody likes being ripped off, but we all are sometimes and there's no point in letting the loss of a few cents spoil our day. Where philosophy fails (and it certainly doesn't work for me), a scientific approach is better than losing your temper. Ask other passengers what they are paying, or tactfully query the price and prevaricate about whether you really like the look of the bus. If you're being asked too much, a gentle bluff will usually suffice to rectify matters.

A similar approach is useful when buying fruit or vegetables at markets. Visit a couple of stalls to feel the situation out before you actually buy anything. If someone is unwilling to drop their price, the likelihood is that they were asking a fair price in the first place. Above all, keep things in perspective. In my experience, small fruit stalls and the like rarely ask an absurd price and will quite often lower it through hospitableness or desperation to sell perishable goods before the end of the day. If a price seems reasonable and the person obviously needs the money more than you do, why not just leave it at that?

POST

Mail between Kenya and South Africa normally takes about a week, as does post to most European countries. Letters to North America and Australia take longer. Surface mail parcel post from Nairobi is cheap and reasonably reliable.

There are poste restante services at post offices in most large towns. Poste restante at Nairobi's main post office is well organised, though it's advisable to look under both your first name and surname. Letters should be addressed with your name (preferably with your surname underlined) then: POSTE RESTANTE, MAIN GPO, NAIROBI, KENYA.

GROCERY SHOPPING

Almost anything you're likely to want can be bought in Nairobi and Mombasa. There are good supermarkets in Naivasha, Nakuru, Kisumu, Eldoret, Kitale, Nyeri and Malindi. In other towns, fruit and vegetables can be bought at markets while small kiosks – known as dukas – sell manufactured goods. The sort of things you can buy in even the smallest towns include pens, cigarettes, sodas, biscuits, toilet rolls and ugali (maizemeal).

BOOKS AND MAPS

Nairobi's best bookshops compare favourably to those elsewhere in the world and are densely stacked with paperback novels, travel books, Africana and maps. The shop next to the New Stanley Hotel is a good place to start. Kenya has a good local publishing industry which produces a selection of cheap and usable field guides and special interest books: it's well worth spending an hour browsing through a bookshop early in your trip. Good commercially produced maps of the major game reserves and mountains are available in any Nairobi bookshop.

There are a couple of reasonable bookshops on Moi Avenue in Mombasa, but few elsewhere in the country.

CURIOS

You can barely walk 100 m in central Nairobi and Mombasa without tripping over curio stalls and shops. Items for sale include copper bracelets, animal carvings, Makonde carvings, batiks, weaved baskets and kikois, colourful cotton cloths worn wrapped around the body. It's worth shopping around a bit before you start buying. Prices vary wildly and it's much easier to bargain once you know the going rate.

RESTAURANTS

Eating out in Kenya is rarely a problem. Nairobi and Mombasa both have several excellent restaurants. Typically these serve Western meat-based dishes but there are good Italian, Indian and Chinese restaurants as well. By international standards, eating out is cheap.

I've not listed restaurants in smaller towns where the choice is predictable. Any tourist-class hotel will serve Western menus of steaks, chicken and fish dishes. Local restaurants, known as hotelis, serve grilled meat (nyama choma) and stews with chips, rice or maize porridge (ugali) for about half the price charged at tourist-class hotels.

DRINKING

Wherever possible, avoid drinking unsterilised water. Sodas can generally be bought at even the smallest villages and fruit juice and mineral water are available in most towns. The main leisure drink in Kenya is lager beer: there are several brands, all good and moderately priced. South African wines are available at tourist-class hotels and licensed restaurants.

PUBLIC HOLIDAYS

Kenya's public holidays are:
1 January – New Year's Day
Good Friday (date varies)
Easter Monday (date varies)
1 May – Labour Day
1 June – Anniversary of self-government
10 October – Moi Day
20 October – Kenyatta Day
25 December – Christmas Day
26 December – Anniversary of independence and Boxing Day

PHOTOGRAPHY

Kenya offers ample opportunities for photographers, though wildlife photography is difficult without a zoom lens (at least 200 mm). For most needs 100 ASA film is adequate and available throughout the country, but more specialised film can be difficult to locate outside of Nairobi, and even there the range is limited. For photography in forests (e.g. gorillas or chimpanzees) film of 400 ASA or higher is recommended and is best brought to Kenya with you.

It is the height of rudeness to photograph East Africans without their permission. If you want to photograph Masai, Samburu or other people in ethnic dress, expect to pay for the privilege. Many tourists take highly vocal offence to this. They have three options: pay up and shut up, don't take photographs, or try a few sneak shots. If you opt for the latter and find a spear attached to your lens, don't say you haven't been warned. How would you feel about an endless succession of minibuses arriving at your doorstep to photograph your family?

It is illegal to photograph government installations such as railway stations, bridges and military bases, and prudent to keep your camera tucked away in the vicinity of such places.

THEFT

Theft is a considerable problem for tourists, not because Kenya is a particularly dishonest country, but because even the most budget-conscious visitors are wealthy by local standards and because most tourists stand out in a crowd by virtue of their skin colour. With a bit of common sense, the risk of theft in Kenya is quite small, and very localised. Muggings are largely confined to Nairobi and to deserted beaches and quiet coastal roads. Con artists are only really a problem in Nairobi.

The problems specific to Nairobi are covered in the Nairobi chapter, and known trouble spots on the coast are mentioned under the relevant section.

Away from Nairobi and the coast, the only problem is minor theft and pickpocketing, which mainly occur in bus stations and markets. There are several ways to counter casual theft. When you arrive in any town, walk out of the bus station quickly and confidently; the time to establish whether you have walked out in the right direction is once you are away from the crowds. Avoid carrying large amounts of money or valuables in crowded places. Where this is impossible, for instance when you are about to catch a bus, at least ensure that you have nothing valuable in your pockets or any other accessible place. Spectacles and sunglasses are popular with snatch thieves.

Give some thought to where you carry your valuables. The best solution is to stash your passport and travellers cheques in a money belt, preferably a cotton belt that can be discreetly tucked under your clothing (though you should wrap your passport and money in plastic bags to keep them from becoming sweaty). Never advertise your wealth. Large externally worn money belts may be fashionable, but they positively scream out to be snatched, as does expensive jewellery. Carry some local currency in a wallet or pocket so that you never have to reveal your money belt in public – rather let a few dollars' worth of local currency be taken than everything you possess.

Kenya is a law-abiding country. Theft is frowned upon by ordinary citizens, so much so that known thieves are regularly beaten to death by angry mobs. Thieves and con artists prey on people who look edgy or confused, and many experienced travellers believe that by simply looking confident and alert, rather than lost and nervous, they will greatly reduce the risk of being robbed. What's more, indiscriminate paranoia can only divert your attention from genuinely suspicious characters.

SECURITY

Roads in northern Kenya, an area which few tourists visit, are plagued by sporadic outbreaks of armed banditry. At the time of writing, the main risk areas appear to be the coast north of Malindi, the road north of Samburu National Reserve towards Marsabit, and the road between Nairobi and the coast via Garissa. Anyone heading to the northeast should make enquiries as to the current situation. Where a risk is perceived, vehicles are generally forced to travel in armed convoys.

A handful of incidents of armed banditry elsewhere in the region (the murder of Julie Ward in the Masai Mara in 1988 and the killing of a tourist with a poisoned arrow in northern Tanzania in 1994) have received a great deal of publicity but they are too isolated to be a serious cause for concern – the risk of contracting malaria or being killed in a car accident is infinitely greater.

3 ITINERARY AND SAFARI PLANNING

Kenya is a diverse country and few people have the time to explore it thoroughly. Add to Kenya the various attractions in northern Tanzania and Uganda and there's enough to keep anyone going for six months or longer.

Bearing this in mind, it's worth giving some thought to exactly what you want from Kenya. Even the normal sort of itinerary, a split between the coast and the major game reserves, can take several forms, depending on your tastes and interests. On the coast, the beach hotels near Mombasa are ideal for sun worshippers, Lamu is more suitable to those with an interest in culture and history, while the reefs, forests and creeks around Watamu and Malindi will interest natural history enthusiasts. As for the game reserves, there are numerous options in Kenya alone, without including neighbouring Tanzania and Uganda.

In addition to considering which places best meet your interests, reflect upon the style of travel that suits your temperament and budget. Would you prefer to cram as much as possible into your time, or to explore a few selected places at leisure? Do you want every detail of your holiday planned ahead, or would you rather leave things to chance? Are you looking for places where tourists congregate, or would you prefer to get away from the crowds?

We all have different needs and interests. The perfect itinerary for one person may hold little appeal for another. My aim, then, is not to dictate itineraries, but to help readers make an informed choice that reflects their budget, interests and preferred style of travel.

This chapter is divided into five sections. The first gives some general tips for itinerary planning and details of organised safaris. The second is a synopsis of major attractions. The third suggests a few itineraries which can be combined or tailored to suit your needs. The fourth gives an overview of game reserves and organised safaris. The fifth contains specialised information for visitors with special interests such as hiking, fishing and birdwatching.

GENERAL TIPS

When planning your itinerary, resist the temptation to cram in too much. I don't know how often I've seen travel guides recommend itineraries which, realistically, would see you spend most of your holiday dashing around in a car or bus. Many safari operators assume that tourists want to see as many reserves as possible, and so they compile itineraries that allow little time to relax and absorb the surroundings. When you arrive at a game reserve in the late afternoon after a long, dusty drive, your first requirements are likely to be a shower and cold beer, not a mad dash to see game before heading off elsewhere the following morning. You should allow at least two nights (in other words a full day) in any place that you particularly want to visit.

Travellers who are dependent on public transport should be especially conscious of timing. Long bus trips are very draining and an overambitious schedule won't be any fun. Use overnight trains wherever possible: they are comfortable enough to allow you a good night's sleep and by travelling overnight you effectively add a day to your holiday. If your budget is more flexible, you might want to think about the odd internal flight. A return flight to Lamu from Malindi saves two long bus trips, and if Lamu is the only place you want to see on the coast, a return flight from Nairobi will effectively add four or five days to your holiday.

Independent travellers are less isolated from local culture than people on organised tours. A night in a local bar or a few days walking off the beaten track can teach you more about a country than any number of safaris. A flexible itinerary will allow you to exploit opportunities to interact with local people.

SAFARIS

The types of safari on offer are budget camping trips, overland truck safaris and lodge or luxury camping safaris. Some safaris could be double or more the price of others, depending on where you arrange the safari, which company you use, where you intend to go, and the group size.

The main centres for organising safaris are Nairobi and Arusha (Tanzania), with smaller industries operating in Mombasa and Malindi. You can organise a safari to anywhere in East Africa from Nairobi, and it is definitely the best place to arrange safaris to Amboseli and reserves north and west of Nairobi and in Uganda. Safaris to northern Tanzania are best arranged in Arusha or Nairobi. Safaris from Mombasa go all over Kenya, but they tend to be much more expensive than those out of Nairobi. Trips to Tsavo East and West and Shimba Hills are best arranged in Mombasa. Malindi is very close to Tsavo East so day trips are a possibility from there. Safari companies are recommended under the relevant town listings.

Before you select a safari, bear in mind that travelling between reserves takes up a lot of time. Masai Mara is six hours' drive from Nairobi. A three day drive-down safari gives you one and a bit days in the reserve, a four day safari gives you two and a bit days. Unless you have a penchant for whizzing along rutted, dusty roads in a minibus, it's hard to see the appeal of the three day Tsavo West/Amboseli safaris that run out of Mombasa. As a rule, select a safari itinerary that allows you at least one full day in each major reserve you are visiting.

Safari companies will generally quote rates inclusive of park fees, food, transport and accommodation or camping, but it's always advisable to clarify who is paying for what in advance. Prices are negotiable, particularly at the competitive budget end of the scale so never settle for the first price you are quoted.

Which country, which reserves?

It's worth commenting on the differences between safaris in Tanzania and Kenya. Budget safaris in Kenya tend to have fixed departures with up to eight people in a minibus, while safaris in Tanzania tend to leave on request with up to five people in a Landrover. Budget safaris in Kenya are around 30 per cent cheaper than those in Tanzania, but there is more emphasis on personalised itineraries in Tanzania.

At the luxury level, the biggest contrast is in the standard of facilities. Lodges in Kenya are generally well maintained, smoothly run, and up to international standards, whereas lodges in Tanzania tend to be run-down and often suffer from water or electricity cuts. Standards in Tanzania improve every year, but they are likely to lag behind Kenya for some time yet.

Another factor is relative congestion. Kenya's more popular game reserves carry a high tourist volume, whereas those in Tanzania are still relatively uncongested. This is striking when you contrast Masai Mara in Kenya with the adjoining Serengeti in Tanzania. Serengeti is ten times the size of Masai Mara yet it carries only a fraction of the tourists; as a consequence it retains more of a wilderness atmosphere.

With an understanding driver, you can avoid the few crowded areas completely.

If it's the wildebeest migration you want to see, your choice of country will be determined by when you visit. The wildebeest migration follows a reasonably predictable pattern, with slight variations from year to year. The migration normally reaches Kenya in late July, when the wildebeest disperse onto the plains of Masai Mara for a couple of months. The animals migrate back into Tanzania in October, arriving in the Seronera part of the southern Serengeti in November or December in time for the calving season in January. The wildebeest disperse (if you can call herds of up to 10 000 animals a dispersion) into the southern Serengeti for several months before gathering to head back to Kenya in April or June.

Safaris in northern Tanzania all follow a similar itinerary, as all the main reserves are bunched together. The options are discussed in further detail in the chapter on Tanzania, but a five or six day safari could comfortably take in the three main reserves: Ngorongoro Crater, Serengeti and Lake Manyara.

The main reserves within Kenya are spread throughout the country and the choice of itinerary is less obvious than in Tanzania. The most popular long safari is a six- or seven-day trip to Masai Mara and Samburu, usually punctuated by an overnight stop at Lake Nakuru or one of the tree hotels in the central highlands. An itinerary of this sort offers a good general introduction to Kenya's wildlife and an observant tourist could expect to see up to 40 mammal species, including most of the northern specials. The most popular destinations for shorter safaris are Masai Mara and Amboseli.

If apes are a priority, you might incline towards a safari heading west to Uganda. Most such itineraries focus on mountain gorillas, perhaps with a side trip to the chimpanzees at Kibale Forest, but longer overland truck trips allow time to explore Uganda's game reserves.

Budget safaris

Budget camping safaris are geared to independent travellers, so they concentrate on places that are difficult to reach with public transport. The most popular itineraries out of Nairobi are three- or four-day trips to Masai Mara and six- to seven-day trips combining the Masai Mara and Samburu with an overnight stop at Lake Nakuru. Organising a safari to Masai Mara and Samburu is straightforward. There is no need to pre-book from your home country as several companies in Nairobi have daily departures: ask around when you arrive and you can be off the next day. Amboseli and Tsavo appear to have fallen out of favour with camping safari operators in recent years, presumably because game viewing is more erratic, but if you're prepared to pay a bit extra, most budget safari operators have them on their books. Camping safaris from Mombasa to Tsavo West or East are far more expensive than safaris organised in Nairobi.

Nairobi operators can organise safaris to Tanzania, but it will be cheaper to make your own way to Arusha and arrange a safari there. See the chapter on Tanzania for further details.

Overland trucks

Overland truck trips differ from camping safaris in that group sizes are larger (around 20 people) and they cater mainly to budget travellers who do not feel comfortable with the idea of independent travel. A popular round trip from Nairobi, normally a month in duration, is to the mountain gorilla reserves of Uganda and eastern Zaïre, returning via Lake Victoria and Serengeti.

There is probably no better way of seeing a large number of East African reserves affordably and in a short space of time than on an overland truck trip. Nevertheless, you should think carefully about doing a trip of this sort – imagine spending a month holidaying in the constant company of any 20 people you know and you'll recognise the pitfalls. It's really a question of temperament. An overland truck trip might be great fun if you are naturally gregarious, have no desire for autonomy and primarily want to see the sights. They will be hell-on-wheels if you are strongly individualistic, relish the unexpected, and want to meet local people on a one-to-one basis.

These reservations do not apply to overland truck trips to Lake Turkana. These are too short for group tensions to become a real problem, and the area they pass through is difficult to reach independently. Most Turkana trips include a day or two in Samburu, so they can be seen as an alternative to a conventional camping safari.

Several companies run overland truck trips from Nairobi. These work on fixed departure dates. There is nothing preventing you from arriving in Nairobi and making arrangements once you arrive – you'd be unlikely to have to wait more than a few days – but if your timing is tight it's advisable to book in advance so you can match your flights to the trucks' departure date.

Lodge and luxury camping safaris

There are two types of upmarket safari: drive-down and fly-in. Fly-in safaris are the more expensive option, but by cutting travel time, they allow you to fit more into your itinerary.

Upmarket safaris cater to tourists who would be unlikely to use public transport under any circumstances, so the range of itineraries is far greater than with budget safaris. The most popular options revolve around Masai Mara and Samburu. A typical, and recommended, seven-day driving itinerary would see you spending one night at a tree hotel, two nights at Samburu, a night at a Rift Valley lake, then two nights at Masai Mara. With a couple of extra days available you could append Amboseli to this.

Shorter safaris include a three-day trip to Masai Mara, a four-day trip to Masai Mara and one of the Rift Valley lakes, and a similar length trip that combines a night in a tree hotel with Samburu. Another popular option is a three- or four-day trip to Amboseli and Tsavo West.

Safari itineraries from Mombasa revolve around Tsavo East and West and Amboseli. However, it's hard to see how a two-day trip to Amboseli via Tsavo West (offered by several companies) could be much more than a rally drive. Some companies offer packages to Tsavo West and Amboseli starting in Mombasa and ending in Nairobi.

Self-drive safaris

All of Kenya's national parks can be visited in a hired vehicle. You will see less animals this way, as the drivers of organised tours generally know the region well and communicate with other drivers to check out recent sightings, but this will be more than compensated for by not being part of a large group and having the freedom to escape crowded areas. Even in a highly visited reserve such as Samburu, the minibuses tend to stick to a few favoured spots. You also have access to reserves such as Meru and Tsavo East, which carry low tourist volumes and thus offer more of a wilderness experience.

In theory, most Kenyan reserves can be visited in a saloon car, and it's a fact that most tour operators use two-wheel drive minibuses. All the same, I would hesitate to recommend anything but a 4x4 to someone who isn't familiar with the roads or with their particular vehicle. Bear in mind that minibuses have exceptionally high clearance for a non-4x4 vehicle, and that the drivers are very experienced in local conditions. I needed to switch to four-wheel drive at some point in every large reserve where I drove myself. Only in some of the smaller reserves such as Hell's Gate, Lake Nakuru and Nairobi National Park is a saloon car adequate.

HITCHING AND PUBLIC TRANSPORT

Hitching or bussing to reserves may be an attractive option to people who would feel constrained on an organised safari but who cannot afford to hire a vehicle. The problem with hitching is that private vehicles are thin on the ground and most safari drivers are instructed not to pick up hitchhikers. Even if you do get a lift it will probably be directly to a lodge, where a night's acccommodation will cost more than a budget safari would have. Neither of these factors is a problem if you're reasonably philosophical and you have enough time on your hands, but the recent nearly tenfold hike in park fees means that if you get stuck in a park for a few days you could end up spending a lot of money without seeing many animals.

Of the larger parks, the best for hitching to are Tsavo East and Amboseli. Aruba Lodge in the former is easy to get to, it has camping and affordable rooms, and it overlooks a dam where large numbers of animals congregate. Amboseli is small and heavily visited, and all vehicles must pass through Ol Tukai village where there is cheap accommodation alongside the lodges. Samburu, Masai Mara, the developed part of Tsavo West and all the large reserves in Tanzania are more problematic. In contrast, the two main game reserves in Uganda, Queen Elizabeth and Murchison Falls National Parks, are fairly accessible to non-motorised travellers – and what's more, Uganda is the only East African country to charge a single entrance fee as opposed to a daily fee, so getting stuck is less financially risky.

There are several places in East Africa where game can be seen on foot and which can be reached either by public transport or by walking. Recommended are Hell's Gate National Park, Green Crater Lake, Lakes Bogoria and Baringo, Saiwa Swamps National Park, Arusha National Park (Tanzania), Kakamega Forest (and several forests in Uganda), the Voi Gate of Tsavo East, Lake Jipe on the Tsavo West border, Olorgasailie and all the major mountain reserves except Mount Elgon.

Finally, Lake Nakuru and Nairobi National Parks are both near towns and they have good enough roads for saloon cars. You can visit them relatively cheaply and with a high level of autonomy by hiring a taxi for a morning or afternoon.

HIGHLIGHTS

The first step in planning an itinerary is deciding which places you absolutely must visit. You will then have a basic route to which you can add places along the way. A brief synopsis of East Africa's main attractions, described in further detail in the main text, follows.

Aberdares National Park: The forested Aberdare Range is best known for its tree hotels, Treetops and The Ark, both of which offer an excellent but expensive opportunity to observe animal behaviour at close quarters.

Amboseli National Park: Amboseli is one of Kenya's more crowded reserves, but it's the place to head for if your dream is to have a herd of elephants and Kilimanjaro's snowcapped peaks in your viewfinder at the same time.

Arusha: The largest town in northern Tanzania is the main base for organising safaris to Serengeti, Ngorongoro Crater etc.

Bwindi National Park (Uganda): Along with the Virunga mountains, this is the last remaining mountain gorilla stronghold. Organised gorilla viewing is the main attraction, but there's plenty more to see: chimpanzees, monkeys, forest birds and stunning views.

Gedi Ruins: These mysterious, jungle-clad ruins of a 13th century Swahili city are a must for anyone with an interest in African history. An easy day trip from Malindi or Watamu.

Kakamega Forest: This is Kenya's largest stand of West African-type rain forest, protecting primates, butterflies and birds which are rare elsewhere in Kenya. Experienced guides and ample footpaths make it Kenya's finest birding spot.

Kibale Forest (Uganda): This wonderful forest supports ten primate species and countless birds and butterflies. The main attraction is organised chimpanzee tracking.

Lake Baringo: Any natural history enthusiast could settle here indefinitely. It has varied birdlife, abundant hippo and crocodiles, and walking opportunities in every direction.

Lake Bogoria National Reserve: Bogoria has a dramatic setting and it often hosts large flocks of flamingo. Other attractions include hot springs and wildlife.

Lake Manyara National Park (Tanzania): This reserve en route to Serengeti is noted for a spectacular setting, tree-climbing lions and sporadic influxes of flamingos.

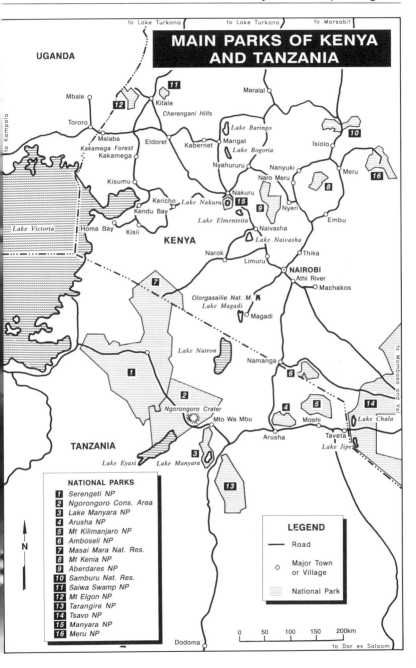

MAIN PARKS OF KENYA AND TANZANIA

NATIONAL PARKS

1 Serengeti NP
2 Ngorongoro Cons. Area
3 Lake Manyara NP
4 Arusha NP
5 Mt Kilimanjaro NP
6 Amboseli NP
7 Masai Mara Nat. Res.
8 Mt Kenia NP
9 Aberdares NP
10 Samburu Nat. Res.
11 Saiwa Swamp NP
12 Mt Elgon NP
13 Tarangire NP
14 Tsavo NP
15 Manyara NP
16 Meru NP

LEGEND

— Road
o Major Town or Village
National Park

0   50   100   150   200km

Lake Naivasha: The closest Rift Valley lake to Nairobi is a perfect first stop in Kenya. The scenery epitomises East Africa, the birdlife is spectacular and several nearby reserves offer the opportunity to confront large mammals on foot.

Lake Nakuru National Park: This lake supports up to two million flamingos. The surrounding forest is dense with game, including rhino, but there is little chance of seeing large predators.

Lake Turkana: This large lake in northern Kenya supports the largest crocodile population on the continent. The surrounding desert is home to people who are virtually untouched by Western influences. Turkana is difficult to reach unless you have plenty of time.

Lamu: The most profoundly traditional Swahili town on the coast has managed to adapt to tourism without losing any of its charm. Lamu seduces everyone who visits it. It's well worth flying up if your time is limited.

Masai Mara National Reserve: This extension of Tanzania's Serengeti plains is famed for the number and diversity of large mammals it supports. Large predators are particularly common. It is also one of the most crowded reserves in the country.

Malindi: This ancient Swahili town offers fine snorkelling and fishing, but it lacks the character of Mombasa or Lamu.

Meru National Park: This park is recommended to self-drive tourists. Wildlife is less prolific than in other reserves, but the wilderness atmosphere is untainted by mass tourism.

Mombasa: The largest town on the East African coast is at least 700 years old. The lively city centre is counterbalanced by the Old Town, much of which dates to the turn of the century, and Fort Jesus, built by the Portuguese in the 16th century.

Mount Kenya: Africa's second highest mountain is popular with hikers and climbers. The forest zone protects several localised animals, most readily seen from Mountain Lodge, a less publicised but I think superior version of the tree hotels in the Aberdares.

Mount Kilimanjaro (Tanzania): Africa's highest mountain can be climbed over five or six days from Moshi. The peaks tower over Kenya's Amboseli National Park and over some parts of Tsavo West.

Mount Meru (Tanzania): Africa's fifth highest mountain can be climbed in three days from Arusha. There's plenty of game on the lower slopes and good views across to neighbouring Kilimanjaro.

Nairobi: Kenya's capital is the focal point of tourism in East Africa and a bustling modern city.

Ngorongoro Crater (Tanzania): The wildlife that lives in this, the largest intact volcanic caldera in the world, has been the subject of countless television documentaries. Crowded due to its confined nature, but still absolutely dazzling.

Olduvai Gorge (Tanzania): This gorge between Ngorongoro Crater and Serengeti is where Mary Leakey discovered the first known hominid skull over a million years old.

Olorgasailie prehistoric site: Two hours south of Nairobi, this peaceful spot is rich in stone tools and the surrounding bush holds a surprising amount of wildlife. A superb itinerary filler if you've a couple of days spare and don't mind basic facilities.

Saiwa Swamp National Park: This obscure national park is the one place where you can to see the localised sitatunga antelope. It also supports several types of monkey and a wide range of swamp and forest birds. All game viewing is on foot.

Samburu complex: The adjoining Samburu, Buffalo Springs and Shaba National Reserves are notable for the contrast between desert plains and lush riverine forest. The area is of special interest as it protects several mammal and bird species rarely seen further south.

Serengeti National Park (Tanzania): This is Africa's best-known reserve, and arguably its finest. It adjoins Masai Mara, but it's much larger and less affected by mass tourism.

Shimba Hills National Reserve: The nearest reserve to Mombasa is the only place in Kenya where sable antelope are found. Forest animals include leopard, elephant, bushpig and black-and-white colobus monkeys. The tourist focal point is Shimba Lodge, a tree hotel that is the equal of the more famous ones in the Aberdares.

Tarangire National Park (Tanzania): This is a good alternative to Serengeti in the dry season, when large herds of plains animals are drawn to the baobab-studded bush along the Tarangire River.

Tsavo East National Park: Although this vast, arid reserve receives relatively few tourists, it's one of the easiest to visit with public transport. Wildlife includes most large predators, several northern species, and a dense elephant population.

Tsavo West National Park: Separated from Tsavo East by the main Mombasa road, it is more moist and hilly than its neighbour. Attractions include a well-developed tourist circuit, good game viewing and magnificent volcanic landscapes.

Virunga Mountains (Uganda/Zaïre/Rwanda border): This volcanic range is one of two remaining mountain gorilla strongholds. Organised gorilla viewing is at present only possible in the Zaïrian part of the range.

Watamu: This resort village offers some of the best snorkelling and diving in Kenya and there are several local excursions for natural history enthusiasts.

SOME POSSIBLE ITINERARIES

The following itineraries, all of which form a loop from Nairobi, are planning aids, not rigid suggestions. They will give you an idea of what you can realistically fit into your time in the country, but they can easily be modified, extended or combined to suit your interests.

Itinerary one: Two weeks coastal

This itinerary assumes a general interest in coastal history, wildlife and underwater activities. It would be equally suitable done on public transport or with a hired vehicle. If you only have a week on the coast, you would either have to leave out Lamu or else miss everything else and fly directly to Lamu from Mombasa, Malindi or Nairobi.

Night 1	:	Overnight train, drive or fly to Mombasa
Night 2-3	:	Beach near Mombasa/Shimba Hills National Park
Night 4	:	Watamu
Night 5	:	Watamu (spend day snorkelling, diving or fishing)
Night 6	:	Watamu (day trip to Sokoke Forest or Mida Creek)
Night 7	:	Malindi (via Gedi Ruins)
Night 8-11	:	Lamu
Night 12	:	Malindi
Night 13	:	Mombasa town (visit Old Town and Fort Jesus)
Night 14	:	Overnight train, drive or fly to Nairobi

Itinerary two: One week Rift Valley lakes

This relaxed trip through a beautiful part of Kenya is suitable for motorised tourists, but is of special interest to people using public transport as it offers ample opportunities to see wildlife on foot.

Night 1-3   :   Naivasha (walks to Hell's Gate and Green Crater Lake)
Night 4   :   Nakuru (drive or hire a taxi to Lake Nakuru National
                 Park)
Night 5-6   :   Lake Baringo
Night 7   :   Nairobi

Itinerary three: Two/three weeks Rift Valley and western Kenya

This itinerary is aimed at independent travellers and concentrates on
areas where you can see wildlife on foot. To expand it to three weeks,
spend a night at Lake Bogoria on your way to Baringo, visit more than
one of the options given for night 8-9, and explore Lake Victoria from
Kisumu.

Night 1-6   :   As for itinerary two
Night 7   :   Kitale via Eldoret
Night 8-9   :   Saiwa Swamps National Park, Cherengani Hills or
                 Mount Elgon
Night 10-12:   Kakamega Forest
Night 13   :   Kisumu
Night 14   :   Nairobi

Itinerary four: Seven days Mount Kenya climb

Night 1   :   Nairobi to Chogoria or Naro Moru
Night 2-5   :   Climb Mount Kenya
Night 6   :   Return to Chogoria or Naro Moru
Night 7   :   Nairobi

Itinerary five: One week northern safari

This safari itinerary is for self-drive tourists wishing to see the unusual
animals of northern Kenya. A 4x4 vehicle is necessary. You could omit
the night at Mountain Lodge if you're trying to cut costs.

Night 1   :   Mountain Lodge
Night 2-3   :   Meru National Park
Night 4-6   :   Samburu complex
Night 7   :   Return to Nairobi

Itinerary six : Eight days Mara/Rift Valley safari

Another safari itinerary for self-drive tourists, again requiring a 4x4.
Note that the return route via Kericho should be enquired about after
rain; if it is impassable, there is a more direct route between Masai Mara

and Lake Nakuru. If you want to combine this itinerary with itinerary five, bypass Nairobi by travelling between Samburu and the Rift Valley via Naro Moru, Nyahururu and Nakuru.

Night 1	:	Lake Naivasha
Night 2-4	:	Masai Mara (via Narok)
Night 5	:	Kericho (via Kisii and Mau escarpment)
Night 6	:	Lake Nakuru
Night 7	:	Nairobi

Itinerary seven: One week Mombasa to Nairobi safari

Another safari itinerary aimed at self-drive tourists, again requiring a 4x4. It can be done in the reverse direction or, with a bit of tinkering, as a round trip from either Mombasa or Nairobi.

Night 1-2	:	Tsavo East (the best route is via Malindi)
Night 3	:	Tsavo West (developed area)
Night 4	:	Tsavo West (Lake Jipe)
Night 5-6	:	Amboseli (via Taveta, Lake Chala and Oloitokitok)
Night 7	:	Nairobi

Itinerary eight: Four week driving safari

A flexible itinerary to give an idea of what would be realistic over four weeks. To cut it to around three weeks, depending on your interests, you could either remain in Nairobi after day 18 or return there from Amboseli on day 21, or else omit days 6-10 (using the direct route between Masai Mara and Nakuru) and cut a couple of days elsewhere.

Night 1-2	:	Lake Naivasha
Night 3-5	:	Masai Mara
Night 6	:	Kericho
Night 7-8	:	Kakamega Forest
Night 9	:	Lake Baringo (via Eldoret and Kabernet)
Night 10	:	Lake Bogoria
Night 11	:	Lake Nakuru
Night 12-14:		Samburu (via Nyahururu and Naro Moru)
Night 15-16:		Meru National Park
Night 17	:	Mountain Lodge or elsewhere in the Mount Kenya area
Night 18	:	Nairobi
Night 19-20:		Amboseli
Night 21-22:		Towards Malindi via Tsavo East and West

Night 23-25:   Malindi and Watamu
Night 26 :   Shimba Hills
Night 27 :   Mombasa
Night 28 :   Nairobi

Itinerary nine: Two/three weeks gorilla/chimpanzee safari

This is aimed at budget travellers journeying independently, wishing to see the mountain gorillas in Uganda. Because the situation regarding the best gorilla reserve to visit changes from time to time, it's impossible to predict exactly how long you will need. I've allocated five days, which should be ample.

This trip could be expanded to three weeks by returning from Kampala in stages via the Rift Valley lakes. A more adventurous option would be to return through northern Tanzania. This would involve staying overnight in Masaka on night 13, then heading on to Bukoba on the Tanzanian shore of Lake Victoria. From Bukoba you can catch an overnight ferry to Mwanza. Direct buses from Mwanza to Arusha pass through Serengeti and Ngorongoro Conservation Area and offer good game viewing at the right time of year.

Night 1   :   Overnight train/bus to Kampala
Night 2   :   Kampala (get current information on the best reserve to visit)
Night 3   :   Kabale
Night 4-8 :   Getting to and from gorilla reserve
Night 9   :   Kabale
Night 10   :   Fort Portal
Night 11-12:   Kibale Forest (chimpanzee tracking)
Night 13   :   Kampala
Night 14   :   Overnight train/bus to Nairobi

Itinerary ten: Three weeks northern Tanzania safari

This gives an idea of what you might reasonably expect to do in three weeks in northern Tanzania. Obviously you can extract a portion of the itinerary if you plan a safari or Kilimanjaro climb only.

Night 1   :   Arusha (a day's travel from Nairobi)
Night 2   :   Arusha (spend the day organising a safari)
Night 3-7 :   Six-day safari to Serengeti, Ngorongoro and Manyara
Night 8   :   Arrive back in Arusha

Night 9   :   Moshi (organise Kilimanjaro climb)
Night 10-14:   Six-day Kilimanjaro climb
Night 15   :   Arrive back in Moshi
Night 16   :   Dar es Salaam
Night 17-19:   Zanzibar
Night 20   :   Dar es Salaam
Night 21   :   Arusha
Night 22   :   Nairobi

NATIONAL PARKS AND RESERVES

East Africa supports the most varied mammalian fauna anywhere in the world, and the greatest population densities, with Tanzania alone estimated to contain 20 per cent of Africa's large mammals. There are well over 100 national parks and reserves in the region which together protect a wide diversity of habitats.

In this book, the term game reserve is used specifically to refer to reserves which protect savannah habitats and the big game species that most tourists come to Kenya to see. For example, Samburu and Masai Mara are considered to be game reserves, but Mount Kenya is not. This may appear to be a rather arbitrary distinction – Mount Kenya is, after all, a national park and it does protect large amounts of game – but it is nonetheless useful. Game reserves are essentially the province of traditional safaris, while forest and mountain reserves tend to attract hikers and people with a more specialised interest in natural history.

Game reserves

The game reserves of East Africa can be grouped into four loose geographical regions: the mixed miombo-acacia woodland reserves of southern Tanzania; the open savannah reserves of northwest Tanzania and southwest Kenya; the light acacia woodland reserves of northeast Tanzania and southeast Kenya; and the dry country reserves of northern Kenya. In wildlife-viewing terms, these regions have much in common: the big five (lion, leopard, elephant, buffalo and rhinoceros) occur in most major East African game reserves, and many other large mammals are found in suitable habitats throughout the region – at least where human activity has not interfered with natural distribution patterns.

The inter-regional differences in fauna deserve some comment, as they will be of special interest to those who want to see species that don't occur further south. As you might expect, the miombo reserves of southern Tanzania have most in common with other southern African parks, with antelope species such as sable, roan, Lichtenstein's hartebeest and greater kudu far more common than they are further north. Many of these reserves still support large herds of elephant. The relatively dense vegetation is reminiscent of national parks such as Kruger and Hwange: large predators, although abundant, are less readily seen than elsewhere in East Africa. The major reserves of southern Tanzania (Selous Game Reserve and Mikumi, Ruaha and Katavi National Parks) lie beyond the normal orbit of Nairobi-based tourists.

The contiguous savannah reserves west of the Rift Valley and east of Lake Victoria are Serengeti, Ngorongoro and Masai Mara. The open grassland of this area supports larger animal populations than reserves further south. Large predators such as lion and cheetah are common and highly visible, but elephant and giraffe are more thinly distributed than elsewhere. Large herds of wildebeest and Burchell's zebra are a feature of this region, as are Thomson's and Grant's gazelle, Coke's hartebeest, topi and defassa waterbuck.

East of the Rift Valley, reserves such as Tsavo East and West and Tarangire (Tanzania) consist mainly of dry acacia woodland. As in southern Tanzania, predators tend to be difficult to see, but elephant are found in profusion: before the poaching of the 1970s and 1980s, some 30 000 elephant lived in Tsavo. Animals associated with this region include lesser kudu, gerenuk, common waterbuck and fringe-eared oryx. The olive baboon found west of the Rift Valley is replaced by the yellow baboon.

The semi-desert reserves of northern Kenya are the most alluring to visitors hoping to see rarer animals. Samburu, the most accessible of these reserves, supports such animals as Grevy's zebra, reticulated giraffe, Beisa oryx, Guenther's dik-dik and gerenuk. This area is also particularly good for predators. In addition to more widespread species such as lion and leopard, it is the best place in East Africa to see nocturnal creatures such as golden jackal, small-spotted genet, striped hyena and aardwolf. The moister Meru National Park lies in a transitional zone and thus supports a mix of northern and southern species.

Forest reserves

Forest reserves offer a different sort of wildlife viewing to the traditional game reserves. The forests of East Africa can be divided into three broad types: coastal, montane and West African. The most accessible coastal forests are Sokoke and Shimba Hills. Montane forest is generally found at altitudes between 2 000 m and 3 000 m and occurs on the slopes of Mounts Kenya, Kilimanjaro, Meru, Elgon and the Aberdares, as well as several less well known ranges. Forests with West African affinities include Kakamega in Kenya, the forests around Lake Tanganyika and most Ugandan forests.

The beautifully marked black-and-white colobus monkey is perhaps the most characteristic animal of the East African forest, and quite awesome when seen swinging between trees with its white tail streaming behind. Another common and widespread primate is the blue monkey (also called Syke's or samango monkey), various races of which are found in most forests in the region. Other animals which commonly occur in forests are buffalo, elephant, leopard, bushbuck, giant forest hog, bushpig, several types of duiker, bushbaby and small predators. The beautifully marked bongo antelope, a West African species, is found in a few Kenyan forests: the Cherengani Hills, the Aberdares and Mount Kenya.

Many of East Africa's montane and coastal forests have been isolated from each other for thousands of years and so they exhibit a high degree of endemism. This is particularly notable in birds and plants: the Taita Hills in Kenya, for instance, support a thrush and white-eye never recorded elsewhere, and there are at least three birds whose range is restricted to Sokoke Forest. In the remote Udzungwa mountains of Tanzania, three new species of bird have been discovered in the last decade and a new genus of francolin was discovered as recently as 1993! Endemicity is also noted in mammals: the selfsame Udzungwa mountains support two unique races of monkey; Ader's duiker and Zanzibar red colobus monkeys are restricted to Sokoke and one forest on Zanzibar.

Primate diversity is greatest in West African-affiliated forests. In western Kenya, redtailed and De Brazza's monkeys are found alongside the more widespread blue monkey and black-and-white colobus monkey, and at night you may also see the sloth-like potto. In Uganda's Kibale Forest, these species are supplemented by red colobus monkey, grey-cheeked mangabey and L'Hoest's monkey.

Western Uganda is home to two of Africa's three ape species. The common chimpanzee is widespread west of Lake Victoria, where it lives in forests such as Kibale, Chambura, Bwindi, Budongo and Semliki, as well as on the slopes of the Ruwenzori and Virunga mountains and the Tanzanian shore of Lake Tanganyika. The mountain gorilla is restricted to Bwindi and the Virunga mountains, while the eastern lowland race of gorilla may occur in the Semliki Forest.

For upmarket tourists, the best way of seeing forest animals is to stay at one of the tree hotels in the Aberdares or at Mount Kenya. These no longer offer frequent sightings of real forest rarities such as bongo antelope and giant forest hog but they do allow one to watch animal behaviour at close quarters.

For budget travellers, the best way to see these reserves is on foot. Forest reserves where walking is permitted include Kakamega Forest, Saiwa Swamps (also the place to see the localised swamp-dwelling sitatunga antelope), Mount Kenya, Mount Kilimanjaro, Mount Meru, Sokoke Forest, Green Crater Lake (near Lake Naivasha) and Kibale Forest (Uganda).

SPECIAL INTERESTS

Mountains

Kilimanjaro, the highest mountain in Africa, lies on the Kenya-Tanzania border, though its peak is in Tanzania and it may only be climbed from that side of the border. East Africa also contains Africa's second, third and fifth highest mountains: Mount Kenya (in Kenya), Margherita Peak (in the Ruwenzoris on the Uganda-Zaïre border) and Mount Meru (in Tanzania).

Any reasonably fit adult can hike to the top of Mount Meru or Mount Kilimanjaro, but the peaks of Mount Kenya and the Ruwenzoris require some technical climbing ability. Hikers can reach Lenana Point, the third highest peak on Mount Kenya, and there is a six to seven-day hiking trail through the forest and moorland zones of the Ruwenzoris.

It is more expensive to organise hikes in Nairobi than from the base of the mountains, but the advantages of doing so will outweigh the costs if your time is limited or you don't want to use public transport.

Technical climbers seeking further information should contact the Mountain Club of Kenya at PO Box 45741, Nairobi; tel: (02) 501747. Their *Guide to Mount Kenya and Kilimanjaro* (Ed. Iain Allen, 1991) is highly recommended to climbers and hikers alike and is available in any good Nairobi bookshop. Technical climbs of Mount Kenya and other more obscure ranges can be organised through most Nairobi tour operators.

Anyone intending to climb one of these mountains is strongly advised to read the section on mountain health in chapter two.

Hiking and walking

Most hikers visiting East Africa stick to the well-established trails up the mountains covered above, but the opportunities for off the beaten track (and less single-mindedly vertical) hiking are enormous. There must be few people who know the back hills of Kenya as well as David Else. His *Mountain walking in Africa 1: Kenya* (Robertson McCarthy) could keep you busy for months. For hiking further afield, the most useful book is Hilary Bradt's *Backpackers Africa: eastern and southern* (Bradt, 4th edition 1994).

East Africa offers unlimited opportunities for unstructured rambling. Lake Naivasha is a good base for day walks, with Hell's Gate National Park, Green Crater Lake and Mount Longonot all nearby. But you can walk anywhere in Kenya outside of the game reserves; there is no more delightful way to see a country than wandering casually off the beaten track. Rural Kenyans are remarkably friendly and there's little to worry about in terms of security. There's little point in recommending individual spots: as you page through this guide, you can easily pick out the sort of places you'd like to spend a day or two exploring on foot.

History and archaeology

The Rift Valley is thought to be where human life evolved. Sites like Olduvai Gorge in Tanzania and Koobi Fora near Lake Turkana have produced fossil remains of hominids that date back more than three million years, and dozens of sites in the region are rich in Stone Age tools. The best places to see early hominid skulls are the national museums in Nairobi and Dar es Salaam. Accessible Stone Age sites include Hyrax Hill near Nakuru and Olorgasailie south of Nairobi.

The two most significant East African civilisations of the early half of this millennium were the Swahili city-states of the coast and the legendary Bachwezi kingdom of southern Uganda. Ample evidence of the Bachwezi kingdom remains in the form of earthworks and fortifications, and although these sites are poorly known among tourists they are reasonably accessible; see my *Guide to Uganda* (Bradt 1994) for details.

The coastal city-states are far easier to see. Many of them are still active cities (Mombasa and Malindi were both notable centres in pre-Portuguese times, though little physical evidence of this remains), and the East African coast is dotted with ruins of mosques and cities dating back to between the 10th and 15th centuries. The easiest of these to visit, and one of the finest examples of the period, is Gedi, near Watamu, an extensive jungle-bound ruin containing several large semi-intact mosques. The ancient town of Lamu is also of interest to historians, not so much for any particular antiquities (though the nearby Takwa Ruins are well worth a look) but because it has retained so much of its traditional atmosphere.

There are dozens of other interesting sites in Kenya. Serious scholars or enthusiastic tourists are advised to contact the national museum in Nairobi or Fort Jesus Museum in Mombasa for further information.

Birds

East Africa has a marvellously rich avifauna, with over 1 000 bird species recorded in Kenya alone and about 1 500 in the whole region. Dazzling it may be, but the diversity can prove daunting to the first-time visitor trying to identify species, a situation which isn't helped by the lack of a truly comprehensive field guide. Serious birdwatchers will need at least a day in any given habitat merely to familiarise themselves with the more common species.

It's fair to say that almost anywhere in East Africa offers rewarding bird-watching to the first-time visitor. Even in the suburbs of Nairobi one can see turacos, forest hornbills and a variety of weavers and robins. Nevertheless, a few places stand out.

A good starting point for bird-watchers would be itinerary three through the Rift Valley and western Kenya. It's difficult to think of a better introduction to Kenya's birdlife than Lake Naivasha. More than 400 species have been recorded in the area and the field guides' bias towards species found near Nairobi makes identification easier than in most parts of the country. Lake Baringo is even better in terms of diversity as it lies in a transitional zone (even on my fifth visit to the lake I added 10 species to my life list) but the presence of northern species can make identification difficult. The checklist on sale at the Lake Baringo Club is an invaluable aid.

The most alluring and frustrating of East Africa's bird habitats is forest. The forests on Mount Kenya and in the central highlands are excellent, but species diversity increases further west as East African birds are supplemented by those more typical of West Africa. For this reason, Kakamega Forest in western Kenya should be on every bird-watcher's itinerary. The forests of western Uganda are even better than Kakamega, but the lack of experienced guides makes them difficult going for first-time visitors, and access can be a problem. The exception is Kibale Forest, where there are reasonably knowledgeable guides, though it will be some years before they catch up with the guides at Kakamega.

Many of Kenya's upmarket lodges have staff members who are competent to lead bird walks in the lodge grounds or, by arrangement, accompany visitors on drives. Block Hotels are particularly good in this respect, with resident ornithologists at the Lake Baringo Club, Outspan and Lake Naivasha Hotels, and good part-time guides at most of their other lodges.

All of Kenya's game reserves offer good bird-watching and they are especially rich in raptors. Samburu is perhaps the most rewarding game reserve in birding terms. Not only is it the best place to see unusual northern desert species such as vulturine guineafowl and Somali bee-eater, but the riverine forest supports a rich variety of woodland and forest species.

As a bird enthusiast who has had his name muddied by the acts of less considerate devotees, I am bound to point out that when you travel on an organised safari it is unreasonable to expect your companions to share your priorities. For most visitors to East Africa, a safari is a once in a lifetime opportunity to see lions and elephants in their natural habitat. Larks and pipits fall a very poor second. It is possible to see plenty of birds without annoying everyone in sight (I saw over 100 species on a recent safari to Masai Mara without once asking the driver to stop) but if you don't think you can restrain your twitching, then for your own sake, the sake of your potential companions, and for the good name of bird-watchers worldwide, hire a vehicle or pay the extra to do a customised safari. Most safari companies will supply you with a knowledgable guide if you specify your interest. Nairobi companies that specialise in upmarket ornithological safaris are Bateleur Safaris, PO Box 42562; tel: (02) 227048; fax: (02) 891007 and East African Ornithological Safaris, PO Box 48109, tel: (02) 48772.

Fishing

Kenya's coast is rated highly by game fishermen. The most sought after fish are similar to those found off the Zululand coast (though known by different names), but here they are found in much greater profusion. The best fishing is in the Pemba Channel off Shimoni near the Tanzanian border. There is also excellent fishing in the Watamu and Malindi areas. The major tourist hotels in all these places can organise fishing trips by motorboat.

Rusinga and Mfangano islands in Lake Victoria both have upmarket game fishing resorts which do fly-in trips from Nairobi and Masai Mara. The main attraction here is the introduced but now abundant Nile perch, the largest freshwater fish in the world (the Lake Victoria record is 86 kg). There is also good fishing in many of the rivers in the Central Highlands: the Naro Moru Lodge in Naro Moru and Izaak Walton Inn in Embu are useful contacts here.

Mountain biking

Mountain biking is an increasingly popular way of travelling, opening up all sorts of exciting possibilities which are effectively off-limits to travellers using public transport. Taking a bike with you to Kenya may present difficulties: airlines have erratic attitudes to this sort of thing and you should discuss packing requirements and charges well in advance. Alternatively, you could rent or buy a second-hand bike in Nairobi, and sell it when you leave. Try Gitonga Cycle Dealers, Landhies Road, Nairobi; tel: (02) 761573 for second-hand bikes or Bike Treks (see address below) for rental.

Once in the country, biking around should present few difficulties. When you are covering large distances, buses and matatus will carry bikes on the roof for a small charge. A book called *Cycling Kenya* (Bicycle Books, San Francisco) contains all sorts of useful advice for cyclists as well as suggesting several routes.

Several Nairobi companies now run mountain bike safaris, perhaps a more realistic option than bringing or buying a bike if your time in the country is limited.

Bike Treks, PO Box 14237; tel: (02) 891007 or book through Let's Go Travel

Hiking and Cycling Kenya, Arrow House, Koinange Street, PO Box 39493; tel: (02) 218336; fax: 224212

Safaris Unlimited, Jubilee Insurance Building, Mama Ngima Street, PO Box 24181; tel: (02) 891168; fax: 891113

Snorkelling and diving

The reefs off the East African coast are rated by enthusiasts to be surpassed only by the Red Sea and Great Barrier Reef. Not having snorkelled elsewhere, I cannot make comparisons, but what I can say without reservation is that swimming amid a dazzling swirl of colourful reef fish is a spectacle equal to any offered on the mainland. Many divers also see sand sharks, skates, octopi and squids.

There are coral reefs on most accessible parts of the Kenyan coast, generally within a kilometre or so of the shore, and it is never a problem to locate a snorkel, mask and flippers. They can be hired for a few dollars at any tourist beach – just ask around. Although you can snorkel virtually anywhere, the best reefs are in the Watamu Marine National Reserve, reached from either Watamu or Malindi. It's possible to combine a snorkelling trip at Watamu with a cruise on a glass-bottomed boat.

Scuba diving can be arranged through hotels on the beaches around Mombasa, Watamu and Malindi. Inexperienced divers can do three-day courses with qualified instructors, and will receive a certificate at the end of it.

When snorkelling or diving, care should be taken not to damage the coral in any way. Coral is razor sharp and there are several coral-dwelling creatures which inflict painful, or even lethal, bites. Wear flippers or beach shoes, and don't poke about in the coral with your hands. Wear a T-shirt to stop your back from getting sunburnt.

A guide to the common reef fishes of the western Indian ocean and Kenya coast (K. Bock, Macmillan, 1978) includes good background information, tips on underwater photography, excellent colour photographs and descriptions of almost 200 species. It's available in most Nairobi bookshops. Buy it! The national parks booklet *Marine national parks of Kenya* is also useful, with species descriptions and sound practical advice.

Arts and crafts

A great variety of local craftwork is sold in the multitudinous curio stalls found in Nairobi, Mombasa, Arusha and every other tourist centre worth its salt. Among the more attractive items are the colourful hand-woven vyondo (baskets), copper bracelets, kikoi cloths, Ethiopian crosses, Masai beadwork necklaces and all manner of batiks. Most of the carvings are generally mass-produced trinketry. Look around, though, preferably at proper curio shops, and you'll find wonderful Makonde wood carvings from southern Tanzania and absorbingly grotesque masks from West Africa.

Prices at curio stalls are always negotiable, so ask at a few and haggle a bit to get a feel for the going rate before you actually buy anything. Contrary to many people's expectations, you can buy most things cheaper at the city market in Nairobi than at curio stalls along safari routes. If you are going to Tanzania, Arusha is the cheapest place to buy curios in East Africa, and the curio shops generally stock merchandise of reasonable quality.

4 NAIROBI

Telephone code: (02)

Kenya's capital city is a lively and cosmopolitan place, said to be the largest town between the Sahara and South Africa. Nairobi is reminiscent in some ways of a scaled-down but more frenetic and less parochial version of Johannesburg: both cities were founded in the late 19th century, and as a result they have a slightly rootless air and a compressed sense of history. Both cities also have an improbable setting, though in the case of Nairobi the reason for this lies not in any mineral wealth but in its strategic position on the Uganda railway.

Nairobi shares with Johannesburg a pleasantly temperate climate, determined by its altitude of about 1 800 m, and while the moist, forested highlands around Nairobi have far more intrinsic scenic appeal than the South African highveld, neither city boasts much in the way of tourist attractions. Nairobi is the main funnel for tourism into East Africa, but few people spend more time there than they have to.

As much as anything, tourists flee Nairobi because it is such an overwhelming introduction to East Africa. Tourists are the lifeblood of the city's many thieves and con artists, and of the plagues of safari touts and curio sellers who prowl the city centre. There's no denying that the incessant hassle and the risk of theft are enough to reduce the most phlegmatic soul to a paranoid wreck, but the instinct to flee is an overreaction. Curio sellers and safari touts can be deflected with a touch of humour, and, while one should never underestimate the ingenuity of Nairobi's thieves, a bit of common sense goes a long way towards minimising the risk of theft.

Frankly, I like Nairobi. There is a cavalier good humour about the place, an air of relaxed hedonism, which I find irresistible. I'm definitely in the minority on this score, but I'm by no means alone. Come to Nairobi overland from Europe or southern Africa, or return there after a dusty safari or climbing Mount Kenya, and the glitter outweighs the squalor. The excellent restaurants, ubiquitous cold beers and well-stocked shops alone make Nairobi stand out from the rest of Africa. Nairobi has its share of slums; the poverty of many of its residents is evident; but it is no tinpot capital. This is a busy, lively, exciting city. Such places are rare in Africa.

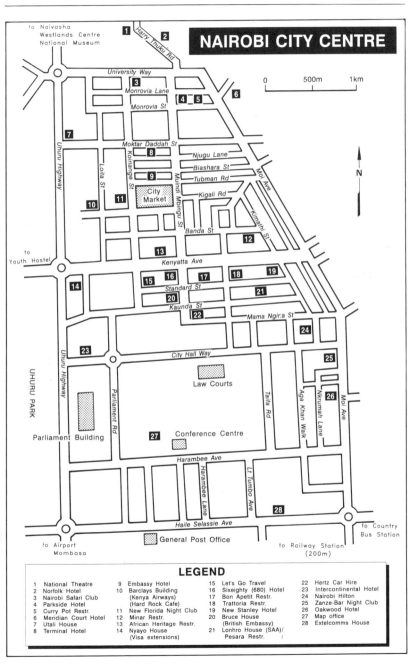

NAIROBI CITY CENTRE

to Naivasha
Westlands Centre
National Museum

0   500m   1km

N

UHURU PARK

Parliament Building

Law Courts

Conference Centre

General Post Office

to Youth Hostel

to Airport
Mombasa

to Railway Station
(200m)

to Country
Bus Station

University Way
Monrovia Lane
Monrovia St
Moktar Daddah St
Njugu Lane
Biashara St
Tubman Rd
Kigali Rd
Banda St
Kenyatta Ave
Standard St
Kaunda St
Mama Ngir.a St
City Hall Way
Harambee Ave
Haile Selassie Ave

Harry Thuku Rd
Uhuru Highway
Loita St
Koinange St
Muindi Mbingu St
Moi Ave
Kimathi St
Uhuru Highway
Parliament Rd
Taifa Rd
Aga Khan Walk
Nkrumah Lane
Moi Ave
Harambee Lane
Lt Tumbo Ave

City Market

LEGEND

1 National Theatre	9 Embassy Hotel	15 Let's Go Travel
2 Norfolk Hotel	10 Barclays Building	16 Sixeighty (680) Hotel
3 Nairobi Safari Club	(Kenya Airways)	17 Bon Apetit Restr.
4 Parkside Hotel	(Hard Rock Cafe)	18 Trattoria Restr.
5 Curry Pot Restr.	11 New Florida Night Club	19 New Stanley Hotel
6 Meridian Court Hotel	12 Minar Restr.	20 Bruce House
7 Utali House	13 African Heritage Restr.	(British Embassy)
8 Terminal Hotel	14 Nyayo House	21 Lonhro House (SAA)/
	(Visa extensions)	Pesara Restr. :

22 Hertz Car Hire	
23 Intercontinental Hotel	
24 Nairobi Hilton	
25 Zanze-Bar Night Club	
26 Oakwood Hotel	
27 Map office	
28 Extelcomms House	

CRIME AND THEFT

A remarkable number of tourists get ripped off in some way or another within a day or two of arriving in Nairobi. Don't let this put you off – personally, I've never felt that threatened there – but do read the following advice. With a bit of common sense and forethought, Nairobi is no more dangerous than any large city.

While such things are difficult to quantify, anecdotal evidence suggests that the worst area for mugging is the triangle of streets between Moi Avenue and River Road. Many budget travellers are drawn to this area for the cheap accommodation and earthy atmosphere, and a high proportion get mugged. Walking around this area isn't particularly risky in daylight, but towards dusk and after dark it verges on asking for trouble. My advice is simple: find a room elsewhere, certainly until you've settled into East Africa.

Nowhere in Nairobi can be considered safe at night. Taxis are cheap, safe and easy to locate, and I advise any short-stay visitor to make liberal use of them. Even if you are only going a couple of blocks, you should always take a taxi at night or if you are carrying valuables or large sums of money.

As a matter of course, whenever and however you arrive in Nairobi, catch a taxi from your arrival point to your hotel. Many travellers would consider this an extravagance, and it's probably true that the chance of being mugged in a crowd is small. But the thieves who proliferate at places such as bus stations do have legs – they can follow you to a quiet spot. They also have brains: carrying a rucksack is as good as announcing that you have all your valuables on your person. During my last trip to Kenya, I met three people who were mugged while carrying their luggage between a bus station and their hotel.

There are plenty of con artists in Nairobi. The most blatant are the money-changers who work the area around the New Stanley Hotel. Don't deal with them, and bear in mind that any communication beyond a blunt "No" – or, better, a KiSwahili "Sitaki" (I don't want) – marks you out as a new arrival. A more underhand category of trick involves bogus policemen offering you the option of arrest or a large fine. In any situation like this, demand to be taken to a police station to sort it out. Do not, however, allow yourself to be led up a quiet alley. A typical scenario is that you're approached in the street by a stranger who suggests you both go for a cup of coffee and a chat, then when the stranger departs you are descended on by "policemen" who claim you've been talking to a subversive.

Much as I hate to encourage distrust, Nairobi is the one place in East Africa where there is cause to be suspicious of anyone who approaches you on the street. Without being rude (they may, after all, be sincere) I would tell them I am busy. And remember that successful con artists must appear to be trustworthy: I'd be more wary of a smooth talker in a business suit than a drunk in rags.

One final thought. Everyone fancies their chances with new arrivals. You are less likely to be hassled if you are mistaken for an expatriate. A few words of Swahili will go a long way towards creating the right image, as will avoiding touristy clothes like a khaki safari suit or shorts and a T-shirt, and instead opting for trousers and a collared shirt or a skirt and blouse.

ACCOMMODATION

Accommodation is discussed under two headings: tourist class and budget.

Tourist class

Tourist class consists of luxury, upmarket and modest brackets.

Luxury bracket

Nairobi has several luxury hotels of international standard. The Norfolk Hotel, Harry Thuku Road, Lonhro Hotels; tel: (02) 335422 is the oldest, opened in 1904, and the favoured haunt of celebrities visiting Kenya. Although nothing of the original hotel remains (the oldest surviving wing dates to 1937), the hotel is strong on atmosphere and the service and food are impeccable.

The Nairobi Safari Club, University Way, PO Box 43564; tel: (02) 330621, is the Norfolk's closest rival in the city centre, with an exclusive atmosphere and all-suite accommodation. The other luxury hotels in central Nairobi are more transatlantic. The Nairobi Hilton, Mama Ngima Street, PO Box 30624; tel: (02) 334000, is affiliated with the international Hilton chain and is a distinctive landmark in the city centre. The Hotel Intercontinental, City Hall Way, PO Box 30353; tel: (02) 335550, also part of an international chain, has nice grounds but is rather bland.

The Nairobi Serena, Nyerere Road, Serena Hotels; tel: (02) 725111, a short walk from the city centre, is the most expensive option in Nairobi, but the elaborate decor and beautiful grounds opposite Central Park place it a notch or two above most of the city centre hotels.

About 15 km out of town, the Safari Park Hotel, Thika Road, PO Box 54038; tel: (02) 802493, is an unabashedly over the top hotch potch of African and international influences, and attractive in a vaguely surreal way, with large grounds, 21 restaurants (which between them leave few corners of the globe untasted), discos, piano bars and a couple of casinos. The nearby Windsor Golf and Country Club, Kigwa Road, Windsor Hotels; tel: (02) 802149, is altogether more mellow and countrified, a mock-Victorian building set in a large forested estate with an 18-hole golf course and immaculate facilities. Though a bit inconvenient if you're only passing through Nairobi, both these hotels are far better value than their central competitors.

Upmarket bracket

The New Stanley Hotel, Kimathi Street, Sarova Hotels; tel: (02) 333233, is one of the older hotels in town, and the Thorn Tree Café on its ground floor is the best known tourist landmark in central Nairobi. The New Stanley perches comfortably at the top of the upmarket bracket, both in quality and price. It's good value for money and a convenient place to spend a first night in Nairobi.

The more modest Sixeighty Hotel, Kenyatta Ave, PO Box 43436; tel: (02) 220592, is an unpretentious and functional tower block perfectly positioned for exploring downtown Nairobi. Similar in standard, but less shabby and not so convenient, is the Boulevard Hotel, Harry Thuku Road, PO Box 42831; tel: (02) 334071.

There are also a few options away from the city centre. The Panafric Hotel, Kenyatta Avenue, Sarova Hotels; tel: (02) 720822, is the most upmarket and closest to town, but for atmosphere you can't beat the Fairview Hotel, Bishops Road, PO Box 40842; tel: (02) 723211, a sensibly priced family-run place that was established in the 1930s and still retains something of a country flavour. Another established favourite, reasonably priced though due a spot of refurbishment, is the Jacaranda Hotel, Block Hotels; tel: (02) 448713, near the busy Westlands shopping mall.

Modest bracket

Two of the cheapest tourist-class hotels in the city centre, both acceptably comfortable and very convenient, are the bland Hotel Ambassadeur, Moi Avenue, Sarova Hotels; tel: (02) 336803 and the atmospheric creaky Oakwood Hotel, Kimathi Street, PO Box 40683; tel: (02) 332170. Even cheaper and also reasonably central is the Meridian Court Hotel, Murangu Road, PO Box 30278; tel: (02) 333916, with comfortable, apartment-like accommodation including cooking facilities. About 2 km out of town, the Silver Springs Hotel, Argwings Kodhek Road, PO Box 61362; tel: (02) 722451, is quietly unpretentious and reasonably priced.

Budget

There is no shortage of cheap accommodation in Nairobi, though budget travellers may need to look around before finding a vacant room. The Youth Hostel or, if you have a tent, Mrs Roche's are reliable fallbacks. Better still, especially if you are arriving after dark, make an advance booking at a modest hotel for your first night. When you arrive at the airport, catch a taxi to wherever you plan to stay.

Hostels

If you arrive in Nairobi on your own, there's a lot to be said for heading to a hostel. Nairobi is more fun (and safer) when explored in a group, and the hostels have an atmosphere conducive to meeting drinking mates or long-term travelling companions, and for catching up on the latest travel information.

Two hotels in the River Road area have dormitory facilities and a predominantly traveller clientele. The Iqbal Hotel, Latema Road, PO Box 11256; tel: (02) 220914, is clean, secure, and very popular (it's often booked up a day or two ahead). The New Kenya Lodge, River Road, PO Box 43444; tel: (02) 222202, is decidedly more low-life and security can be a problem. One reservation about staying at either hotel, at least until you are attuned to Nairobi, is that they are located in prime mugging territory.

Of the out of town hostels, the pick is the Youth Hostel, Ralph Bunche Road, PO Box 48661; tel: (02) 723012. Previously rather claustrophobic, it has recently been rebuilt and now boasts several large dormitories and a great rooftop with views over the surrounding leafy suburbs. Facilities include lockers (provide your own padlock), an equipped kitchen (food can be bought at a supermarket 500 m away) and a room where you can store luggage for a nominal fee. Alcohol is banned and no food is served, but the Silver Springs Hotel around the corner serves inexpensive food and cold beer, and there is also a good Indian restaurant in a nearby office block. There is no curfew.

Mrs Roche's, in a private garden on Third Parkland Avenue, is, apparently, something of a legend among travellers. The shaggy-haired, my-air-ticket-was-cheaper-than-yours atmosphere feels a little anachronistic, but it's unquestionably very relaxed and the private rooms, dormitories and campsite are all very cheap.

The YMCA, State House Road, PO Box 63063; tel: (02) 724066, is another good place to meet travellers. The private rooms are reasonably priced and facilities include a swimming pool and an inexpensive restaurant.

Cheap hotels

The best cheap hotels are west of Moi Avenue, near the market and Jevanjee Gardens. They're all a bit scruffy, but clean and secure, with self-contained rooms and hot water. These hotels tend to fill up early in the day, so get there early or book in advance. Recommended are the Terminal, Moktar Daddah Street, PO Box 43229; tel: (02) 228817; the Embassy, Tubman Road, PO Box 47247; tel: (02) 224087; and the Parkside, Monrovia Street, PO Box 53104; tel: (02) 333445.

The dozens of cheap hotels east of Moi Avenue are, as a rule, more down-market than the hotels listed above. There are, however, several exceptions: the Africana, Dubois Street, PO Box 47827; tel: (02) 220654; the Dolat, Mfangano Street, PO Box 45613; tel: (02) 222797; the Hermes, Haile Selassie Ave, PO Box 62997; tel: (02) 340066; the Paris, Mfangano Street, PO Box 72632; tel: (02) 337483; Sagret, River Road, PO Box 18324; tel: (02) 333395; and Samagat, Taveta Road, PO Box 10027; tel: (02) 220604.

Recommended cheap hotels out of the town centre include the Westview, PO Box 14680; tel: (02) 448471 near Westlands Shopping Mall, the Sagret Equatorial, PO Box 18324; tel: (02) 21786; and Heron Court, PO Box 41848; tel: (02) 720740, both on Milimani Road. The Heron Court is particularly worth looking at for long stays.

RESTAURANTS

One of the joys of Nairobi is the quality, diversity and relative cheapness of its restaurants. A variety of Asian, African and European cuisines are represented, and vegetarians and hardened carnivores are both well catered for. With so many places to choose from, the following listing serves to highlight a few of the more unusual restaurants, and those which offer particularly good value. It's by no means comprehensive, and new restaurants open and established ones close: don't be afraid to experiment.

Eating out in Nairobi is inexpensive by any standard. Even if you are on a budget, don't make the mistake of bypassing places with a plush exterior and bow-tied waiters on the assumption that they will be out of your price range.

African Heritage, Kenyatta Avenue. Large African buffet lunches, Ethiopian food on Friday evenings and arguably the best chicken tikka and naan bread in the city centre. An added attraction at Sunday lunches is the live African music.

Alan Bobbe's Bistro, Caltex House, Koinange Street. One of Nairobi's top restaurants, established in 1962, this serves matchless French cuisine.

Bon Apetit, Standard Street. Better than average curries and steaks. There's no skimping on the portions and it's cheap even by Nairobi's standards – thoroughly good value.

The Carnivore, Langata Road. Nairobi's most famous restaurant, and a popular place to conclude a safari. The main draw is an all-you-can-eat buffet centred around game meat, but rather surprisingly the vegetarian dishes have received a big thumbs-up from several vegetarians I've spoken to. There's more moderately priced food and a cosmopolitan disco at the *Simba Grill* next door. The Carnivore is about 5 km out of town: there are plenty of taxis hanging about outside.

Curry Pot, Monrovia Street. Inexpensive Indian food, popular with locals and budget travellers alike.

Daas Ethiopia Restaurant. Not to be missed if you have yet to try Africa's most distinctive cuisine. Ethiopian food consists of spicy stews eaten with a vast pancake-like expanse of sour-tasting njera bread. At the Daas, your meal is accompanied by exuberant traditional Ethiopian singers and dancers. Previously in the defunct Grosvenor Hotel, the Daas is now in a remote suburban house. Take a taxi.

Garfunkel's, Kenyatta Ave. Relatively pricey but good Chinese food.

Hong Kong, Fedha Towers, Standard Street. Cantonese dishes.

Ibis Grill, in the Norfolk Hotel. One of Nairobi's best restaurants, serving international cuisine with an African flavour.

Lord Delamere Terrace, in the Norfolk Hotel. Worth visiting as much for the swanky atmosphere as the food, though the pizzas are the best

I've had in Nairobi and surprisingly moderately priced. It sells draught beer on tap.

Malindi Dishes, Gaborone Road. Nairobi's leading Swahili restaurant, especially worth visiting if you're not going to the coast.

Mandy's, Emperor Plaza, Koinange Road. More than adequate curries and meat dishes, dirt cheap.

Maneaters and *Lobster Pot*, Imenti House, Moi Avenue. Good, up-market restaurants sharing premises and specialising in game meat and seafood respectively.

Mayur, in the Supreme Hotel, Keekorok Road. Superb and inexpensive Indian vegetarian buffets.

Minar, Banda Street. Good affordable Indian food, with a wide selection of vegetarian and meat dishes. Convenient if you are staying in the city centre.

Pesara Sandwich Market, Lonhro House, Standard Street. A snackery serving the best coffee in central Nairobi, yummy wholewheat sandwiches and good salads.

Safari Park Hotel, Thika Road. Boasting over a dozen restaurants serving a wide variety of cuisines (African, Chinese, French, Indian, Italian, Japanese, Korean) and a Carnivore-style carvery, this is an interesting place to spend an evening away from the city centre. A free shuttle bus service runs between Kenyatta Ave (around the corner from Woolworths) and the Safari Park Hotel every hour or so.

Steak House Ltd, Chester House, Koinange Street. A well-above average steakery, with 1,2 kg T-bones likely to set alight the eyes of any hardened carnivore.

Thorn Tree Café, in the New Stanley Hotel. A popular central meeting point, and a good place to stop for cake and coffee, but meals are overpriced.

Trattoria, Standard Street. This Italian restaurant is one of the most popular places in the city centre, with a varied menu and excellent food at reasonable prices.

Wimpy, Kenyatta Avenue. Exactly what you would expect: burgers and French fries, all very cheap.

NIGHTLIFE

Nightlife for most visitors to Nairobi revolves around eating out, and it's an excellent place to do this. There are dozens of places in the city centre where you can round off a meal with a cold beer. Of the larger hotels, the first floor open-air bar of the Sixeighty Hotel lacks atmosphere, but it's central and pleasant. The Lord Delamere Terrace in the Norfolk Hotel is livelier and there's draught beer. The Pub, a local businessmen's hangout on Standard Street, is also worth checking out.

There is live Zaïrian and Kikuyu music most nights somewhere in Nairobi, but it can be difficult to track down. Look for advertisements in the entertainment pages of the *Daily Nation*. Places which sometimes host live music in the city centre are the Zanze-Bar, Moi Avenue and Garden Square Restaurant, City Hall Way. There's usually more going on out of town: the Bombax Club, Ngong Road; tel: (02) 565691; Cantina Club, Wilson Airport, Langata Road; tel: (02) 506085 and Sportsview Hotel, Thika Road; tel: (02) 803890 are all worth giving a ring.

A popular out of town nightspot is the Simba Grill next to the Carnivore Restaurant. It gets very loud and lively as the evening progresses and attracts a mixed crowd of well-to-do locals, expatriates and tourists. There's occasional live music but normally it's a disco. You need to get there by taxi; there will be plenty waiting outside when you want to leave.

Otherwise, Nairobi's nightspots run the gamut from a bit tacky to utterly squalid: in many, prostitutes and wannabees (they can't all be making a living?) outnumber the conventional clients. This shouldn't dissuade you from exploring – it's all pretty good humoured and, in terms of safety, there's far more to worry about on the streets outside – but you should know what to expect. You're less likely to receive unwanted attention if you go in a group, preferably of mixed gender.

Starting with the merely tacky, Buffalo Bill's, in the Heron Court Hotel on Milimani Road, is an unabashed pick-up joint, but there are plenty of other tourists and the open-air bar is a relatively sedate introduction to Nairobi's nightlife. The Florida 2000 on Moi Avenue is louder and brasher, but some relief from the sound system can be found at an open-air bar and restaurant behind the dance floor. Its sister club, the New Florida on Koinange Street, is even louder and sleazier; great for a reggae mindblast perhaps, but conversation tends to be limited. The newly-opened Hard Rock Café in the Barclays Plaza on Loita Street sounds like it's worth a visit.

There are plenty of bars in the River Road area, of which the Modern Green Day and Night Club on Latema Road has acquired a slightly self-perpetuating reputation with budget travellers. The atmosphere is friendly, boozy and slightly frantic, and there is certainly no shortage of local colour, but it's difficult not to feel a little voyeuristic.

BUSES AND TAXIS

You can be assured of finding a taxi within minutes wherever you are in Nairobi. The largest concentrations are outside the Sixeighty, Norfolk, New Stanley and Hilton hotels, and at the railway station, airport and most bus stations. Bargaining is the order of the day. Any hotel will be able to ring for a taxi if none is available outside.

Numbered buses and matatus cover every conceivable route in Nairobi. The driving is lunatic, but serious accidents are unlikely in Nairobi's ponderous traffic. One should, however, be wary of pickpockets. Otherwise, buses and matatus are a cheap, straightforward and efficient way of getting around, at least if you are spending some time in Nairobi. Short-stay visitors are advised to stick to taxis.

SAFARI COMPANIES

There are over 500 tour operators in Nairobi, offering a wide variety of packages. A very useful, well-organised first contact, at least to get a feel for current prices and itineraries, is Let's Go Travel, Caxton House, Standard Street, PO Box 60342; tel: (02) 340331/213033; fax: 336890, which acts as an agent for dozens of operators and has prices for virtually every tourist-class hotel and safari option in Kenya.

Upmarket

The following are all respected and well-established upmarket safari companies.

Abercrombie and Kent, Bruce House, Standard Street, PO Box 59749; tel: (02) 334955; fax: 215752

Big Five Tours and Safaris, Phoenix House, Kenyatta Avenue, PO Box 30471; tel: (02) 29803

Flamingo Tours, Harambee Plaza, City Hall Way, PO Box 27927; tel: (02) 27927

Ker and Downey, cnr Busia and Enterprise Roads, PO Box 41822; tel: (02) 556466; fax: 552378

Pollman's Tours, Arrow House, Koinange Street, PO Box 45895; tel: (02) 337952; fax: 337171

Star Travel, New Stanley Hotel, Standard Street, PO Box 48225; tel: (02) 226996/220165; fax: 214371

United Touring Company (UTC), Kaunda Street, PO Box 42196; tel: (02) 331960; fax: 216181. UTC has desks at Jomo Kenyatta Airport, Intercontinental Hotel, Jacaranda Hotel, Nairobi Safari Club, New Stanley Hotel and Norfolk Hotel.

Universal Safari Tours (UST), Cotts House, Wabera Street, PO Box 49312; tel: (02) 221446

Budget

There are a number of good, well-established budget safari companies in Nairobi, but it can be difficult to distinguish them from the shoddy, fly-by-night operators who spring up and go bankrupt all the time. The following companies are all reputable, which doesn't mean that they are immune to error or don't return the odd dissatisfied client, but they are reliable and prepared to discuss refunds or extra time if things go wrong. Bear in mind, too, that the budget safari scene tends to be fast moving. The staff of cheaper hotels and hostels will recommend companies that offer them a good commission: other travellers are a more reliable source of current information.

Dallago Safaris, Mercantile House, Koinange Street, PO Box 75260; tel: (02) 212936; fax: 212936. Too new to recommend without slight reservation, but reasonable rates and daily departures make them worth a visit. All the reports I've heard are good.

Gametrackers, Kenya Cinema Plaza, Moi Avenue, PO Box 62042; tel: (02) 338927; fax: 330903. Standard game-viewing safaris plus camel trekking, cycling trips and climbing on Mount Kenya and the Aberdares.

Kenia Safaris, Jubilee Insurance Building, Kaunda Street, PO Box 19730; tel: (02) 223699; fax: 217671. Reliable, well-priced camping safaris on all the standard itineraries.

Safari Camp Services, cnr Koinange and Moktar Daddah Street, PO Box 44801; tel: (02) 228936; fax: 212160. Best known for their Turkana Bus, which has been running for close on two decades and remains good value. Their Wildlife Bus is also highly rated.

Savuka Safaris, Pan-Africa Insurance Building, Kenyatta Avenue, PO Box 20433; tel: (02) 215256/214904/225108; fax: 215016. A recommended first port of call for standard itineraries, with daily departures on several routes, a well-organised tented camp in Masai Mara and rates that compete with anyone.

Worldwide Adventure Ltd, Nginyo House, cnr Koinange and Moktar Daddah Street, PO Box 76637; tel: (02) 210024; fax: 332407. In addition to the usual itineraries, this company specialises in Turkana trips and 14 to 35 day mountain gorilla safaris.

Yare Safaris, Moi Avenue, PO Box 63006 Nairobi; tel: (02) 214099; fax: 213445. Specialists in trekking in northern Kenya. I've heard plenty of good reports about their week-long camel safari in the Maralal district. Departures are from Nairobi every Saturday – definitely worth checking out.

CAR RENTAL

Virtually any safari company can arrange car rental and there are also several specialist car hire firms. Cars can either be rented on a self-drive basis or with a driver. Most companies will only rent self-drive vehicles to people over 23 years of age in possession of a valid driving licence. Special arrangements must be made to take the vehicle out of the country.

Although there are several local car hire firms, there is a lot to be said for going to an international company such as Hertz or Avis. Rates are generally higher but the vehicles are normally properly maintained and backup is more extensive: Hertz, for instance, issue all customers with a list of garages countrywide licensed to maintain their vehicles. With several less reputable garages operating scams on unsuspecting tourists (they will go so far as to pretend to phone the rental company, let you ask for permission to have repairs done, only for you to find out when you return to Nairobi that you weren't speaking to the rental company at all and there will be no compensation) this sort of service is invaluable.

A list of recommended car hire firms follows:

Hertz/UTC, Fedha Towers, Muindi Mbingu Street, PO Box 42196; tel: (02) 214456; fax: 216871. There is a Hertz office at Jomo Kenyatta Airport; tel: (02) 822339

Avis, College House, University Way, PO Box 49795; tel: (02) 229576; fax: 215421

Glory Car Hire, Tubman Road, PO Box 66969; tel: (02) 225024

Europcar, Bruce House, Standard Street, PO Box 40433; tel: (02) 334722

Habib's Cars, Agip House, Haille Selassie Avenue, PO Box 48095; tel: (02) 220463; fax: 220985

EMBASSIES

For a full list of embassies in Nairobi, see *What's On,* a free pamphlet available from any tourist-class hotel. The embassies of countries covered in this guide are:

Rwanda: International House, Mama Ngima Street; tel: (02) 334341

Tanzania: Continental Towers, cnr Uhuru Highway and Harambee Road; tel: (02) 337618

Uganda: Phoenix House, Kenyatta Ave; tel: (02) 330801

Zaïre: Electricity House, Harambee Road; tel: (02) 229771

MAPS, NEWSPAPERS AND BOOKS

A good selection of local and foreign novels is available from the two bookshops on the corner of Kimathi Road and Kenyatta Avenue. These shops also stock a good range of field guides, travel guides to neighbouring countries and maps of the more popular game reserves and mountains. Several street vendors along Kimathi Road sell foreign newspapers.

CURIO SHOPPING

Curio shops are almost as prolific as safari companies. If you're prepared to bargain, though, you'll get better deals at markets. The largest concentration of curio kiosks is around the city market; take your time and you'll get curios very cheaply. The Masai market which takes place every Tuesday on the open area on the corner of Uhuru Highway and Kenyatta Avenue is also recommended.

MEDICAL PROBLEMS

For blood tests, visit Nairobi Laboratories in Pioneer House on Moi Avenue. The Nairobi Hospital, Argwings Kodhek Road; tel: (02) 722160, is rated the best in the city. Your hotel or embassy will be able to recommend doctors. There are pharmacies all over the city centre, most of them well stocked.

AIRLINES

A full list of airlines is included in the *What's On* booklet. The most likely to be of use to visitors are:

Kenya Airways, Barclays Plaza, Loita Street; tel: (02) 210771; fax: 337252

South African Airways, Lonrho House, Standard Street; tel: (02) 229663; fax: 227488

Air Tanzania, Chester House, Koinange Street; tel: (02) 214936

Uganda Airlines, Uganda House, Kenyatta Avenue; tel: (02) 221354; fax: 214744

BANKS AND FOREIGN EXCHANGE

There are banks dotted all over the city centre. The main branch of Barclays on Kenyatta Avenue has the only foreign exchange counter open on Saturday mornings. The foreign exchange counter at Jomo Kenyatta Airport is open 24 hours a day, seven days a week.

INTERNATIONAL PHONE CALLS AND FAXES

These can be made with an acceptable degree of success from Extelcomms House, Haile Selassie Avenue or, more expensively but with less fuss, at any tourist-class hotel.

VISA AND VISITOR'S PASS EXTENSIONS

This can be done while you wait at Nyayo House on the corner of Kenyatta Avenue and Uhuru Highway. How long you wait can be anything from five minutes to a couple of hours, depending on the length of queues – an early arrival helps (it opens at 8h30).

SIGHTSEEING IN AND AROUND NAIROBI

The National Museum

Definitely worth a visit, the National Museum houses an excellent pre-history section, with interesting reproductions of rock art from Tanzania. There isn't much in the natural history section you won't have seen if you've visited any other African museum before, though the marine life and bird sections are both very good. Also of interest are the ethnographic displays and paintings by Joy Adamson on the first floor, and the Lamu Gallery, which covers coastal history from the 9th to the 19th century. The snake park and aquarium outside are utterly missable.

The Railway Museum

A must for rail buffs, this is signposted and a 10-minute walk from the railway station. The more interesting displays relate to the building of the Uganda railway in the 19th century.

Nairobi National Park

This 117 square km reserve is the source of those publicity shots of lion or rhino with skyscrapers shimmering in the background. Remarkably, considering it is less than 7 km from the city centre, there is nothing artificial about Nairobi National Park: it is fenced on one side only, and animals move freely across the other designated boundaries to the adjacent Athi Plains. Almost every species of plains animal is found here – elephant are the only notable exception – and it is rated the best park in the country for seeing lion kills and black rhinoceros. More than 400 bird species have been recorded.

The main entrance to the park is at the Kenya Wildlife Services head-quarters on Langata Road. It can be visited in an ordinary saloon car; bird-watchers in particular would find it rewarding to hire a vehicle for a day's slow exploration. If you don't have a vehicle, half-day tours can be organised with any Nairobi operator. Hitching is also possible, especially on weekends when Nairobi residents are most likely to visit. There is no accommodation in the park.

Karen Blixen's house

The Danish baroness Karen Blixen moved to Kenya in 1918, where she farmed for several years. Her book *Out of Africa*, published in 1937, relates her experiences in Kenya and was the basis for the film of the same name. The house where she lived was restored and furnished in period style for the filming of *Out of Africa* and it is now a museum, with accompanying coffee shop, restaurant and nature trail. A must for Blixen cultists (they exist!). The house is 8 km out of town in the suburb of Karen; either catch a number 24 bus or else join one of the numerous guided tours available through Nairobi operators.

Ngong Hills

The Ngong Hills south of the city centre support substantial areas of forest, large mammals including buffalo, bushbuck and, reputedly, leopard, and a good variety of birds. The easily reached peaks offer great views back to Nairobi and across the Rift Valley. Unfortunately, mugging has become a serious problem in the area and what used to be a popular unescorted day walk can no longer be considered safe. You can, however, still drive to the highest peak (2 459 m), and the police station in Ngong village will generally provide an armed escort for walkers. Ngong lies on the D523 to Narok about 12 km from Nairobi. Buses numbered 111 and 126 travel between Nairobi and Ngong.

5 BETWEEN NAIROBI AND THE COAST

This chapter covers the arid, thinly populated and superficially unin-teresting part of Kenya which lies between Nairobi and the coast. Most tourists sleep through the region on the comfortable overnight train between Nairobi and Mombasa. The only major tourist attractions are Amboseli, Tsavo West and Tsavo East National Parks, but there are several possible diversions which will be attractive to visitors who have their own transport. There is probably no other part of Kenya that illustrates so clearly the truism that even in the most well-visited coun-tries a small sidestep off a well-travelled route can remove you com-pletely from the milieu. Travellers who are short of time but wish to stray from the beaten track will find this a rewarding area to explore.

THE NAIROBI-MOMBASA RAILWAY LINE

The most popular and straightforward way to get between Nairobi and Mombasa is on the daily train service which leaves in each direction at 19h00 and arrives at around 8h00 the next morning. This is easily the best train service in East Africa, with well-maintained first and second class sleepers. Bedding and excellent three course meals are included in the ticket price.

Trains from Mombasa cross the Athi Plains shortly before they arrive in Nairobi: herds of plains animals are guaranteed and a friend who travels on the train regularly has seen black rhinoceros on a number of occasions.

ALONG THE NAIROBI-MOMBASA ROAD

The 500 km tar road which connects Nairobi to Mombasa is in fair condition though badly potholed in parts. If you don't have a vehicle, you can travel directly between the towns on one of several overnight bus services for about half the price of a second-class rail ticket.

The only settlements of note along the Nairobi-Mombasa road are Athi River, Mtito Andei and Voi. Between Mtito Andei and Voi the road is flanked by Tsavo East and West National Parks, which together form the largest conservation area in Kenya. The area is rich in wildlife, particularly elephant, but few people see anything more exciting than baboons from the main road.

Machakos

Machakos lies in the Mau Hills 19 km east of the Mombasa road. It is the capital of Ukambani, the home of the Akamba, a Bantu-speaking group closely related to the Kikuyu and renowned for their industry and business acumen. In past times of drought, the Akamba supported themselves by bartering produce such as honey, metal tools and baskets for food grown in the neighbouring Kikuyu highlands. Surrounded by dry plains, Machakos defies expectations with its shady avenues and general appearance of fertility and activity. There is little in the way of tourist development, but it's a pleasant easy-going town and well worth a minor diversion. It is also the best place in Kenya to buy vyondo (baskets) – try Machakos Craft Centre (to your left as you enter the town along the main Nairobi road) or the craft shop opposite the market.

A steady stream of matatus and buses connects Machakos to Nairobi. There are several local lodgings in the town centre and a couple of more idiosyncratic options just outside. The Machakos Inn, 500 m along the Thika road, has rustic accommodation in bandas (local lodging rates) and a campsite. The newer and classier Five Hills Lodge is a comfortable cheap hotel less than 1 km out of town on the Kitui Road.

Hunter's Lodge

Named after John Hunter, the hunter turned conservationist who opened it, this was once a popular stop between Nairobi and Mombasa. Patronage and upkeep have declined in recent years – it's too far from Tsavo to be a viable base for exploring the park, and the speed of modern cars has nullified its original purpose – but the lodge is an attractive option if you are looking for a place to break the trip, or if you just feel like relaxing for a day in well-wooded grounds with a reed-fringed lake, rich in birdlife. Hunter's Lodge lies 160 km from Nairobi near Mikundu village. The tariffs put it in the cheap hotel bracket, which makes it very good value. Bookings can be made through Empress Fashion, Kimathi Street, PO Box 40683, Nairobi.

Mtito Andei

Mtito Andei lies halfway between Mombasa and Nairobi at the main entrance to Tsavo West National Park. Really no more than a village, Mtito Andei is nevertheless as glitzy as things get on this road, making it the obvious place to pull over for a cold drink, a bite to eat and a tankful of petrol. Otherwise, it's decidedly short on charm; the only reason you might want to prolong your stay is if you're heading into the national park. There is a campsite at the park entrance gate 500 m from the main road, and there are a few lodgings in the village. The only tourist-class accommodation, the modest Tsavo Inn, is booked through the Kilimanjaro Safari Club.

Voi

The largest town on the Mombasa road is the base for independent visits to Tsavo East and the place to pick up transport towards Taveta and the Taita Hills. There's no shortage of lodgings: Vuria Lodging and Sagala View Lodge are recommended. Alternatively, head out to the Tsavo East gate (an hour on foot) for camping or banda accommodation.

TSAVO EAST NATIONAL PARK

This comparatively obscure national park is the largest in Kenya: an 11 000 square km expanse of dry acacia scrub divided into two unequal parts by the Galana River. Tsavo East is famous for its large elephant herds and, until recently, it was the focus of Kenya's poaching war. The two-thirds of the park north of the Galana was closed to the public for several years due to the danger posed by poachers, while south of the river it was not unusual to come across tuskless elephant carcasses left to rot where they had been shot.

The elephants of Tsavo were controversial even in the 1970s, long before poaching took its toll. Cut off from their normal migration routes by cultivation, some 20 000 elephants crowded into the area, resulting in widespread environmental destruction, signs of which are still visible today. Some conservationists advocated selective culling, others preferred to let nature run its course. The poachers settled the issue. Tsavo East now has a population of about 4 000 elephants; even though poaching has ceased and the population is growing, it will be many years before it reaches the unmanageable proportions of the 1970s.

Tsavo East has a harsh and remote character. In all but the most developed areas you can drive for hours without seeing another vehicle. The characteristic red soil is covered by a thin acacia scrub, broken only along the wooded banks of the perennial Galana and seasonal Voi rivers. During the dry season the watercourses offer excellent game viewing, but animals tend to disperse after rain. Two particularly good spots for animals are the small lake below Mudanda Rock, which often attracts large herds of elephant during the dry season, and Kanderi Swamp near the Voi entrance gate.

Elephants are still present in herds of 50 or more, and herds of up to 1 000 buffalo are common. Other large herbivores include giraffe, Grant's gazelle, gerenuk, lesser and greater kudu, impala, fringe-eared oryx, Coke's hartebeest, eland and warthog. Lion are common in the vicinity of Aruba Dam, as are spotted hyena. Leopard, cheetah, striped hyena, hunting dog and smaller predators are seen infrequently.

Tsavo East offers surprisingly varied bird-watching. The comparatively lush riverine woodland, such as at Voi Gate, holds a selection of acacia-related barbets, hornbills, weavers and starlings. In the dry scrub deeper in the park you can expect to see a variety of birds such as raptors, shrikes and bee-eaters. Golden pipits are common. Birds favouring open water are most likely to be seen at Aruba Dam, while Kanderi Swamp is good for waterbirds that prefer cover.

How to get there

Organised safari

Tsavo East is increasingly popular with coastal tour operators. As it's only 110 km from Malindi to the Sala Gate, day trips are a viable option, though staying overnight will give you more chance of seeing a variety of animals.

Self-drive

The main access point is Voi Gate, 5 km from the Mombasa Highway. There is also a gate at Mtito Andei. It's worth noting that from Tsavo East you can continue on good dirt roads via Aruba Dam and Sala Gate to Malindi, a more interesting and direct route than the tarred road via Mombasa. Voi is 215 km by road from Malindi. The park north of the Galana River can be visited with permission from the park headquarters at Voi Gate. Self-drive visitors will be required to take a ranger with them.

Public transport/hitching

Tsavo East is accessible to travellers using public transport and there are plenty of good wildlife-viewing opportunities which don't involve finding lifts around the park. The main gate and campsite are an hour's walk from Voi town. From the gate you can make a day visit to Voi Safari Lodge using the staff bus, which passes the gate at 8h00 and returns from the lodge in the mid-afternoon.

The wardens at Voi are helpful with finding lifts further into the park. The obvious target is Aruba Lodge (see below): the lodge vehicle, which visits Voi most days, will provide a lift if there is space. Aruba Lodge is a magnet for safari vehicles so it is possible to line up a lift to Malindi; but bear in mind that tour drivers are understandably loath to pick up hitchers.

Accommodation

The upmarket Voi Safari Lodge (AT&H) is perched on a cliff a 10-minute drive from Voi Gate. A small waterhole below attracts a constant stream of antelope, as well as herds of buffalo and elephant during the dry season.

Tsavo Safari Camp (Kilimanjaro Safari Club) is a luxury tented camp 25 km from Mtito Andei Gate. It is reached by crossing the Athi River on a dinghy. The surrounding area is notable for birds as much as big game.

The modestly priced Crocodile Tented Camp, PO Box 500, Malindi; tel: (0123) 20481, lies in a shady stretch of woodland along the Galana River outside Gala Gate. Except at crocodile feeding time, when the minibus hordes descend, it's a pleasantly low-key retreat in an area abounding with game. Camping is permitted under a ramshackle shelter outside the camp's fence.

Aruba Lodge, PO Box 14982, Nairobi; tel: (02) 721382, is on the shore of Aruba Dam, the park's largest stretch of open water. The area teems with large mammals, especially in the dry season, and game viewing from the lodge is always good. There's plenty of birds around too. Accommodation is in comfortable but run-down cottages (cheap hotel rates) and there is a large campsite. A shop sells basic foodstuffs, beer and sodas.

Voi Gate Campsite is in a patch of acacia woodland teeming with birds and wildlife. Elephant pass through daily. Cheetah and lion are sporadic visitors. There are a few bat-infested bandas which campers can use at no extra charge – advisable under the circumstances. Basic provisions and sodas are sold at the staff canteen. If you have a vehicle, you can drive to Voi Safari Lodge after dark; this is one of the few places where night driving is allowed in a Kenyan national park. Taken slowly, it's a great opportunity to see nocturnal predators.

About 1 km outside Voi Gate, Lion Hill Camp, PO Box 298 Voi; tel: (0147) 2647, has a campsite and cottages, similarly priced to Aruba Lodge.

TSAVO WEST NATIONAL PARK

Separated from Tsavo East by the artificial barrier of the Mombasa Highway, Tsavo West is quite different in character to its neighbour. Here, dry plains give way to an undulating, volcanic landscape covered in tall grass and dense bush, and crisscrossed by an established and well-defined tourist circuit.

Tsavo West is crossed by several streams and rivers, and its animal population tends to be dispersed. The tall vegetation makes game spotting more challenging than in reserves such as Amboseli and Masai Mara; nevertheless, the full range of predators is present, as are other large mammals such as elephant, buffalo, Masai giraffe and Burchell's zebra. Commonly seen antelope include impala, fringe-eared oryx, waterbuck, bushbuck, Coke's hartebeest, Kirk's dik-dik and lesser kudu. When game viewing is erratic in the Ngulia and Kiligani areas, head for the roads around the Tsavo River near Kiteni.

Tsavo West is most memorable for its scenery. The vaguely unreal volcanic landscapes are in turn intimate and panoramic; even in the most developed part of the park, badly rutted roads and dense foliage ensure that a visit never feels like a milk run. A walking trail on the slopes of Chiamu Crater leads across a recent lava flow; no vegetation has yet taken hold, leaving it with the crumbling, black appearance of a slag heap. Chiamu is a good place to see lesser kudu darting into the undergrowth.

At Mzima Springs, a pair of clear pools are fed by underground water filtered by the volcanic rock of the Chyulu Hills. The pools are linked by a pipeline to Mombasa, and supply most of the town's water. Fringed by riparian forest and raffia palms, Mzima has an oasis-like quality. The pools are reached by a short nature trail from which you are likely to see vervet monkeys and a variety of birds. The top pool hosts a population of hippo and the bottom pool is frequented by crocodiles. Mzima's most attractive feature is a submerged viewing tank where you can watch large numbers of fish circle anti-clockwise. You may also see hippo from a fishy perspective, though they generally stay on the other side of the pool.

Birdlife in Tsavo West is less exciting than in other national parks, perhaps because there are few focal points, but you can expect to see a selection of raptors, ground birds and acacia-related species. Tsavo West lies on a major bird migration route and Ngulia Lodge attracts large numbers of migrants between October and January, especially after misty nights. A display in the lodge shows ringing operations performed there.

Lake Jipe, on the southwest border of Tsavo West, is discussed later in the chapter under the Taveta Road.

How to get there

Organised safari

Tsavo West is visited by several tour operators in Mombasa and Nairobi, often in conjunction with Amboseli National Park.

Self-drive

The main gate to Tsavo West is on the Mombasa Highway at Mtito Andei. It is supposedly possible to visit the park in a saloon car, but many of the roads are terrible: I wouldn't like to try it. The route between Tsavo West and Amboseli is discussed under Amboseli National Park.

Public transport/hitching

Any vehicle travelling between Nairobi and Mombasa can drop you off at Mtito Andei, where you can camp at the main gate. Hitching into the park shouldn't prove too difficult, but bear in mind that most vehicles will be heading for a pricey lodge.

Accommodation

There are two excellent upmarket lodges in Tsavo West, both booked through AT&H. Kilugani Lodge overlooks a busy waterhole with the Chyulu Hills and, on a clear morning, Kilimanjaro in the background.

Ngulia Lodge, the better of the two, is on a sheer cliff with wonderful views across the Yatta Plateau. A few metres from the bar, a waterhole attracts antelope and birds throughout the daylight hours. Lion, leopard and elephant are regular nocturnal visitors. All rooms face the waterhole and most have private balconies.

Finch-Hatton's Safari Camp, PO Box 24423, Nairobi; tel: (02) 882744, is named after the Robert Redford character in the film *Out of Africa*. This extremely luxurious tented camp lies next to a hippo pool (which, like Mzima, is fed by underground springs) with Kilimanjaro in the background.

Ngulia Safari Camp and Kitani Lodge each consist of half a dozen large cottages (cheap hotel rates) with equipped kitchens and bathrooms. Ngulia Camp is on a small cliff above a waterhole which, judging by the well-worn paths leading to it, should produce excellent nocturnal game-viewing. Kitani Lodge's setting – in a tranquil grove of acacia trees – may seem rather ordinary upon arrival, but you'll do a double take when the clouds lift and you realise that the mass rising on the horizon directly in front of your verandah is none other than Kilimanjaro. Bookings, not normally necessary, can be made through Let's Go Travel.

The little-used campsite 2 km from the park headquarters (junction three) has showers and running water. The surrounding woodland is rich in birds, and the water tank in the middle of the campsite bodes well for nocturnal animal visits. The campsite at Chyulu Gate isn't as nice. Travellers without a vehicle are allowed to camp at Mtito Andei Gate.

About 50 km south of Mtito Andei, a five-minute walk from the Mombasa road, there is a free campsite (no facilities) on the Tsavo River near Tsavo Gate.

THE TAVETA ROAD

Taita Hills

This isolated 2 205 m range, south of the Mombasa Highway, is excellent walking country, offering cool relief from the surrounding plains. Taita is the northernmost part of a chain of montane forest "islands" stretching from Gorongoza in Mozambique through ranges such as the Udzungwa and Usambara in Tanzania. Taita supports several localised bird species and two endemics: the Taita white-eye and Taita olive

thrush. The white-eye is common throughout the hills, but the thrush
is rare and possibly even extinct. It is confined to less than 5 square km
of forest on the slopes of Ngaongao and Mbololo, where it was last
seen in 1965. The forest is a good place to see a variety of warblers,
robins and greenbuls. Elsewhere, look out for the localised Taita falcon.
Mwasungia Guesthouse, 2 km from Wundanyi town and 5 km from
the Ngaongao Forest, is a good local lodging and a useful base for day
walks.

Taita Hills Wildlife Sanctuary

Despite the misleading name, this private sanctuary lies on the plains
south of the Taita Hills and holds similar species to Tsavo West. There
are two luxury lodges in the sanctuary and a luxury tented camp, all
run by Hilton Hotels. The best-known of these, Salt Lick Lodge, is a
fantastic cluster of raised cottages, linked together by suspension bridges
and connected to the outside world by a drawbridge. The nearby salt
lick and waterhole attract large numbers of animals, most notably elephant, especially during the dry season. This is Treetops transplanted
from the forest to the bush: the architecture falls distinctly along love
it or hate it lines, but the game viewing can be excellent.

Taveta

This dusty, rather isolated town lies near the Tanzanian border on the
scrubby plains below Kilimanjaro. What little tourist traffic Taveta sees
is mainly transient – people passing though on their way from the
Tanzanian border – but the wild west frontier town atmosphere is
unusual enough to make it a pleasant base from which to visit the
nearby lakes of Chala and Jipe. There are a few lodgings to choose
from, and cheap hotel rooms at the new Chala Lodge.

Lake Chala

This beautiful crater lake on the slopes of Kilimanjaro is hidden from
view until you're virtually at it. The sheer crater walls are heavily wooded
and the lake itself has startlingly clear water – local fishermen sit on
the side and look for fish, then dangle their rods to catch them. Swimming is safe, provided you're prepared to brave the mythical monsters
and the harmless – and quite possibly extinct – introduced pygmy
crocodiles that are said to inhabit the lake. Lake Chala is 8 km from

Taveta on the Oloitokitok road. You can walk there and back in a day and there's a fair chance of hitching a lift, but if you are hoping fc an early morning glimpse of Kilimanjaro, you might want to camp o the crater rim. There are a couple of suitable spots and it's said to b safe.

Lake Jipe

In direct contrast to Chala, Lake Jipe is large, shallow and fringed b dense papyrus beds. It lies on the little-visited southern border of Tsav West, with the Pare Mountains in Tanzania providing a backdrop. Ele phants are frequent visitors to the shore, especially in the dry season and hippo are everywhere, necessitating a certain amount of cautio when walking along the roads near the lake. Birdlife is good: in additio to typical acacia- and water-related species, the reed beds protect severa more localised birds such as black heron, black coucal and pygmy goose Less encouragingly, the mosquitoes are terrible and lake flies are abun dant. There is a motorboat for hire at the gate, but it's cheaper to mak a private arrangement to go out on a dugout and experience the at mosphere with one of the fishermen who live in the village 2 km from the gate.

Unless you time your trip to tie in with market days in Tavet (Wednesday and Saturday), reaching Lake Jipe can be problematic with out your own wheels. The lake lies on the Tsavo West and Tanzanian border about 30 km from Taveta; the only public transport is a bus to the village 2 km from the Tsavo entrance gate on market days. It's also worth looking out for the Jipe Lodge vehicle, which shows up to buy provisions on market days and whose driver is normally happy to give travellers a lift.

There are a few cheap basic bandas at the entrance gate, or you can camp. Warm sodas are sometimes available at the gate, and you can buy tilapia from local fishermen at the nearest village. Otherwise you should be self-sufficient. The only facility of note is a rudimentary shower.

The upmarket Lake Jipe Lodge, PO Box 31097, Nairobi; tel: (02) 227623, is good value and well off the minibus circuit.

AMBOSELI NATIONAL PARK

No image evokes the popular essence of East Africa so clearly as that of an elephant herd sweeping across a dusty plain with the perfectly formed, snowcapped peak of Kilimanjaro rising majestically in the background. And it is the desire to capture this image on film which makes Amboseli one of Kenya's most popular national parks. When Kilimanjaro appears from its cloudy mantle – normally in the early morning – t towers over Amboseli: this is the highest free-standing mountain in he world, rising an incredible 5 km above the surrounding plains.

On maps, Amboseli's dominant feature is the lake after which it is named. But Lake Amboseli is dry for years on end, and it is only transformed into a large shallow pan after exceptional rains, as happened in early 1993. There are two permanent swamps in Amboseli, Enkongo Narok and Olokenya, both near Ol Tukai village in the centre of the park. The remainder of the park is flat and dusty, thinly-vegetated, and prone to both drought and swamping. The bleak landscape has probably been degraded by the high level of tourism – the park is only 400 square km in area – and the environmental destruction caused by off-road driving. Scenically, Amboseli is at its best towards dusk, when the harsher aspects of the landscape are softened by a reddish glow as the sun filters through the dust, while a will-they, won't-they shroud of clouds offers tantalising glimpses of Kilimanjaro.

Amboseli offers excellent game viewing. The park's abundant elephant are often to be found foraging shoulder deep in the swamps alongside Burchell's zebra and buffalo, a fantastic and unusual sight. Other animals you can expect to see are waterbuck, Thomson's gazelle, wildebeest, Masai giraffe, hippo and warthog. Large predators are rare (lion and cheetah have been hunted out by local Masai, whose livestock they attack) and only spotted hyena are seen with any frequency.

The swamps hold a remarkable variety of water-related birds: greater and lesser flamingo, greater jacana, and a variety of herons, ibises, waterfowl and plovers (the localised long-toed lapwing is common). Between November and March you can also expect to see a variety of migrant waders and, with luck, any of the three migrant harriers hawking above the swamps. A series of causeways allows good access to the swamps. Elsewhere in the park, the near absence of cover vegetation makes for relatively poor bird-watching, though the acacia woodland around the lodges can be rewarding.

Amboseli is served by a good network of roads: it's too small to get lost in. The best game-viewing roads are those through the swamps. The viewpoint on Observation Hill overlooks Enkongo Narok Swamp and gives a panoramic view of the park.

How to get there

Organised safari

Amboseli features regularly on tours departing from Nairobi and Mom basa, often in tandem with Tsavo West. The park's relative proximit to Nairobi and small size make a one night safari from Nairobi a viabl option.

Self-drive

Amboseli is 200 km from Nairobi and 60 km from Namanga on th Tanzanian border. The tarred Nairobi-Namanga road is in good con dition. The dirt road between Namanga and the park is heavily rutted and comfortable only at lunatic speed, but dozens of vehicles drive along it every day.

Amboseli can be reached from Tsavo West via a monumentally awfu and disconcertingly changeable 120 km stretch of dirt road. The roac is sandy in parts, covered in volcanic rock elsewhere, and liberally sprinkled with potholes throughout. The moment you think you've mastered the situation it throws up something new. The minibuses tha hurtle along it at breakneck speed are not to be emulated unless you're familiar with the road. Taken slowly in a 4x4, you may not have the most enjoyable drive, but you'll get there. At least there is welcome relief halfway, near the junction with the Oloitokitok road, where a couple of curio stalls sell lukewarm tea and soda. Security in the area has been slightly suspect since a tourist vehicle was attacked in 1989 There has been no repeat of this incident, but vehicles travelling be tween Tsavo West and Amboseli are required to travel with an armed policeman (arranged for free at the park entrance gates).

Public transport/hitching

Amboseli is a realistic target for travellers without a vehicle, if only because the concentration of facilities in Ol Tukai reduces the risk of getting stuck or having to spend the night in an expensive lodge. Never theless, if you do get stuck in the park for a couple of days, you'll stil be forking out park fees without necessarily seeing a great deal of game.

There are regular minibuses from Nairobi to Namanga. The road to Amboseli forks from the town centre so it's easy to find a hitching post. The best bet for lifts is either a supply truck or park vehicle. There are several local lodgings in Namanga. The cheap Namanga River Hotel lates back to the colonial era and allows camping in its wooded grounds. Once in the park, the entrance to Ol Tukai village forms a funnel through which all transport must pass at some point.

Accommodation

There are two luxury lodges in Ol Tukai, a village-like conglomeration of buildings in a patch of acacia woodland in the centre of the park. Despite having attractive grounds, Amboseli Lodge is very ordinary for the price. Kilimanjaro Safari Lodge, though identically priced and under the same management, seems better. Both lodges are booked through the Kilimanjaro Safari Club.

The luxury Amboseli Serena Lodge (Serena Hotels) is an altogether more attractive prospect. It is well situated, overlooking a small swamp frequently visited by elephants, with flowering gardens designed to make it blend into the surrounding bush.

There are a couple of cheaper options in Ol Tukai village. Ol Tukai Lodge consists of several well-maintained cottages all with kitchen, shower and verandah. Charges are comparable to cheap hotel rates. Bookings can be made through Let's Go Travel, though the cottages are mainly used by expatriates, so there's little need to book except perhaps over long weekends. Budget travellers might want to ask about staying in the nearby and more basic drivers' bandas, where charges are similar to local lodgings.

There is a fenced campsite just outside Amboseli's southern boundary, about 15 km from Ol Tukai. It's an attractive spot, under-utilised by safari companies and set in an acacia thicket with individually cleared sites. There's a lot of game in the area. The only facilities are running water and longdrop toilets.

If you are staying in cottages or bandas at Ol Tukai, you can eat at either of the luxury lodges – there's no restriction on walking within the village. You can also get a solid three-course meal at the drivers' canteen for less than 10 per cent of the price of a lodge meal!

6 THE COAST

The East African coast conforms effortlessly to every travel brochure archetype of a tropical paradise; it is a seemingly endless succession of white sandy beaches, fringed by swaying coconut palms and lapped by the warm blue waters of the Indian Ocean. No big surprise, then, that the coast, as much as the game reserves, is a magnet for tourism in Kenya.

If your idea of a perfect holiday is lounging by the sea with a deck chair and book, you'll love Kenya's beaches. But there is more to the coast than a stock seaside holiday in tropical surroundings. Offshore, a string of reefs teems with a kaleidoscope of colourful fish, offering some of the best snorkelling and game fishing in the world. Forests like Sokoke are rich in endemic birds and mammals.

The East African coast has a strong sense of place and history, determined by the cultural cohesion of the Swahili people. The towns have a depth of character that is often lacking in their upcountry cousins, while mysterious jungle-bound ruins provide testimony to an ancient trade that has flourished intermittently since before the birth of Christ. The old-world pace of Swahili life is intertwined with a relentless humidity that makes even the slightest excursion take on the dimensions of a marathon race.

Most people arrive at the coast at Mombasa, the largest port in East Africa. Mombasa is on an island which is linked to the mainland by Nyali Bridge to the north and Likoni ferry to the south. On the mainland near Mombasa are Kenya's most popular and developed beaches: Nyali, Bamburi and Shanzu to the north; Shelly, Tiwi and Diani to the south. Other attractions on the south coast are Shimba Hills National Reserve and Wasini Island.

The coast north of Shanzu Beach is less developed for tourism. The most popular resorts, Watamu and Malindi, are more low-key and cheaper than the beaches around Mombasa. But the real gem of the north coast is the remote island town of Lamu, an ancient settlement which has changed little in the last few decades.

MOMBASA

Telephone code: 011

From a distance, Kenya's second most important city and largest port might appear to be a major tourist magnet. In fact, it is more of a funnel, as most visitors head directly to one of the nearby beaches. This is a shame. Mombasa's historical continuity and tropical languor are a world away from the breezy modernity of Nairobi. The town feels truly indigenous, as opposed to a Western transplant which has been Africanised almost by default.

Mombasa is a historical town. It has been the site of a trading centre since the time of the ancient Phoenicians and Romans, who knew it by a different name, while medieval Arab and Chinese documents indicate that it had become one of the major coastal trading centres at least as early as the 14th century. Since then it has passed through the hands of Portugal, Oman and Britain, all the time retaining its position of importance and developing a strongly individual character. It is well worth setting aside time to explore Mombasa before you head out to the beaches.

How to get there

Air

Kenya Airways fly daily between Nairobi, Mombasa and Zanzibar. Their office is on Nkrumah Road; tel: (011) 221251. An increasing number of international flights now arrive in Kenya at Mombasa. Kenya Airways flights from Johannesburg stop at both Nairobi and Mombasa.

Prestige Air Services on Nkrumah Road; tel: (011) 221443, fly daily to Lamu as well as having charter flights elsewhere.

Rail

The most popular way of travelling between the capital and the coast is by overnight train. Trains depart daily in both directions at 19h00 and take about 13 hours. It's advisable to book a day or two in advance, although I've managed to get same-day bookings on several occasions.

Road

There is plenty of transport along the Mombasa-Nairobi road, and also between Mombasa and Malindi. There are daily buses between Mombasa and Tanga and Dar es Salaam in Tanzania.

Sea

There are sometimes ferries between Mombasa and Zanzibar, but the situation changes regularly. Ask around for current information.

Dhows travel between several points along the coast, but they are neither safe nor comfortable for long journeys. In any event, it's increasingly difficult to find captains who are willing to take travellers.

Accommodation

Tourist class

Tourist-class accommodation on Mombasa Island is modestly priced and relatively rudimentary. For a reasonably central upmarket base the best bet is Nyali Beach Hotel (see Beaches north of Mombasa), ten minutes' drive from the city centre.

The best tourist-class accommodation on the island is the modestly priced New Outrigger Hotel, PO Box 82345; tel: (011) 220822, on Kilindini Harbour. Better value perhaps, and a lot more central, is the Hotel Sapphire, Kenyatta Ave, PO Box 1254; tel: (011) 494841, which offers tourist-class accommodation at cheap hotel rates. Rooms are spacious and have a private verandah, with a few other attractive touches television, fridge and music system.

There are three older hotels in town. The oldest, built in 1908, is the Castle, Moi Avenue, PO Box 84231; tel: (011) 223403, which is centrally positioned but poorly maintained and overpriced considering the options. The Lotus, Cathedral Road, PO Box 90193; tel: (011) 313207, is better, on a quiet road near Fort Jesus and the Old Town. The Manor Hotel, Nyerere Avenue, PO Box 84851, tel: (011) 314643, the ex-residence of the British Governor, is the best of the three.

Budget

The pick of the cheap hotels is the New Palm Tree, Nkrumah Road PO Box 90013; tel: (011) 311756. New it is not, but the self-contained rooms are clean, comfortable, spacious and have fans. The hotel has an inviting first-floor courtyard and serviceable ground-floor bar and restaurant. The Splendid Hotel, Meru Road, PO Box 90482; tel: (011) 220817, is similar in price and vintage, but the scruffy, musty rooms get a firm thumbs down.

Fitting in between cheap hotel and local lodging, the Glory Guesthouse, Kwa Shibu Road, PO Box 85527; tel: (011) 313204, may be

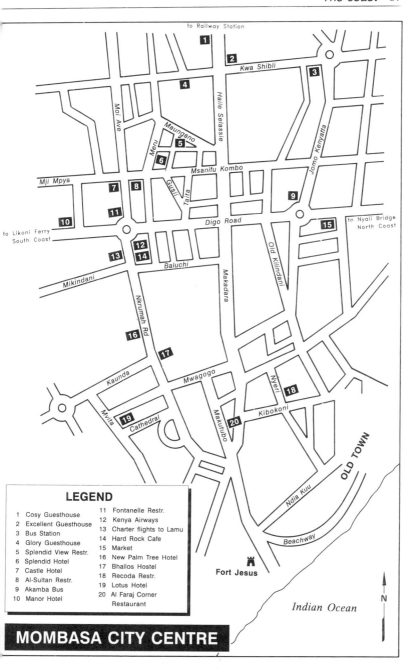

LEGEND

1 Cosy Guesthouse
2 Excellent Guesthouse
3 Bus Station
4 Glory Guesthouse
5 Splendid View Restr.
6 Splendid Hotel
7 Castle Hotel
8 Al-Sultan Restr.
9 Akamba Bus
10 Manor Hotel
11 Fontanelle Restr.
12 Kenya Airways
13 Charter flights to Lamu
14 Hard Rock Cafe
15 Market
16 New Palm Tree Hotel
17 Bhallos Hostel
18 Recoda Restr.
19 Lotus Hotel
20 Al Faraj Corner
Restaurant

Fort Jesus

Indian Ocean

N

MOMBASA CITY CENTRE

bereft of character, but it's clean and safe and some of the self-contained rooms have air-conditioning. The similar Excellent Guesthouse on Haille Selassie Road has clean, freshly-decorated self-contained doubles with fans – excellent is stretching a point perhaps but it's good value.

There are dozens of lodgings scattered around the city centre. First stop should be the Cosy Guesthouse, Haile Selassie Road, PO Box 83011; tel: (011) 313064, where most rooms have fans and balconies. The New People's Hotel, Abdul Nassir Road, PO Box 85342; tel: (011) 312831, is acceptable – and convenient if you want an early morning start to Lamu. Bhallos Hostel, Nkrumah Road, PO Box 88825; tel: (011) 313833, is secure, comfortable and usefully positioned between the city centre and the Old Town.

Restaurants

At the top of the range, the Tamarind Restaurant is a taxi ride from the town centre on the mainland opposite Nyali Bridge. Rated the best seafood restaurant in Mombasa, it is advisable to make a reservation, tel: (011) 471747. Also recommended is the Al Sultan Restaurant on Meru Road where first-class Indian meals are supplemented by seafood, Italian dishes and anything else you can think of. Air-conditioning is not the least of its attractions.

The Hard Rock Café on Nkrumah Road lacks authenticity, but if you've been in East Africa a while it will be difficult to resist the ice-cold draught beer, blasting air-conditioning and splendidly tacky Western decor. Between pop videos, the screens show muted wildlife documentaries, the sole concession to the fact you're in Africa. It's questionable whether the sight of animals tearing each other to shreds will do much to enhance your appetite; anyway, the food is very overpriced. But it's a good place for a pre- or post-meal drink.

The best of the more modest eating places is the Splendid View Restaurant on Maungano Road, which specialises in Indian food and is worth visiting for its chicken tikka and naan bread alone. Opposite the Splendid View, the Splendid Hotel is notable less for its scenic qualities than for a rooftop bar which offers cold beer and breezy relief from the muggy streets below. Also recommended is the shady courtyard of the Fontanelle Restaurant at the junction of Moi Avenue and Nyerere Street. For Cantonese cooking, the Chinese Overseas Restaurant, also on Moi Avenue, is recommended.

For genuine Swahili cooking at dirt cheap prices, the Recoda on Nyeri Street, established in 1942, is the top spot. It doubles as a juice bar and butchery by day, and closes early, so the time to visit is the early evening. The Al Faraj Corner Restaurant on Makadara Road serves cheap and tasty biriani dishes – a good place for lunch if you're coming from the Old Town. For upmarket Swahili food, try the Swahili Curry Bowl on Tangana Road.

Around Mombasa town

Dozens of safari companies and tourist-oriented shops, stalls and restaurants line Moi Avenue and the adjoining back roads. Also on Moi Avenue is Mombasa's best-known landmark, the highly unexciting metal elephant tusks which regularly feature on postcards, and the nearby tourist information office.

The Portuguese-built Fort Jesus, now a national museum, is at the end of Nkrumah Avenue overlooking the harbour. Despite several renovations and additions over the years it has largely retained its original 1593 plan. It deserves a couple of hours' exploration. Clambering around the fortifications is great fun, and your understanding will be enhanced by studying the booklet on sale at the gate. The ruined dwellings in the large courtyard suggest it may well have served as a fortified village during times of siege. A small museum displays indigenous and imported pottery discovered at various coastal archaeological sites, and there are some restored Omani living quarters in a turret overlooking the Old Town. After leaving the fort, wander around the corner to view the sheer 16 m high walls of the seaward projection.

A visit to the adjacent Old Town follows naturally from a tour of Fort Jesus. The Old Town has been settled for centuries, and even though there were few stone houses before 1850, several of the mosques are ancient. The oldest is Mhandry Mosque (1570), but Basheikh Mosque is built on the foundations of a mosque dating to the 14th century. Many other buildings date to the turn of the century and show a Zanzibari influence in their ornate balconies and carved wooden doors. Ali's Curio Market, opposite the fort, was built in 1898 and has served as a police station and bar. Photographs taken in 1910 show many buildings which are still standing today.

The Old Town has a striking sense of community. It is a residential area of small family-run businesses, at least one of which, the scent emporium on Bachuma Street, has been run by the same family since 1850. Children play in the narrow alleys and everyone knows everyone else. It feels more like a self-contained village than the suburb of a large city.

The labyrinthine alleys of the Old Town invite casual exploration broken by the occasional stop at a roadside coffee stall or juice shop For detailed historical coverage, a good map, and notes on over 5(buildings, buy the booklet *Old Town Mombasa: a historical guide* (com piled by the Friends of Fort Jesus and available in most Mombasa bool stores).

The Old Town is strongly Muslim. Visitors should dress so as not to give offence.

Car hire

Glory Car Hire, Moi Ave, PO Box 85527; tel: (011) 221159

Hertz Car Hire, Moi Ave, PO Box 84782; tel: (011) 316333

THE COAST SOUTH OF MOMBASA

Shelly Beach

Shelly Beach, immediately south of Mombasa, has a suburban characteu and is less attractive than the beaches further south. The turn-off to the beach is near the Likoni ferry terminal.

Accommodation

Tourist-class accommodation can be found at the Shelly Beach Hotel, PO Box 96030; tel: (011) 451001, which is rather dithery and run-down, but pleasant and very modestly priced. There are self-contained rooms with fans at cheap hotel rates at the CPK Guesthouse, PO Box 96170, tel: (011) 451619, 300 m from the Likoni turn-off. The Children's Holiday Resort, PO Box 96048; tel: (011) 451417, is an older self-catering establishment popular with families.

Tiwi Beach

Telephone code: 0127

This beautiful, palm-fringed beach is extremely popular with budget travellers, mainly because of Twiga Lodge, by far the best budget accommodation on any of the beaches. It's easy to arrange snorkel hire if you want to explore the reef. Diving courses are run from a diving centre between Twiga and Minilets.

How to get there

The turn-off to Tiwi is clearly signposted 17 km south of the Likoni ferry; any southbound matatu will drop you there. It is possible to walk the 2 km to the beach from the junction, but the high incidence of mugging along this road makes it inadvisable. Wait for a lift or get a taxi: a service has recently been established at the junction.

Accommodation

Twiga Lodge, PO Box 80820, Mombasa; tel: (0127) 2457, has been popular with travellers for years and it retains a congenial atmosphere that seems rooted in the sixties. Up to 100 travellers congregate here at any one time, partly because it's the starting point for several overland truck companies. Most people pitch a tent, but there are four-bed bandas (local lodging rates) and self-contained double rooms with fans (cheap hotel rates). There is an on-site shop and a lively bar and restaurant.

Less rudimentary self-catering accommodation can be had at Coral Cove Cottages, PO Box 96455, Mombasa; tel: (0127) 2555; and Minilets, PO Box 96242, Mombasa; tel: (0127) 2551. Prices fall between cheap hotel and modest tourist-class rates.

Diani Beach

Telephone code: 0127

Diani Beach is the most developed beach on the south coast, with 20-odd hotels and self-catering establishments along its length. There are several restaurants, banks, curio shops and supermarkets in the shopping centres along the beach road. For bicycle or car hire, try Glory Car Hire in the Diani Shopping Centre opposite the Trade Winds Hotel. Most of the hotels hire out equipment for windsurfing, sailing, snorkelling and diving.

Although Diani is among the most developed beaches in East Africa, there are remnants of the forest which once ran its length that still hold typical lowland forest birds and primates. The Tiwi River north of the beach near the Indian Ocean Beach Club is also rich in birds. The disused 16th century Kongo Mosque is hidden in the baobab forest near the river.

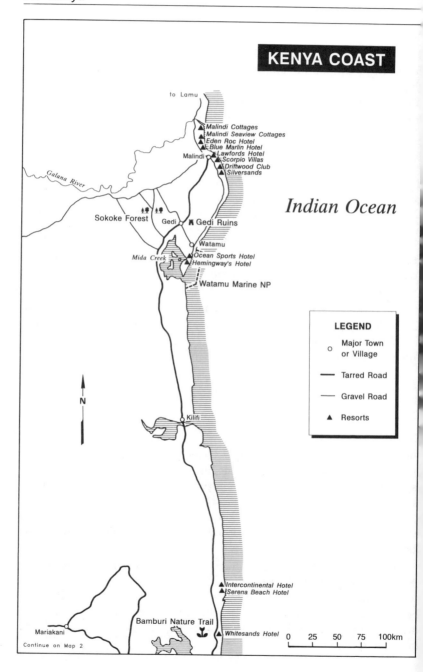

KENYA COAST

to Lamu

Malindi Cottages
Malindi Seaview Cottages
Eden Roc Hotel
Blue Marlin Hotel
Lawfords Hotel
Malindi
Scorpio Villas
Driftwood Club
Silversands

Galana River

Indian Ocean

Sokoke Forest   Gedi   Gedi Ruins

Watamu
Mida Creek   Ocean Sports Hotel
Hemingway's Hotel

Watamu Marine NP

N

Kilifi

LEGEND

○ Major Town
   or Village

— Tarred Road

— Gravel Road

▲ Resorts

Intercontinental Hotel
Serena Beach Hotel

Bamburi Nature Trail

Mariakani   Whitesands Hotel   0   25   50   75   100km

Continue on Map 2

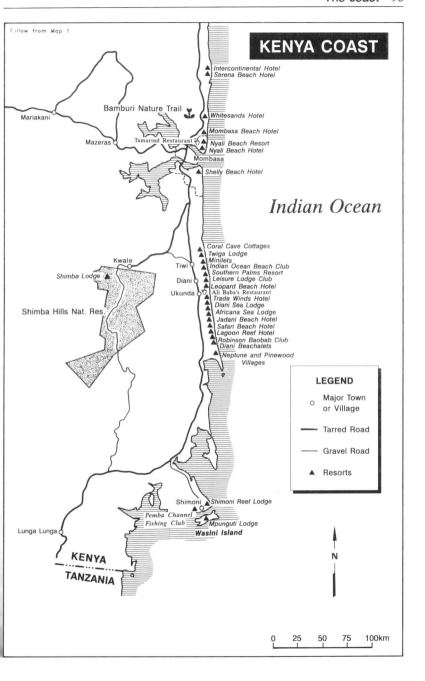

Follow from Map 1

KENYA COAST

Mariakani

Mazeras

Bamburi Nature Trail

Tamarind Restaurant

▲ Intercontinental Hotel
▲ Serena Beach Hotel

▲ Whitesands Hotel

▲ Mombasa Beach Hotel
▲ Nyali Beach Resort
▲ Nyali Beach Hotel

Mombasa

▲ Shelly Beach Hotel

Indian Ocean

Kwale

Tiwi

Diani

Ukunda

Shimba Lodge ▲

Shimba Hills Nat. Res.

▲ Coral Cave Cottages
▲ Twiga Lodge
▲ Minilets
▲ Indian Ocean Beach Club
▲ Southern Palms Resort
▲ Leisure Lodge Club
▲ Leopard Beach Hotel
▲ Ali Baba's Restaurant
▲ Trade Winds Hotel
▲ Diani Sea Lodge
▲ Africana Sea Lodge
▲ Jadani Beach Hotel
▲ Safari Beach Hotel
▲ Lagoon Reef Hotel
▲ Robinson Baobab Club
Diani Beachalets
▲ Neptune and Pinewood
Villages

LEGEND

○ Major Town
   or Village

— Tarred Road

— Gravel Road

▲ Resorts

Shimoni ▲ Shimoni Reef Lodge

Pemba Channel
Fishing Club ▲ Mpunguti Lodge
Wasini Island

Lunga Lunga

KENYA

TANZANIA

N

0   25   50   75   100km

How to get there

The turn-off to Diani is about 10 km past Tiwi Beach at the village of Ukunda. There is plenty of traffic along the tar road between Ukunda and the beach. Muggings are commonplace in this area. Walking along the beach road during daylight hours is said to be reasonably safe, but it would be tempting fate to carry any valuables.

Accommodation

For top of the range luxury accommodation, the Indian Ocean Beach Club, Block Hotels; tel: (0127) 3730, is highly recommended. The hotel is set on a lovely stretch of baobab-studded coast near Kongo Mosque and the Tiwi River mouth, remote from the main cluster of hotels. The architecture combines Swahili and colonial elements; rooms are large with fine attention to detail. Sailing and windsurfing are included in the room rates.

Upmarket hotels on Diani are generally of high quality. The Southern Palms Resort, PO Box 363, Ukunda; tel: (0127) 3721, is a new hotel with a good pool and Swahili architecture. Leisure Lodge, PO Box 84383, Mombasa; tel: (0127) 2011; and Leopard Beach Hotel, PO Box 34, Ukunda; tel: (0127) 2111, are older hotels built around a low cliff. Kaskazi Beach Hotel, PO Box 135, Ukunda; tel: (0127) 3170, has a ruined mosque in the grounds and a spacious Swahili design, making it one of the more atmospheric options. Trade Winds Hotel (AT&H), the oldest and one of the cheapest hotels on the beach, is relaxed as opposed to flashy, and a popular meeting place for expatriates. Jadani Beach Hotel; tel: (0127) 2622; Africana Sea Lodge; tel: (0127) 2624; and Safari Beach Hotel; tel: (0127) 2726, are co-managed by Alliance Hotels. Guests at any one hotel can move freely between all three. Lagoon Reef Hotel, PO Box 83058, Mombasa; tel: (0127) 2627, has large grounds, landscaped gardens, a great pool and an intimate atmosphere. The Robinson Baobab Club, PO Box 84792, Mombasa; tel: (0127) 2026, is also well established, with developed gardens laid out on a rocky cliff.

More modestly priced accommodation can be found at Neptune Village, PO Box 696, Ukunda; tel: (0127) 3061, south of the main cluster of hotels, on a quiet beach where there is some indigenous vegetation remaining. Accommodation is in well-equipped self-contained cottages. The nearby Pinewood Village, PO Box 90521, Mombasa; tel: (0127) 3720, offers accommodation in large villas. There's a restaurant or you can cater for yourself. Food can be bought from the on-site shop. Nomads, PO Box 1, Ukunda; tel: (0127) 2155, is the cheapest and one of the oldest hotels on Diani, with self-contained cottages and bandas right on the shore.

The best genuine budget option is Diani Beachalets, PO Box 26, Ukunda; tel: (0127) 2180, which lies well away from the centre of activity at the southern end of the beach road. Accommodation is in bandas and self-contained cottages, or you can camp. Vindigo Cottages, PO Box 77, Ukunda; tel: (0127) 2192, are similar, though no camping is permitted and the rates are higher. Dan's Camping; tel: (0127) 3529, is the only traveller-oriented place on Diani, with dormitory accommodation and camping in a small garden. Once very popular, Dan's has seen better days and security is suspect, but it's very cheap and convenient.

Restaurants

All tourist-class hotels have restaurants and snack menus. Prices are high by Kenyan standards. There are some specialist restaurants along the beach road. A good mid-range option is Sher-e-punjab, an Indian restaurant in the Diani Complex Shopping Centre. At the top of the range Ali Barbar's, built in a coral cave next to the Diani Sea Lodge, is very expensive but is rated one of the best seafood restaurants in Kenya.

Shimoni and Wasini

Telephone code: 0127

Wasini Island and the nearby mainland village of Shimoni lie north of the Tanzanian border near the Pemba Channel, an area renowned for game fishing and snorkelling. Wasini has supported a small Swahili settlement for centuries and the modern village is built around old ruins. The Shimoni Caves, in a patch of forest near the jetty, are thought to be over 20 km long and were used in the 19th century for holding slaves. The forests near Shimoni and mangroves on Wasini support a range of forest birds and monkeys. Also of interest is Shimoni's market, which is built over an old British colonial outpost.

How to get there

Shimoni lies 14 km off the main tar road between Mombasa and the Tanzanian border. There are frequent buses and matatus from Mombasa. Wasini Island Restaurant runs a motorboat service between Shimoni and the island (except in May and June when the restaurant is closed). Smaller local boats make the trip regularly, and more cheaply.

Accommodation

The luxury Pemba Channel Fishing Club, PO Box 86952, Mombasa; tel: (011) 313749, is a highly professional organisation with an emphasis on big game fishing (it closes in the off-season between April and July). Sea Adventures, PO Box 56, Shimoni; tel: (0127) Shimoni 12, is a luxury house-stay run by a family with extensive fishing experience. Rates include meals and fishing trips. The upmarket Shinomi Reef Lodge, PO Box 61408, Nairobi; tel: (0127) Shimoni 9, is less extravagant than the Fishing Club and the emphasis is more on scuba diving than fishing. Accommodation is in self-contained cottages.

Budget travellers should cross to Wasini Island, where you can camp or rent a banda (cheap hotel rates) at Mpunguti Lodge. Meals are available, but water is often restricted and there is no electricity. Snorkelling trips can be arranged through the Wasini Island restaurant.

SHIMBA HILLS NATIONAL RESERVE

The Shimba Hills lie about 20 km inland from Diani Beach. Densely forested, biologically diverse and surprisingly little visited, the national reserve is a welcome contrast to the crowds and humidity at sea level. Shimba Hills is most famous for Kenya's only population of sable antelope (300 individuals). It is also a coastal stronghold for 500 elephant which once migrated between Shimba and Mkomazi in Tanzania. Other common animals are giraffe (reintroduced), buffalo, bushbuck, blue monkey and black-and-white colobus monkeys. The reserve's last lion disappeared in 1992, leaving leopard as the only large predator. Over 200 species of bird have been recorded, many of them coastal forest specials. The views from the hills across to the Indian Ocean are fantastic on a clear day.

How to get there

Visitors to Shimba Lodge can arrange transfer from any beach hotel near Mombasa. In addition, most Mombasa tour operators can arrange day trips to the reserve.

It is possible to get to Shimba independently. Matatus run from Mombasa to the village of Kwale, 5 km from the gate. From there you can walk to the gate and try for a lift into the park. If you get stuck, there are basic lodgings in Kwale.

Accommodation

The upmarket Shimba Lodge (Block Hotels) is arguably the most underrated lodge in Kenya: a Treetops-style construction with an atmosphere and intimacy that is sadly lacking in the original. The rooms are small but perfectly adequate and they all have private balconies which, like the lodge's open areas, overlook a floodlit waterhole. Regular nocturnal visitors include elephant, bushpig, marsh mongoose, bushbuck, genet, civet, monitor lizard, blue monkey, bushbaby and leopard. Birdlife around the lodge is disappointing, though palmnut vulture and fish eagle appear to be resident, and crested guineafowl make regular appearances. The best place for viewing birds is the raised walkway which leads through the forest canopy to a platform above a marshy clearing. Sundowner game walks (leopard are regularly seen on this), morning game drives (best chance of seeing sable) and guided bird walks can be arranged at reception.

In the reserve, about 3 km from the entrance gate, the attractively positioned and little-used campsite has cheap banda accommodation.

BEACHES NORTH OF MOMBASA

Telephone code: 011

Three beaches stretch between Mombasa town and Mtwapa Creek. Nyali Beach, immediately north of Nyali Bridge, is the closest to Mombasa and the easiest to visit if you're staying in central Mombasa. The other beaches are Bamburi and Shanzu.

How to get there

Regular matatus to Nyali leave Mombasa from Haile Selassie Avenue. Ask to be dropped at Nyali Beach Hotel for access to the public beach. The hotels on Bamburi and Shanzu beaches are accessible from the main Malindi road. Any northbound vehicle can drop you at the entrance to one of these hotels.

Accommodation

The luxury accommodation is on Shanzu beach. Serena Beach Hotel, Serena Hotels; tel: (011) 485721, is recommended for its design, spacious grounds, and excellent facilities. The Intercontinental, Intercontinental Hotels; tel: (011) 485811, is characterless by comparison.

The upmarket hotels are Whitesands (Sarova Hotels); tel: (011) 485926, on Bamburi Beach, and Nyali Beach Hotel (Block Hotels); tel: (011) 471567. Whitesands is very attractive, with spacious public areas centred around lily-covered pools, as well as an excellent beach, good restaurants, a well-equipped watersports centre and a huge variety of non-water-related activities. Nyali Beach Hotel, built in the 1940s but much renovated and expanded, is a little more staid but equally attractive.

Modestly priced accommodation can be found at Tamarind Village, PO Box 95805, Mombasa; tel: (011) 471279, a Swahili influenced apartment complex overlooking Mombasa harbour and Nyali Beach Resort, PO Box 1874, Mombasa; tel: (011) 226521, which consists of fully-equipped apartments with sea views. Both complexes have on-site restaurants.

Bamburi Nature Trail

This is a popular excursion from Mombasa town or the north beach hotels. Run by the Bamburi Cement Factory, the trail runs through a rehabilitated quarry where large enclosures protect a variety of antelope and birds, as well as more unusual animals such as crocodiles and servals. The indigenous birdlife is good.

WATAMU

Telephone code: 0122

This ramshackle fishing village and the adjoining string of incongruously flashy hotels seem the most contrived of Kenya's main resorts. But Watamu's Turtle Bay is also the most scenically memorable beach in Kenya, an idyllic stretch of fine white sand given character by a group of large, ragged coral formations that burst from the sea like giant mushrooms. Watamu is an excellent base from which to explore such diverse attractions as Watamu Marine National Park, Gedi Ruins, Mida Creek and Sokoke Forest. There is more to the resort than first impressions might suggest.

Watamu Marine National Park offers perhaps the finest snorkelling in Kenya. Turtle Bay is a maze of underwater coral gardens, and the number of fish these support is mind-boggling. Any of the hotels can organise trips in glass-bottomed boats, combined with snorkelling, or you can make your own arrangements with boat owners – if you're prepared to negotiate, this option works out more cheaply. The scuba diving centre at the Ocean Sports Hotel offers full diving courses as well as excursions for experienced divers. Fishing is prohibited in the national park, but the larger hotels can arrange game fishing further out to sea.

When I first visited Watamu in 1986, it was a scruffy fishing village. Now the village has become something of a sideshow to the big hotels: misplaced (bogus?) Masai strut the streets looking appropriately photogenic; mock German beer halls and flashy curio stalls nestle between the dukas and small homesteads. Notwithstanding concerns about cultural destruction, I got the impression the villagers are enjoying it all. And even after wandering through the less salubrious and more obviously Muslim sidestreets, the place certainly looked more prosperous than it did a few years ago.

Although Watamu is small, the recent tourist boom has ensured that facilities are good: a bank and several shops and restaurants can be found in the village.

How to get there

Watamu lies about 5 km off the main Mombasa-Malindi road. The turn-off is signposted at the village of Gedi about 20 km south of Malindi. Buses between Malindi and Watamu leave every half hour or so, and cover the full length of the Watamu beach road so they can drop you off wherever you want. Coming from Mombasa, ask a Malindi-bound vehicle to drop you at the Gedi turn-off, where you should quickly find transport on to Watamu.

Accommodation

The tourist-class accommodation in Watamu stretches along the 4 km beach road between the village and Mida Creek. The top hotel is Hemingway's, PO Box 267; tel: (0122) 32624, which has a great seafront position about halfway between the creek and the village. The restaurant is good and service is excellent. All rooms are sea-facing with air-conditioning; rates are in the luxury bracket.

The upmarket Barracuda Inn, PO Box 59; tel: (0122) 32070, is a new Italian-owned place with a good seafront position a short walk from the village. All rooms have air-conditioning. The highly recommended Ocean Sports Hotel, PO Box 100; tel: (0122) 32008, which shares an entrance with Hemingway's, is a modest family-run hotel built in 1957.

The atmosphere is very down to earth, and the water sport facilities are the best on the beach. Rooms have fans and air-conditioning.

A modestly priced house-stay at Mrs Simpson's House, PO Box 33; tel: (0122) 32023, is the obvious choice for natural history enthusiasts. Mrs Simpson is an elderly Kenyan resident with a strong interest in conservation. Her house is on a quiet stretch of beach near Mida Creek. Experienced guides can take guests bird-watching in the Sokoke Forest or snorkelling on the reefs. Heading towards the cheap hotel bracket, Paradise Lodge, PO Box 249; tel: (0122) 32062, on the outskirts of the village, is nicely laid out with comfortable-looking rooms and a good restaurant. It is functional rather than luxurious, but good value. Nearby, Peponi's, PO Box 25; tel: (0122) 32246, is firmly in the cheap hotel bracket and equally good value. The feel of the place is quite upmarket with comfortable rooms (no fans) and compact grounds populated by a clientele that is overwhelmingly young, chic and Italian.

Facing each other on the main road fringing the village, the Dante, PO Box 183; tel: (0122) 32243; and Villa Veronika, PO Box 57; tel: (0122) 32083, have self-contained rooms with fans at cheap hotel rates. Villa Veronika is dingier and pricier than the Dante, but it has a nice garden and the atmosphere is a little more welcoming.

The local lodgings in the village are seedier than average but indisputably cheap. If you're looking at this sort of price bracket, the Adventist Youth Centre, PO Box 80, about 1 km from the village, is a more wholesome bet, consisting of a campsite and basic dormitory accommodation, all rather run-down but perfectly positioned above the main bay – and dirt cheap.

Mida Creek

Mida Creek is one of the more accessible bird-watching spots on the coast, and particularly worth visiting between November and March when large numbers of migrant waders line the shore. More than a dozen wader species are regulars, with crab plover, grey plover, terek sandpiper and curlew sandpiper the most common. You should also look out for black heron, reef heron, osprey, Malindi pipit and East Coast batis. If you have snorkelling equipment, the underwater caves at the entrance of the creek support a small population of giant rock cod.

Ocean Sports Hotel runs regular boat trips to the creek. For serious bird-watchers, however, it is preferable to visit on foot. The mouth is about an hour's walk from Watamu village: follow the beach road past Hemingway's and Mrs Simpson's to its end. The north shore, the best place for waders, is more easily reached from the main Malindi-Mombasa road. From Gedi village head towards Kilifi for about 2 km, then take one of the dirt tracks branching to your right; the creek is less than 1 km from the main road. Try to visit at low tide when the sand flats are exposed.

Sokoke Forest

This is the only sizeable expanse of lowland forest in Kenya, a mixture of Brachystegia woodland and dense coastal forest. Isolated from similar habitats, it supports several endemic and localised animal species. Ader's duiker, a less bulky version of the red duiker, is found in one other forest, on Zanzibar Island, while the golden-rumped elephant shrew is endemic to Sokoke.

Sokoke supports a wide range of forest birds; hornbills, bulbuls, bush shrikes and flycatchers are particularly well represented. At least two species, Sokoke scops owl and Clarke's weaver, are found nowhere but Sokoke; other species with a limited distribution include Sokoke pipit, East Coast akalat, spotted ground thrush, and Amani and plain-backed sunbird.

The Sokoke Forest can be visited as a day trip from Watamu or Malindi. The entrance gate to the reserve is on the Malindi-Mombasa road, 2 km south of Gedi. If you want to stay overnight – a good idea, bearing in mind that animals are most active in the early morning – camping is permitted at the entrance gate.

You really need a vehicle to get deep enough into the forest to see a fair selection of the more unusual birds. A guide will help; the rangers at the gate are normally willing to discuss a fee. The rare mammals are most readily seen at the Gedi Ruins, which lie in an extension of the forest.

Gedi Ruins

The Gedi Ruins, one of the most intriguing historical sites on the Kenyan coast, are the remains of a walled city which was founded in the 13th century and occupied for 300 years. The ruins cover 45 acres and the city once housed about 2 500 occupants. The strange thing about Gedi is that, despite its size and proximity to Malindi, its original name has been lost in the mists of time and no contemporary records of it survive. It is equally difficult to explain why the ruins lie 2 km from the nearest access to the sea. Gedi invites speculation.

Gedi has a haunting atmosphere, due in large part to the tangled forest which has engulfed it. The stone town has been cleared of forest growth, but the larger trees are still standing. Of interest in the main ruins is a fluted pillar tomb, a less ornate tomb dating to 1399, a large 15th century great mosque, and a palace. From the main ruins, several well-maintained footpaths lead through the forest to the city wall, where there are several small mosques and discrete houses. At the entrance gate, a small museum displays a variety of artefacts found at Gedi during excavations. The booklet on sale at the gate has details of all the important buildings and a good map of the site.

The footpaths around Gedi allow easy access to the Sokoke Forest. There is a good chance of animal encounters, especially in the early morning. The elusive golden-rumped elephant shrew is more likely to be heard crashing into the undergrowth than seen, as is Ader's duiker. The most visible large mammal is the blue monkey. Birdlife is prolific. With patience and luck you may see some Sokoke specials. Even if you don't, hornbills are raucously abundant and you can expect to see a few good forest birds. Many of the trees around the main ruins are labelled. Look out for the wonderful strangler fig near the House of the Dhow.

The ruins are a straightforward day trip from Watamu or Malindi. The entrance is ten minutes' walk from Gedi village and well sign-posted. Overnight camping is not permitted.

MALINDI

Telephone code: 0123

Malindi has been a major trading centre for centuries and was the base for Portuguese operations on the coast in the 16th century. There is still a nominal Old Town, but it's small and contains few buildings that date much before the Second World War. Malindi today is first and foremost a resort town. Nevertheless, the combination of the Swahili earthiness of the backstreets and the excellent tourist facilities on the beachfront can be rather enjoyable once you settle in.

Malindi does have a few genuine antiquities. On Da Gama Point, at the southern end of Malindi beach, is the cross erected by Vasco da Gama in 1499. Nearby, next to Da Gama's Restaurant, is a small Portuguese church and graveyard. And in the town centre, opposite Uhuru Gardens, there is a large Friday Mosque with two fine examples of pillar tombs.

Scuba diving and game fishing excursions can be arranged through the various beachfront hotels. The Driftwood Club enjoys a good reputation and is relatively cheap. For snorkelling trips on glass-bottomed boats, you can either use a hotel or make private arrangements with boat owners on the beach. The snake park on Casuarina Point is rated the best in Kenya.

If the seaside activities pall, Malindi is a useful base for trips to the Gedi Ruins and Sokoke Forest. For a more organised excursion, Lake Chem Chem, 8 km out of town on the Tsavo road, has recently been proclaimed a nature reserve. White rhino have been introduced and the lake draws large numbers of migrant waders. Day trips, which see you riding around the reserve on a camel, can be booked through Tusker Safaris in the Galana Shopping Centre.

How to get there

Air

There are charter flights most days between Mombasa, Malindi and Lamu. Prestige Air Services' office is in the arcade next to the Blue Marlin Hotel.

Road

A good tar road connects Malindi to Mombasa. Buses between the towns leave throughout the day and the trip takes three to four hours. There are also regular buses from Watamu.

Accommodation

Tourist class

Tourist-class accommodation in Malindi is quite low-key and less costly than the beach hotels around Mombasa. The most upmarket option is Scorpio Villas, PO Box 368; tel: (0123) 20194, a cluster of self-catering cottages in luxuriant surroundings, with an on-site restaurant if you don't want to cook.

There is a choice of modest beachfront hotels in the town centre. The Blue Marlin and Lawfords are co-owned, PO Box 54; tel: (0123) 20440, and there's not a lot to choose between them. The Blue Marlin has a little more character – its claim to fame is that Ernest Hemingway stayed there. The Eden Roc Hotel, PO Box 350; tel: (0123) 20480, is similar but shows its age less obviously.

For modestly priced self-catering accommodation, Malindi Seaview Lodges, PO Box 746; tel: (0123) 20304, are attractively located and good value. The Driftwood Club, PO Box 63; tel: (0123) 20155, 2 km south of town, is a little more expensive but has excellent fishing and water-sports facilities.

Budget

Malindi Cottages, PO Box 992; tel: (0123) 20304, 2 km out of town on the Lamu Road, offers a variety of cottages and semidetached double rooms at cheap hotel rates. It's a little run down to make the tourist-class grade, but it's perfectly adequate, and the on-site restaurant and swimming pool make it good value.

The established traveller's focus is Silversands, PO Box 442; tel: (0123) 20412, 2 km south of town on the beach. The campsite is marred by the absence of shade, but the bandas and standing tents are cheap. A better bet these days is the Fondo Wehu Guesthouse, PO Box 5367; tel: (0123) 30017, a friendly, family-run affair and a good place to meet travellers. Clean double rooms have fans and mosquito nets and there is a large dormitory (nets only). Laundry is free and a huge breakfast is included in the price, which is in the local lodging bracket. Fondo Wehu is 10 minutes' walk from the bus station and signposted.

Other budget options fall on a blurred line between cheap hotels and local lodgings. Euro Gastehuis is a new German-run establishment around the corner from Fondo Wehu. The Glory Guesthouse, PO Box 994, tel: (0123) 30309, has adequate self-contained rooms with mosquito nets and fans. Ozi's Bed and Breakfast, PO Box 60; tel: (0123) 20218, is central, overlooks the beach, and has clean but spartan rooms. The Sea Breeze Guesthouse, PO Box 5333; tel: (0123) 20612, is particularly good value with clean self-contained rooms at rock bottom prices (though ask for a room with a fan). The Beach View Lodge, PO Box 42; tel: (0123) 20268, is a new, centrally positioned high-rise where large self-contained rooms with mosquito nets and fans are excellent value.

Finally, the Lutheran Guesthouse, PO Box 409; tel: (0123) 21098, has self-contained, self-catering bandas which work out very cheaply on a weekly or monthly basis.

Restaurants

The main road through Malindi is lined with restaurants. At the top of the range, Herman's Beer Garden is the place to head for for keg beer or an enormous steak, while Trattoria Pizzeria specialises in Italian food. The best Indian restaurant is the Surahi Restaurant; the cheaper Polka Curry House places greater emphasis on vegetarian dishes.

The Palm Garden is something of a rendezvous spot, and of more interest for the lively, if somewhat seedy, atmosphere and reliable supply of cold beer than for the very ordinary curries and Western dishes it serves. The food at Da Gama's is essentially Western fare (burgers and steaks) but it's tasty and cheap, and the portions are dauntingly generous.

The Travellers Café serves simple meals at rock bottom prices, making it deservedly popular with budget travellers. Even cheaper, and far more interesting, is the small hoteli (eatery) next to the Open View Night Club, which serves Swahili dishes to a predominantly local clientele.

The anonymous juice bar round the corner from the bus station may look shoddy, but it sells wonderful fruit juices, surpassing even those in Lamu. Bawaly and Sons' shop (opposite Uhuru Gardens) offers another must: a marvellous variety of halwa jellies, with coffee on the house.

Car hire

Hertz has an office on the main road near the Blue Marlin Hotel, tel: (0123) 20069.

LAMU

Telephone code: 0121

Lamu is special. Situated on a small island and separated from Malindi by 200 km of dusty roads, it has managed to retain much of its pre-colonial shape and atmosphere. There is something irresistible about

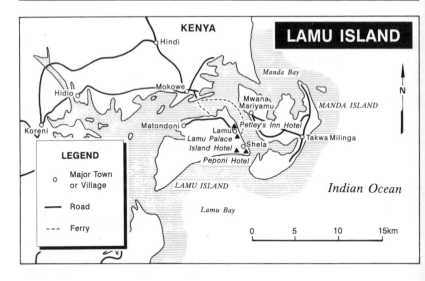

Lamu, a delicious languor and cultural integrity which induce visitors to stay on and on: if you come here planning to spend three days and end up staying a month, you won't be the first person to do so.

There are no cars on Lamu island. Donkeys dawdle along the maze of narrow cobbled alleyways which make up the town. There is no clear division between residential and business districts. Homes, guest-houses, restaurants, mosques and shops are intermingled; children play in the main road; old Muslim men sit on the pavement chatting; women dressed in black buibui veils suddenly appear and disappear through residential doorways. Houses are built to a distinct design: two or three stories high, they enclose an open courtyard and the rooftop is used as a verandah. The rooftops are very much a part of Lamu, the place to catch a breeze while you view the town from an unusual, panoramic angle. And, after dark, they can be hauntingly beautiful: palm trees swaying beneath a pristine night sky, the silence punctuated by gossip from the streets below and the insane braying of the island's many donkeys.

Despite its deep-rooted air of tradition, Lamu also seems to have a very dynamic, open society. Although it is not touristy in any normal sense of the word, the island has been a magnet for travellers since the sixties. As you walk the streets, hippy dirges and reggae vie for attention with the regular Islamic prayer calls. Perhaps the greatest indication of

Lamu's ability to adapt – it has, after all, seen several influxes of new cultures over the centuries – is the way it has managed to retain a distinct character despite the high tourist presence. There are plenty of hustlers in Lamu, but their relaxed approach is a world apart from the hysterical beach boys and taxi drivers around Mombasa and Malindi. Tourism in Lamu isn't about lounging around in luxurious hotels on palm-fringed beaches. It is far more interactive than that; the onus is on you to adapt to Lamu's pace, a task which is not terribly difficult.

Lamu town is built on the channel between Lamu and Manda islands. The latter is unpopulated and edged by low, dense mangroves. The channel lends the town the air of a river port – despite the unmistakable saline smell. The modern waterfront dates to about 1830; before that, the water reached up to Harambee Avenue, the main road through town, where the fort (built 10 years earlier) stands. There are few historical landmarks in Lamu; the interest stems not from individual relics, but from an overall sense of time warp. The entire town is a monument of sorts. The museum on the waterfront is worth visiting for an overview of Lamu's history.

There is plenty to keep yourself busy with around Lamu: donkey trips to the other side of the island, dhow excursions to neighbouring islands or to go snorkelling, or a gentle stroll to the nearest beach. The most attractive option, however, is simply doing nothing. The sticky coastal heat induces a physical and mental torpor; the longer you spend in Lamu the more dreamy it all feels. It is easy to fill the days wandering aimlessly through town, punctuating your drift with frequent stops for a fruit juice or beer, chatting to locals and other travellers, or just lounging on the rooftop of your guesthouse.

Single women should be aware that Lamu has a reputation for sexual harassment. Shela Beach in particular is the one place in Kenya where rape seems to be a cause for concern. It would be a wild overreaction to let this put you off visiting Lamu: many single women do, and one or two incidents can tarnish a place's reputation for years. But it's not difficult to see how the interactive tourist culture in Lamu, combined with the very real cultural gap between tourists and locals, could lead to misunderstanding. Try to avoid dressing in a manner which might be perceived as provocative, and bearing in mind that Lamu has a reputation for holiday romances, deal with unwanted flirtation firmly and immediately.

How to get there

Air

Prestige Air Services in Mombasa fly to Lamu daily via Malindi. If you are on a budget, flying from Malindi isn't prohibitively expensive; at the time of writing the cost was less than US $100 return. The airstrip at Lamu is on Manda Island; motorboat taxis wait to transfer passengers across to Lamu town.

Road

The road between Malindi and Lamu is rough; there are only a couple of buses a day and the trip takes about five hours. It's advisable to visit the bus station a day in advance and make a booking. Bus journeys from Malindi terminate at Mokowe on the mainland, from where motorboat taxis transfer passengers to Lamu town.

In late 1993, a series of armed attacks took place on the road between Malindi and Lamu. Sorting through the inevitable rumours, it seems there were only a handful of incidents, which ceased immediately the government provided an armed escort for all vehicles. It's impossible to say whether this was an isolated outbreak or whether it marks the beginning of an ongoing problem. Make enquiries before taking a bus or driving up to Lamu; if there have been attacks recently, I would seriously recommend you fly.

Accommodation

Tourist class

The new and modestly priced Lamu Palace, PO Box 83; tel: (0121) 33272, is the most upmarket address in town, and the only hotel with air-conditioning. It seems rather disconnected from the rest of the town; hopefully it won't set a precedent for new tourist development. The Palace offers fly-in packages from Malindi and Mombasa (incorporating a dhow trip to Takwa Ruins and inclusive of accommodation, food, transport and fees) which are worth considering if you have time constraints or don't feel like making your own arrangements. Contact any Mombasa or Malindi tour operator for details.

Lamu's oldest hotel is Petley's Inn, PO Box 4; tel: (0121) 33107, a family-run place on the beachfront, recently refurbished and now good value at cheap hotel rates. There are also a handful of tourist-class guesthouses in Lamu, generally at cheap hotel rates and furnished in traditional Lamu style, with fans, mosquito nets and a constant water supply. These include Amu House, tel: (0121) 33420; Haludy, Kishuna and New Mahrus, all PO Box 25; tel: (0121) 33001; Yumbe Guesthouse, PO Box 81; tel: (0121) 33101; and Stone House, PO Box 193; tel: (0121) 33149.

In Shela village, 2 km from Lamu town, Peponi's, PO Box 24; tel: (0121) 33029, is the island's most prestigious hotel, fitting firmly into the luxury bracket. Also in Shela, the modest Island Hotel has immaculate rooms furnished in traditional Swahili style and a good restaurant. Reservations are made by contacting PO Box 70940, Nairobi; tel: (02) 229880.

Budget

Travellers arriving in Lamu should expect to be approached by a horde of touts offering accommodation. Without being offensively aggressive, there's little you can do to resist them, and, all things considered, they are more of a help than a hindrance. Lamu town is confusing on first arrival and the touts will usually know where rooms are available.

Accommodation prices in Lamu depend on the season, the quality of the guesthouse and room, the number of nights you want to stay, and your bargaining abilities. Before taking a room, see if it has a fan or net and check the water pressure. Out of season, tariffs rarely rise above normal local lodging rates; when rooms are in demand, they edge into the cheap hotel bracket.

There are dozens of guesthouses in Lamu. Where you end up will depend largely on where the touts take you. If you would rather not leave things to chance, you can ask to be taken to a specific guesthouse: I can safely recommend the Bahari, Casuarina and Pole Pole Guesthouses and Salama Lodge, all of which have good rooftop verandahs, self-contained rooms with fans and mosquito nets, and a relatively reliable water supply. But guesthouses in Lamu open, close and change hands regularly; ask travellers returning from Lamu for current recommendations.

The Peace Guesthouse deserves a special mention as it is the only place in Lamu with dormitories and a campsite. It also has self-contained rooms with fans. It's a 10-minute walk from the waterfront; anyone can direct you there.

If you'd prefer to stay near the beach, private rooms can be rented in Shela village – just ask around. The Pomme and Shalla Guesthouses fall into the cheap hotel bracket. The only budget accommodation is Hussein's Guesthouse, opposite Shela's mosque; reservations are made by writing to PO Box 330, Lamu; tel: (0121) 33420 or enquiring at the Amu Guesthouse in Lamu town.

Restaurants

Lamu's restaurants are one of its chief delights. Over the years, it has developed a cuisine distinct from that found elsewhere in the country: a combination of traditional Swahili dishes and Lamu peculiarities such as yoghurt, fruit pancakes, fantastic fruit juices, milkshakes and garlic toast. Fish and crayfish dishes predominate, and are generally excellent, but most menus also include some Indian, vegetarian and meat dishes. There are too many restaurants to discuss them all individually, and prices are reasonably uniform, but a few places stand out.

Three of the most popular restaurants along the seafront are the Hapa Hapa, Bush Garden and Labamba. There's not a lot to choose between them: Labamba probably has the edge on seafood and Bush Garden on curries, while Hapa Hapa sells wonderful fruit juice. Still on the seafront, Petley's Inn and Lamu Palace Hotel do reasonable seafood – though pricey by Lamu standards – and are the places to head for if you're after a cold beer.

An old favourite, the Yoghurt Inn, opposite the Bahari Guesthouse, has a similar menu and prices to the seafront restaurants. Rumours Coffee Shop, on Harambee Avenue behind the Lamu Palace Hotel, serves cappuccino and delicious confectionery. The Serendip Restaurant, in the backstreets behind the museum, specialises in Indian vegetarian food. Restaurants in Lamu are forever opening, closing or changing name and/or ownership: try to be adventurous.

Around Lamu Island

Shela and the beach

The village of Shela, 3 km south of Lamu town, is the destination of the island's most popular day excursion, the pristine, uncrowded, 12 km stretch of white sand that is Shela beach. There's no reef here, so the sea is relatively cool and there is even the odd wave. You can walk along the waterfront from Lamu town to the beach, or else take one of the regular motorboat taxis which leave from Lamu town. There's no shade; take along sunblock.

Shela village is worth a pause: an ancient, charming settlement now in obvious decline, it boasts a remarkable mosque dating to 1829. If you've walked from Lamu town, you'll certainly want to drop into the Bahari Restaurant on the seafront, which serves good fruit juice and a variety of meals and snacks.

Shela beach is the main risk area on Lamu for muggings and rapes. Walking between Lamu town and Shela village is reputedly safe – I certainly didn't feel threatened and there are plenty of people around – but, male or female, it would be inadvisable to go much beyond the village unless you are in a group. And under no circumstances should you take any valuables.

Matondoni

This picturesque fishing village lies on the opposite side of the island to Lamu town and is famous as a dhow-building centre. It seems a particularly industrious village: wherever you go people are weaving mats and baskets or crushing maize. The gracious village headman runs a duka that stocks sodas but little else. He is happy to show visitors around and to find a room for anyone who wishes to stay overnight.

The best way to visit Matondoni – easily organised through any of the touts on the waterfront – is on the back of a donkey. The trip takes up to two hours each way, depending on how stubborn the beast is. Wear long trousers and a hat. The interior countryside is hot and dry, and covered in vicious acacias to which the donkeys feel a magnetic attraction. The occasional blissfully shady mango trees offer some relief. The low acacia scrub rattles with birdlife; look out for the dazzling carmine bee-eater.

Around the Lamu archipelago

Day trips by dhow

Several of the touts on the waterfront can organise dhow trips from Lamu. If you want to sail in a dhow, this is a more realistic option than trying to find one to take you between Malindi and Lamu. Prices are cheap and they drop as the group gets larger, but you should clarify in advance exactly where you are going and for how long.

The most popular day trip combines fishing and a lunchtime barbecue based around the morning's catch with an afternoon trip to the Takwa Ruins on Manda Island. Before you visit Takwa, check out the excellent displays in the Lamu museum. Overnight camping is permitted at Takwa; you should be self-sufficient, however, and will have to pay to retain the services of a dhow for a second day.

Another good trip is to the reefs around Mandatoto Island, which teem with fish. Depending on prevailing winds and tides, this trip requires an early start and you can expect to arrive back in Lamu town after dark.

Pate Island

Pate Island is off the beaten tourist track but an interesting place for a few days' exploration. A motorboat taxi runs daily between Lamu town and Pate's main settlements, Pate town and Faza. Pate town is in some ways like a smaller, more low-key version of Lamu town, and just as ancient; the ruins of the old town lie behind the modern one. Near the modern village of Siyu are the remains of the 9th century city of Shangu, with over 300 tombs and a large ruined palace. There is no accommodation on the island; it's normally possible to arrange to stay in private homes in Pate town, Siyu and Faza, but it would be advisable to carry a tent. Neither is there any transport: you'll have to walk between towns. A Surveys of Kenya map would be useful.

Kiwaiyu Island

This pencil-shaped island lies beyond Pate and is notable for its idyllic beach, excellent snorkelling and total sense of separation. It's a wonderful place to spend a few days relaxing, especially if you are interested in snorkelling or fishing. In addition to the obvious water-related activities, the lodges on Kiwaiyu can organise game-viewing safaris to Boni and Dodori game reserves on the mainland opposite Kiwaiyu.

On the mainland opposite the island is the upmarket Kiwaiyu Safari Lodge, PO Box 55343, Nairobi. On the island itself there is modestly priced accommodation at Munira Safari Lodge, PO Box 224, Lamu. Budget accommodation can be found at Kasimu's camp, with basic bandas and a campsite at local lodging rates.

Both lodges can arrange transfer by plane from Lamu, Malindi or Mombasa, or by motorboat from Lamu. Budget travellers will have to make their own way there. There are motorboat taxis from Faza on Pate (two to three hours) or you can negotiate to go by dhow from Lamu Island (eight to 24 hours). You could see if a motorboat is heading to one of the camps and negotiate to ride with that; ask at Petley's Inn or the Salama Guesthouse.

7 THE SOUTHERN RIFT VALLEY AND MASAI MARA

The 8 700 km-long Rift Valley stretches down Africa from the Red Sea to the Zambezi delta and cuts a dramatic 1 200 m chasm into the Kenyan highlands. Studded with beautiful, papyrus-fringed lakes and volcanoes, home to the pastoral Masai and abundant game – the latter sadly depleted in the last century – the Rift Valley floor is archetypal East Africa.

Tourist activity in the southern Rift Valley centres around a string of lakes: Magadi, Naivasha, Elmenteita, Nakuru, Bogoria and Baringo. Kenya's most famous game reserve, Masai Mara, which borders Tanzania southwest of the Rift Valley, is also covered in this chapter.

THE MAGADI ROAD

South of Nairobi and the Ngong Hills, the tarred road to Lake Magadi makes a dramatic descent into a part of the Rift Valley that is harshly beautiful, searingly hot and, especially if you've spent a few days in Nairobi, remarkably wild in character. There are no settlements other than Masai villages along the road, and the region still holds large numbers of wild animals, most visibly giraffe. In the middle of this austere landscape, only a couple of hours from the capital yet completely ignored by the country's tourist machine, lie two wonderfully low-key attractions: the lake itself and Olorgasailie prehistoric site.

Olorgasailie prehistoric site

Half-a-million years ago, Olorgasailie overlooked a large shallow lake, the home to long extinct species of giant elephant and hippo, and also to roving bands of hunter-gatherers, *Homo erectus*. The gorge beneath the site was excavated by the Leakey family in the 1940s, when it was discovered to hold a wealth of Stone Age tools. Along the short guided trail through the gorge there are masses of tools to be seen. You can also see the fossilised leg bone of a giant pachyderm dwarfing the equivalent bone of the African elephant placed alongside it.

Olorgasailie offers more than a glimpse into human prehistory. It is a wonderfully scenic spot, lying adjacent to an extinct volcano and offering commanding views across the bed of the dead lake to the Rift Valley wall. The surrounding bush is rich in wildlife. Giraffe, baboon and eland can be seen all year – the latter regularly stroll into the campsite at night – and hyena and jackal call throughout the night. During the rainy season, large numbers of animals disperse into the area and lion are regularly heard. There are plenty of footpaths through the surrounding bush, and no restrictions on walking.

A range of dry country birds is attracted to the campsite. A resident and very tame pair of red-and-yellow barbets punctuate the calm with their absurd, clockwork-like display and call. Regular visitors include Abyssinian scimitarbill, slaty-coloured boubou, chestnut sparrow, cutthroat finch, silverbill, purple grenadier and Somali goldenbreasted bunting.

Olorgasailie is in the heart of Masai country. Tourists are too infrequent for the hype that spoils Masai contacts in more popular areas; if you speak a bit of Swahili, it's easy to get chatting here and there's no pressure to buy curios or take photos. Tempting as it may be, it would probably be foolish, and certainly very rude, to pull out a camera without feeling out the situation first.

Olorgasailie is a lovely spot, but you'll get little from a hurried visit, and the absence of creature comforts puts it out of reach of all but the most adventurous travellers. But with a little initiative – and an ample supply of food – anyone with an interest in natural history could spend a memorable few days exploring the surrounding bush and absorbing the calm atmosphere.

How to get there

Olorgasailie lies 1 km off the Magadi road, clearly signposted about 60 km south of Nairobi and 3 km past the village of Oltopesi. It's an hour's drive by car or two hours by bus from Nairobi. Buses to Magadi will drop you at the turn-off.

Accommodation

The four basic double bandas at Olorgasailie have mattresses but no bedding. Drinking water and firewood are normally available. Limited food supplies and sodas can be bought at Oltopesi, but it's best to bring all the food you need. It's unlikely the bandas will be full, but you might want to play safe and book through the national museum in Nairobi; tel: (02) 742161. Camping is permitted.

Lake Magadi

Lake Magadi seems a bizarre and inhospitable apparition: not so much a lake as a sludge bed of blindingly white salt and soda deposits, exploited by the Magadi Soda Company since before the First World War and a major source of the soda used in glassmaking worldwide. To get a good look at the lake, ask to walk out on one of the causeways used by the mining company. At the southern end of the lake there are normally large numbers of flamingos, and nearby swamps hold a good variety of waterbirds.

Magadi township is strictly a mining concern. There are no tourist facilities. Travellers are few and far between and you can normally expect a welcome at the company swimming pool and golf course clubhouse, where a small membership fee may be levied.

Experienced 4x4 drivers will find that the area around Magadi repays exploration. There is a lot of game around, including lion, and good bird-watching is ensured by a diversity of habitats ranging from open grassland to riverine forest along the Ewaso Ng'iro River. If you have your own 4x4, Nguruman Game Post, on the Ewaso Ng'iro River 30 km west of Magadi township, can be reached via a reasonable dirt road. Further exploration towards the Nguruman range will depend on the condition of tracks beyond the game post; during the rainy season movement may be restricted. You can camp and ask for current advice at the game post.

How to get there

Magadi township lies 94 km south of Nairobi. The tar road is well maintained; if you have your own vehicle you should be there in one or two hours, making it a perfectly feasible day trip. There are two buses daily between Nairobi and Magadi, leaving Nairobi Country Bus Station at around midday and staying overnight at Magadi before returning in the early morning.

Accommodation

There is no formal accommodation in Magadi, but if you are reliant on public transport, you should expect to spend the night. It's normally possible to camp on the golf course.

MASAI MARA NATIONAL RESERVE

The 1 680 square km Masai Mara is Kenya's most famous and popular game reserve, and arguably its finest. In terms of number and variety of animals, Masai Mara is only rivalled by Tanzania's Serengeti plains, of which it forms the northern extension. Slightly hillier than Serengeti, the Mara plains are predominantly open savannah, interspersed with patches of acacia woodland and, along the Mara River, riparian forest.

Masai Mara offers excellent game viewing at all times of the year. Lion are absurdly common and easily spotted in the open terrain. More than five sightings in a day is far from unusual, and the animals are so used to vehicles that you can approach to within metres of them. Prides are large and kills are frequent: to give some idea, I saw a pride of three males, six females and thirteen cubs bring down three buffalo in the space of an hour; a friend who visited a week later saw a similar spectacle.

The Mara is also a good place to see cheetah, which, when they are not pacing across the plains, are often to be found surveying the surroundings from a termite mound. The long-term survival of cheetah in the area may be threatened by the ever-present minibuses. Cheetah are diurnal hunters, favouring the cooler hours around dusk and dawn, but in the Mara their presence is given away by vehicles on early morning and late afternoon game drives. They have reportedly turned to hunting in the draining midday heat.

Of the other large to medium-sized predators, spotted hyena and black-backed jackal are both common. Leopard are present but as secretive as ever; they are most likely to be seen in the dense vegetation fringing the Mara River. As in many other parts of Africa, African hunting dog numbers are in critical decline. Nocturnal hunters such as bat-eared fox, side-striped jackal, golden jackal, striped hyena and a variety of small felines are seldom seen by casual visitors.

The Mara-Serengeti ecosystem is famous for the annual migration of over one million wildebeest and hundreds of thousands of zebra. Most of the migration is played out on the Tanzanian side of the border, but the herds erupt across the Mara River into Kenya in late July or, more usually, August, before returning south in October. The river crossing is a dramatically grisly spectacle in which thousands of animals perish, creating a field day for scavenging predators. Once in Kenya, the herds to some extent disperse onto the Mara plains; but with so many animals in such a relatively small area, concentrations numbering tens of thousands are regularly seen.

Though impressive at all times of year, the concentrations of plains animals are less dramatic between November and July. Buffalo are common; judging by the number of half-eaten carcasses lying around, they are the favoured prey of the reserve's lions in the absence of wildebeest. Among the more common plains antelope are impala, Thomson's and Grant's gazelle, oribi, topi and Coke's hartebeest. Bushbuck, waterbuck and bohor reedbuck are often seen in association with water. Large numbers of hippo can be seen in the Mara River and giraffe and elephant are both reasonably common throughout the reserve. The small number of black rhinoceros which survived the poaching onslaught of the 1980s are seen by tourists with surprising frequency.

Masai Mara holds a good selection of birds. Large raptors, especially vultures (including Egyptian), are well represented, as are grassland species such as larks, pipits and longclaws. The larger terrestrial birds such as secretarybird, ostrich and the faintly comic ground hornbill will generally make an impression on even the most aviphobic of tourists. For serious bird-watching, acacia woodland and riverine vegetation are particularly rewarding. With your own vehicle, an early morning visit to the riverine forest surrounding the hippo pools on the Mara River is highly recommended, but don't expect to see much later in the day when the minibuses arrive en masse.

The mention of minibuses brings me to Masai Mara's one drawback. It is East Africa's most popular reserve; these days it's not unusual to find yourself among ten other vehicles circling a lion pride. With your own vehicle, this congestion can largely be avoided; on an organised safari you're more or less stuck with it. Personally, I found it less of an irritation than I had expected, but if you want the same experience in a less congested area, Tanzania's Serengeti National Park – almost ten times the area of the Mara and, at a guess, visited by one-tenth the number of tourists – is a recommended alternative.

How to get there

Masai Mara can be reached with an organised safari, in a hired 4x4, or by charter flight. The journey on the main approach road, via the town of Narok (where there is petrol and a selection of cheap hotels and restaurants) takes about six hours. A second, more circuitous route, only viable in good weather, connects Masai Mara to Kisii in western Kenya via the Mau escarpment. Any lodge or travel agent can organise transfer from Nairobi by air.

Accommodation

Tourist class

Masai Mara is dotted with lodges and tented camps. The level of competition ensures that standards are high, but then so are the tariffs. All lodges are able to organise game drives and in many cases the cost of these is automatically included in the price of a room. This will be a waste of money if you are driving yourself.

The following camps and lodges are listed in ascending order of price. They cater to safari companies and package tours and thus do not normally incorporate game drives into the room rates. Prices all fall in the upmarket bracket. Addresses are in Nairobi.

Fig Tree Camp, PO Box 40683; tel: (02) 220592

Mara River Camp, PO Box 48019; tel: (02) 331191

Keekorok Lodge (book through Block Hotels)

Mara Sarova Lodge (book through Sarova Hotels)

Olkurruk Mara Lodge (book through AT&H)

Mara Sopa Lodge, PO Box 72630; tel: (02) 336088

Mara Serena Lodge (book through Serena Hotels)

The following tented camps and lodges are listed in ascending order of price. They cater mainly to private groups and thus their rates, which fall firmly into the luxury bracket, are generally inclusive of game drives.

Talek River Camp, PO Box 74888; tel: (02) 338084

Siani Springs Camp (book through Windsor Hotels)

Kichwa Tembo Camp (book through Windsor Hotels)

Mara Intrepid's Camp (book through Prestige Hotels)

Mpata Safari Lodge, PO Box 58992; tel: (02) 217015

Sekenani Camp, PO Box 61542; tel: (02) 333285

Mara Safari Club (book through Lonrho)

Governor's Camp, PO Box 48217; tel: (02) 331871

Budget

The options for budget travellers who visit Masai Mara independently are rather limited. The only campsite within the park is next to the Mara Serena Lodge. Camping is permitted at Olooloo, Musiara, Talek,

Sekenani and Ololaimutiek gates. Telek and Musiara are rated the best. There is a local lodging in the village of Telek near the gate of the same name.

Balloon trips

A popular and memorable addition to a visit to Masai Mara is a one to two hour balloon trip. Current prices, inclusive of a champagne breakfast, are in the US $300-400 range. Bookings can be made at any lodge or in Nairobi through one of the following companies: Balloon Safaris, PO Box 43747; tel: (02) 502850; Mara Balloon Safaris, PO Box 48217; tel: (02) 726427; and Adventures Aloft, PO Box 40683; tel: (02) 221439.

THE RIFT VALLEY WEST OF NAIROBI

Many people regard this part of the Rift Valley as the most dramatic anywhere between the Red Sea and Mozambique. The valley cuts between the highlands of western and central Kenya like a vast ribbon; the dusty floor, delineated by cliffs up to one kilometre high, is broken up by a string of gem-like lakes and the evocative outlines of extinct volcanoes. The grand scale of the scenery seems to epitomise East Africa, and with ample opportunity to see large mammals on foot, it is an area that begs gentle exploration, especially by non-motorised travellers.

Heading west from Nairobi, whether by road or rail, you will first climb gently through the green highlands around Limuru, an area that is given a decidedly un-African appearance by its pine and eucalyptus plantations. Then, without warning, the Rift Valley floor comes into view more than 500 m below. This is as dramatic an introduction to the Rift Valley as you could hope for, the view from the escarpment sweeping across the ragged crater of Longonot Volcano to the hazy outline of Lake Naivasha 30 km away. When you come by rail or along the old Naivasha road, the descent to the valley floor passes through an area of indigenous forest large enough to still support black-and-white colobus monkeys. The new Naivasha road descends along a gentler slope, and the scenery is more open. However you descend, the temperature rises by a few degrees and the vegetation thins out when you reach the floor.

LAKE NAIVASHA AND SURROUNDINGS

Telephone code: 0311

Lake Naivasha is an ideal first stop in Kenya: arguably the most attractive of the Rift Valley lakes and certainly the most popular, as much for the several day trips in the vicinity as the lake itself. Lake Naivasha has no known outlet and is one of only two freshwater lakes in the Rift Valley. Given to large fluctuations in level – its water volume has varied by over 1 000 per cent since it was "discovered" by Joseph Thomson in 1890 – the nature of the lake shore is forever changing. At present much of it is fringed by dense stands of papyrus. In marked contrast to the dusty euphorbia-studded scrub along the South Lake Road, only a few hundred metres from the lake itself, the shore is swathed in acacia woodland dominated by the large and distinctive yellow fever tree.

The lake supports a large population of hippo. There is also some terrestrial game around – I've seen giraffe along the shore a couple of times. For reliable game viewing, a day trip to Hell's Gate National Park, Crescent Island or Green Crater Lake Reserve (see day trips in the Naivasha area) is recommended.

The Naivasha area is renowned for its diverse and colourful birds. Over 400 species have been recorded and, because the field guides show a marked bias towards birds of south-central Kenya, I would regard it as the top bird-watching spot for first-time vistors to East Africa. A dedicated newcomer to the region could reasonably expect to identify 100 species in two days. Try to visit as many sites as possible: the various lakeside hotels and campsites often hold quite different species.

Look out for the wonderfully colourful and incessantly noisy Fischer's and yellowcollared lovebirds (and hybrids), introduced to the area from Tanzania. Less welcome exotics include the coypu, a large aquatic South American rodent, the floating *Salvinia* fern and Louisiana red crayfish, which between them have made marked changes to the lake ecosystem.

How to get there

Before heading out to the lake, your first goal is Naivasha town, 80 km northwest of Nairobi. On the new Naivasha road, it's about an hour's drive. With your own vehicle – preferably a 4x4 – the town can also be reached via the more scenic but less zippy old Naivasha road. A steady stream of buses and matatus connect Nairobi to Naivasha town. Rail services between Nairobi and Malaba and Kisumu in western Kenya stop in Naivasha town.

The lake is approached along Moi South Lake Road, which branches from the old Naivasha road about 2 km out of town. The South Lake Road, once a driver's nightmare, has recently been surfaced for its first 30 km. Matatus from town run along it on a regular basis, and hitching is fairly easy, especially at weekends.

Accommodation in Naivasha town

Although it's none too exciting in itself, you may find yourself spending a night in Naivasha if you arrive late in the day. It's also the obvious place to stock up on provisions; there are several fruit and vegetable stalls and a couple of good supermarkets on Moi Avenue.

There is no flash accommodation in town. There is, however, a very good cheap hotel, the La Belle Inn, Moi Avenue, PO Box 532; tel: (0311) 20116, a converted 1920s farmhouse which still retains something of a country hotel atmosphere. The excellent and sensibly priced meals and snacks served on the verandah are recommended, even if you are only passing through town. The recently opened Kenvash Hotel, situated off Moi Avenue behind the post office, is a little cheaper than La Belle Inn.

Lake shore accommodation

There is a good selection of accommodation along the South Lake Road, catering to most tastes and budgets.

Tourist class

In the upmarket category, the Lake Naivasha Country Club (Block Hotels) is the top hotel on the lake shore. The main building, which served as Kenya's international air terminal after the Second World War, has a gracious colonial ambience. A path through the attractive grounds leads through huge yellow fever trees to the lake shore where a wooden gazebo is ideally positioned for bird-watching. The buffet lunch is magnificent. This hotel is the base for day trips to Crescent Island.

By comparison, the similarly priced Safariland Hotel, PO Box 72, Naivasha; tel: (0311) 20241, looks increasingly run-down, though it too has wonderful grounds. The large campsite, like the hotel, is poor value for money.

A luxury tented camp has recently opened in the Green Crater Lake Nature Reserve, east of Naivasha. The camp is on the lake shore and surrounded by forest. For further details and reservations contact Safaris Cordon Bleu, PO Box 70560, Nairobi; tel: (02) 882634.

Several private house-stays are possible in the Lake Naivasha area, with tariffs, inclusive of board, mostly falling in the upmarket bracket. Numbers of guests are limited and bookings are essential. Bookings for private house-stays can be made through Let's Go Travel in Nairobi.

Budget

Budget travellers and campers have a wide choice of accommodation around the lake. Coming from Naivasha town along South Lake Road, the first option is the Yellogreen Hotel, about 1 km past the turn-off from the old Naivasha road. There are a few self-contained rooms here at cheap hotel rates and you can camp. A strong disincentive to staying here is that you are separated from the lake by a kilometre or so of private land. The food is reasonable value, however; it's a good place for a meal or cold beer if you're staying at Burch's.

About 2 km further, the poorly signposted Burch's farm (the entrance is next to a dilapidated blue building marked Thitavo Shop and Hotel) is a relaxed family-run establishment where you can sleep in a grounded boat, at local lodging rates, or camp on the lake shore. It caters more to expatriates than to tourists: during the week you'll as often as not have the campsite to yourself, but at weekends it can get a bit hectic. Nocturnal hippo visits are part of the fun, and there's plenty of birdlife around.

The cheapest accommodation on the lake shore is at the YMCA, about 12 km further down the road. Unfortunately it's rather run-down and cramped, and some distance from the lake. Having said that, the walk to the shore via a neighbouring farm passes through extensive papyrus beds teeming with waterfowl and waders. The YMCA is also well positioned for day trips to Hell's Gate. Accommodation is in bandas (local lodging rates). Camping is permitted for a nominal fee.

Just past the YMCA you pass through a small village and the turn-off for Hell's Gate. About 2 km further, Fisherman's Camp is undoubtedly the best budget option on the lake. Accommodation is in papyrus and wood cottages, which are fully equipped for cooking and have hot showers. There is also cheap and very basic dormitory accommodation and a large, beautiful campsite. Fisherman's Camp is set in yellow fever woodland: the birdlife is superb and hippo come into the grounds most nights. Facilities include bicycle, boat and tent hire. An on-site shop sells cold beers and sodas and you can eat at the Fish Eagle Inn next door. Cottages should be booked through Let's Go Travel in Nairobi; there's no need to book for camping and dormitory accommodation.

The adjacent Fish Eagle Inn is similar to Fisherman's Camp but less earthy and more expensive. The bar and restaurant are definitely worth visiting if you're staying next door and the comfortable self-contained rooms fill a real gap between the posh hotels and more rustic options. The dormitory, although it is much nicer than the one next door, is too expensive to appeal to budget travellers at whom it is presumably aimed. The campsite is characterless, overpriced and, as a consequence, normally empty.

Day trips in the Naivasha area

Crescent Island

This island opposite the Lake Naivasha Country Club supports large herbivores such as giraffe and waterbuck (the latter have a reputation for aggression; don't approach them too closely) and a wide range of birds. You may only visit from the country club; the entrance fee includes a motorboat ride across to the island.

Elsamere conservation centre

Originally the home of Joy Adamson, Elsamere is popular for its superb afternoon tea and video show. The centre lies on the lake shore about 2 km past Fisherman's Camp and is open to day visitors between 15h00 and 17h00. A troop of black-and-white colobus monkeys is resident in the grounds. A certain amount of accommodation is available, preferably to visitors with a strong interest in conservation. Bookings and inquiries should be made to PO Box 1497, Naivasha; tel (0311) 30079.

Green Crater Lake Sanctuary

To the east of Lake Naivasha, a small lake lies in the crater of the extinct Songasoi volcano. This was only recently made a sanctuary; plains animals have been introduced and the forested crater rim supports black-and-white colobus monkey, buffalo and a variety of forest birds.

The entrance to the reserve is on the South Lake Road 6 km past the end of the tarmac. Without a vehicle, the best way to get there is to hire a bicycle from Fisherman's Camp. There is a luxury tented camp in the crater (see Lake shore accommodation).

Hell's Gate National Park

Hell's Gate, an impressive sandstone gorge south of Lake Naivasha, was declared a national park in the mid-1980s. Aside from the dramatic scenery, the main attraction of Hell's Gate is that it is one of the few accessible places in East Africa where you can walk or cycle unaccompanied among a wide variety of plains animals. This is the most attractive way to visit Hell's Gate. Bicycles can be hired from Fisherman's Camp. If you've never done so before, encountering large mammals – even antelope – without the protection of a vehicle adds a new and exhilarating dimension to game viewing. The gorge is very hot during the day; an early start is recommended and you must carry plenty of water. There is no restriction on pedestrians and cyclists using the campsites. The most commonly seen mammals are Thomson's gazelle, Coke's hartebeest, klipspringer, zebra and buffalo, but lion, leopard and cheetah are all present and even elephant have been recorded. Fischer's Tower, a striking volcanic plug near Elsa's Gate, is overrun with rock hyrax. The cliffs of the gorge provide nesting sites for several species of raptor, most famously a pair of lammergeyers (bearded vultures) which, despite the hype, have not been seen in a decade and presumably moved on or died years ago.

Elsa's Gate is 1,5 km from the South Lake Road. The turn-off is clearly marked just past the YMCA. There are reasonable roads in the park and, theoretically, you can drive anywhere in a saloon car. You'll have no problems on the main track through the gorge, but I was very glad to have four-wheel drive on the steep, sandy roads of the Buffalo Circuit. The little-used Ol Dubai campsite, where there is running water and a longdrop toilet, is attractively situated above the gorge about 5 km from Elsa's Gate on the Twiga circuit.

Longonot National Park

Mount Longonot is the distinctive ragged-edged volcano which can be seen from the South Lake Road. With a perfect volcanic caldera offering fantastic views in all directions, it's well worth climbing. To do this you need to get to the village of Longonot, about 15 km south of Naivasha town on the old Nairobi road. This is a straightforward drive, but if you don't have a vehicle, you'll probably have to hitch. At Longonot village, visit the Kenya Wildlife Services office to pay the fees and arrange a guide.

The walk from the village to the crater rim takes an hour or so, and is rather steep towards the end. Once at the top, the view down to the forested floor of the crater makes a dramatic contrast to the sparse vegetation on the old lava flows which you've just climbed. You can walk the circumference of the crater rim in about three hours.

LAKE ELMENTEITA

This small lake has a primeval air, surrounded by evocatively shaped volcanic plugs and hills. Thousands of flamingos congregate here at times, and the hippos which abandoned the lake when it dried up in the 1980s have now returned. Elmenteita lies alongside the Naivasha-Nakuru road; the viewing point is easily identified by the presence of the predictable curio stalls. The lake is on the Delamere Estate. It has only recently been developed for tourism, and casual visits are still not encouraged. The only accommodation is the luxury Delamere Tented Camp which has a wonderful position on a cliff overlooking the lake. Night game-viewing drives are available from the camp. For reservations contact PO Box 48109, Nairobi; tel: (02) 335935.

NAKURU

Telephone code: 037

Nakuru, the capital of Rift Valley province, is Kenya's fourth-largest town. It's a dusty, rather nondescript place; cheerfully bustling, but mainly of interest as a transport hub and as a base for visits to Lake Nakuru National Park.

If you have an afternoon to spare, there are a couple of worthwhile day trips in the area. Closest is the archaeological site at Hyrax Hill, about 4 km out of town off the Nairobi road. This has been a site of human habitation for at least 3 000 years, and is of interest for several ancient pit dwellings, a ruined fort and ritual burial sites, all of which are described in detail in a booklet available from the museum at the site. Camping is permitted.

The large mountain which rises behind Nakuru is an extinct volcano called Menengai. The full extent of its 90 square km crater, now partially collapsed, can be seen from a viewpoint at the highest point of the crater rim. To get there, follow the Nairobi road for 2 km, turn left onto the road marked "Hill Climb", then take the second right turn. Once out of suburban Nakuru, a dirt road leads through eucalyptus plantations and grassland for 8 km till it reaches the viewpoint. If you don't have a vehicle, it's a five hour round trip on foot; alternatively, hire a taxi in Nakuru town. There's too little traffic for hitching to be a viable option, except perhaps at weekends.

How to get there

Road

Nakuru is a major transport hub. Buses, minibuses and matatus arrive here from all over the country. There are regular departures to Nairobi, Naivasha, Kisii, Kisumu, Marigat (for Baringo and Bogoria) and Eldoret.

Rail

Trains between Nairobi, Malaba and Kisumu in western Kenya stop at Nakuru.

Accommodation

With two upmarket lodges in the adjoining national park, there is little call for anything fancy in town. There are several cheap hotels though. The Waterbuck Hotel, West Road, PO Box 3327; tel: (037) 40081; and Midland Hotel, GK Kamau Avenue, PO Box 908; tel: (037) 21215, are the most convenient and central. The Kunste Hotel, PO Box 1369, tel: (037) 21214, 2 km out of town on the Nairobi road, is new, clean, reasonably priced and very popular with budget safari operators. The similar Sundowner Lodge, Kanu Street, PO Box 561; tel: (037) 21246, is 3 km from the town centre towards the national park entrance (follow the signposts). It's comfortable, serves good food, and the management can organise day trips into the national park. The Mau View Lodge, Oginga Odinga Avenue west of the town centre, PO Box 1413; tel: (037) 44926, is older and more run-down, but quite pleasant.

Local lodgings are dotted liberally around the town centre, with the choicest clustered on Gusii and Mosque roads. Amigo's Guesthouse, on Gusii Road next to Nakuru Sweet Mart, is cheap, safe, clean, convenient and very popular with travellers. If it's full, the Makoh and

Carnation Hotels, 200 m from Amigo's on Mosque Road, are both acceptable.

If you prefer to stay out of town, there's an anonymous but well-signposted campsite about 7 km from Nakuru on the Baringo road. It has a rustic, farm-like atmosphere and congenial staff. Sodas and beers are available, but not food. Rates are in the local lodging bracket. You can also camp at the entrance to Lake Nakuru National Park (see below).

LAKE NAKURU NATIONAL PARK

The main attraction of this park is Lake Nakuru and its attendant flamingos. Lake Nakuru is a soda lake which, like Naivasha and Elmenteita, is subject to vast fluctuations in water level (it dried up completely in the 1950s). When conditions are right, it supports the largest number of greater and lesser flamingos of any Rift Valley lake – up to two million at any one time! From up close the number of flamingos is daunting, but the full spectacle is best appreciated from the viewpoint on Baboon Cliff, where the flamingos appear as a shimmering pink fringe around the lake.

In addition to flamingos, Lake Nakuru offers good game viewing. The northern shore is fringed by a yellow fever tree forest which is frequented by large numbers of impala, warthog and defassa waterbuck; the animals are fantastically photogenic with the pink-rimmed lake and fever trees as a backdrop. The eastern shore is notable for a giant euphorbia forest below the cliffs east of the main road.

Away from the minibus circuit, the lightly wooded savannah of the southern half of the park is home to herds of Burchell's zebra and Thomson's gazelle. Other animals you can expect to see are Rothschild's giraffe (introduced), buffalo, Grant's gazelle and eland. Lake Nakuru National Park is said to have Kenya's highest density of black rhino, many of them introduced from elsewhere in the country, but in three visits I've yet to see one. Lion are present in small numbers but rarely seen, and the park's sizeable leopard population is as elusive as ever.

Birdlife is varied. Lake Nakuru has a reputation for attracting rare migrant waterfowl, but, unfortunately, the lake is too far from the road for easy identification of smaller waterbirds. Parking for a while at the waterhole between Lion Hill Camp and Lake Nakuru Lodge can be rewarding. Raptors are well represented; secretarybirds seem unusually common in the south of the park. The woodland fringing the eastern and northern shore of the lake is excellent for acacia-associated species.

How to get there

Organised safari

Lake Nakuru is a common fixture on Kenyan safari itineraries, often tagged on to the end of three-day safaris to Masai Mara or as an overnight stop between Masai Mara and Samburu Game Reserve.

Independent visits

The main entrance gate to Lake Nakuru is only 4 km from Nakuru town centre, making it one of the easier parks to visit independently. Many travel agencies and hotels in Nakuru organise day visits there. It is cheaper to make your own arrangements with a taxi driver: the roads are fine for a saloon car and many taxi drivers know the park well. Hitching in from the main entrance gate is not an unrealistic option, but you should make sure your lift will be able to get you out again.

If you are driving yourself, you may encounter a few wildly gesticulating gentlemen along the road to the national park. You don't have a flat tyre, and there's no water or oil leaking from your engine. They are con artists.

Accommodation

There are two upmarket lodges in the park: Lake Nakuru Lodge, PO Box 70559, Nairobi; tel: (02) 224998; and Lion Hill Lodge (Sarova Hotels). Both have attractive grounds, commanding views across to the lake and good facilities including a swimming pool. Lion Hill Lodge is newer and marginally cheaper, but Lake Nakuru Lodge has more character.

If you don't have transport, and you do have a tent, the best place to stay is Backpackers' Campsite at the main gate. The campsite is set in an attractive stand of yellow fever trees away from the lake. A fair amount of wildlife passes through: waterbuck, warthog and – be warned – a troop of very aggressive baboons and another troop of less threatening but equally roguish vervet monkeys. Facilities include cold showers and toilets. Campers without vehicles are not normally charged park entrance fees unless they get a lift into the park.

There are a couple of campsites deeper in the park. The nicest is Njoro campsite, in a secluded patch of yellow fever trees on the western shore, but it was closed when I last visited. In the remote southeast corner of the park, Makalia campsite is set near a waterfall (a dismal trickle would be closer to the mark).

There are cheap dormitory beds and run-down bandas at the Wildlife Club of Kenya hostel about 5 km into the park from the main entrance gate.

LAKE BOGORIA NATIONAL RESERVE

Heading northwards up the Rift Valley along the B4, the grassy farmland around Nakuru gives way to the altogether harsher landscape that is typical of northern Kenya. The baked red soil is crossed by watercourses which rarely flow, and covered in a tangle of dry acacia scrub. At the foot of the Rift Valley wall, some 60 km north of Nakuru and hidden from the main road by a range of low hills, lies the little visited but immensely spectacular Lake Bogoria.

At times, Lake Bogoria's brackish water supports thousands of flamingos, though unlike at Lake Nakuru, here greater flamingo appear to outnumber lesser flamingo. There isn't a great deal of wildlife around other than a small but steadily growing population of greater kudu, which are rare elsewhere in Kenya after they were decimated in a rinderpest epidemic at the turn of the century. Birdlife is varied, with dry country species found in the surrounding scrub and the lake's fringes supporting a variety of waterbirds.

Lake Bogoria is primarily worth visiting for its scenic spectacle. The blue water and green fringe of the lake contrast starkly with the surrounding aridity; nestled in a mountainous bowl, the lake has a primeval quality, amplified when you walk through Maji ya Moto, the hot springs and steaming geysers which leap 2 m into the air from a grassy field on the western shore. These springs, incidentally, should not be treated lightly: they are lethally hot and over the years several tourists have been seriously scalded and even killed after slipping into them.

How to get there

Lake Bogoria is about 20 km by road from the B4 between Nakuru and Lake Baringo. The main turn-off to Loboi Gate is signposted about 3 km south of Marigat. If you have a 4x4, an alternative route is signposted from the village of Mogotio on the B4 about 35 km from Nakuru. This offers a dramatic approach to the lake over rutted dirt roads. It's fairly straightforward; the only possible point of confusion is the fork signposted Bogoria in one direction and Bogoria/Maji Ya Moto the other. Go towards Maji Ya Moto. The lake can also be approached from the Nakuru-Nyahururu road via Lake Solai; again, a 4x4 is necessary.

Until recently Lake Bogoria was difficult to reach without your own transport, but it's a lot easier now there's a hotel near the entrance gate. There are regular minibuses between Nakuru and Marigat. From Marigat there is the occasional matatu to Lobai Gate, but it's probably better to wait at the turn-off south of town for a lift. There are no restrictions on walking in the park. The hot springs are 11 km from Loboi Gate; hitching shouldn't prove difficult, especially at weekends. If you don't have a vehicle and want to reach Fig Tree Campsite, a further 15 km past the hot springs, you'll probably have to walk.

Accommodation

The recently opened Lake Bogoria Hotel, PO Box 208, Menangai West; tel: (037) 42696, 2 km outside Loboi Gate, is a pleasant but rather bland tourist-class hotel with a fair restaurant and a swimming pool. Rates are modest.

The Papyrus Inn Hotel is another recent addition directly opposite Loboi Gate. It's basically a typical local lodging with an unusually smart restaurant, TV lounge and bar with fridge. The pretension to quality, unfortunately, does not extend to the comfort or cleanliness of the rooms, which are acceptable but no more.

It's possible to camp at Loboi Gate. Alternatively, Fig Tree Campsite at the southern end of the national reserve is more attractive, set in a stand of fig trees with a freshwater stream running through, but it's only practical if you have a vehicle or don't mind a long walk.

LAKE BARINGO

The northernmost of Kenya's chain of small Rift Valley lakes, Baringo in many respects resembles a larger, more accessible and less scenically dramatic freshwater version of Lake Bogoria. The area immediately around the lake is flat, dry and apparently overgrazed by goats. Patches of papyrus and well-developed acacia stands line the shore. The Rift Valley wall rises to the west, while a low escarpment lies 2 km back from the lake to the east. There are two small volcanic islands in the lake.

Baringo is not protected in any way and there are several villages on its shore. The largest, Kampi Ya Samaki, has several small guesthouses, shops and bars. Wildlife is scarce, but the lake itself teems with hippo and crocodile, and monitor lizards appear to be common. Because it lies in a transitional zone, the area around Baringo is exceptionally rich in birds and a good place to see northern specials. The Lake Baringo Club has organised bird walks twice a day, led by the knowledgeable resident ornithologist. The club's shop stocks a bird checklist for the area.

If you're spending some time at Baringo, the surrounding area is easily explored on foot. The well-wooded grounds of Robert's Campsite and Lake Baringo Club hold an interesting selection of birds including whitebellied lourie, Taita fiscal, whitecrowned shrike, slaty-coloured boubou, northern masked weaver, whitebilled buffalo weaver, red-backed scrub robin, fantailed raven and a variety of hornbills, starlings and barbets. The open area immediately south of the Lake Baringo Club is a good place to see hippo and it also holds some interesting plovers (Caspian, spurwing and blackhead), migrant wheatears, waders and wagtails. In summer, look out for bluecheeked bee-eater here. The adjacent acacia woodland usually throws up interesting birds; I've regularly seen the white phase of paradise flycatcher here.

The cliffs 2 km from the lake shore are a good destination for a short walk. To get there, follow the tar road back towards Nakuru till you reach the junction, then follow any of several footpaths to the cliffs. Look out for the Verreaux's (black) eagles which nest on the cliff, and the two species of localised hornbills (Hemprich's and Jackson's) which live in the woodland below it. You're unlikely to miss the hyrax which are abundant in the area. Climb one of the footpaths up the cliff for a great view back to the lake.

Boat trips on the lake can be arranged through the main hotels or Robert's Campsite, or by asking around in Kampi Ya Samaki.

How to get there

Air

The Lake Baringo Club and Island Camp organise charter flights to Baringo.

Organised safari

Baringo is a regular feature on upmarket safaris from Nairobi.

Road

Kampi Ya Samaki, Robert's Campsite and the Lake Baringo Club lie 2 km off the B4; the turn-off is clearly signposted about 20 km north of Marigat. The road is tarred the whole way. Coming by public transport from Nakuru, there are regular minibuses as far as Marigat. Transport thins out after that, but there are still several matatus daily to Kampi Ya Samaki and hitching is quite easy.

Accommodation

The upmarket Lake Baringo Lodge (Block Hotels) has a great lake shore position about 1 km before Kampi Ya Samaki. The food is good and there's a swimming pool. Evening slide shows and bird walks with the resident ornithologist give this hotel the edge for bird-watchers: it's very popular with ornithological tours. Hippo are regular visitors at night.

Other tourist-class options are Island Camp (Windsor Hotels), a luxury tented camp situated on Ol Kokwe Island, and the newer Saruni Camp, PO Box 61542, Nairobi; tel: (02) 333285, also on Ol Kokwe, which is more modest and places a strong emphasis on birds.

For budget travellers, the nicest place to stay is Robert's Campsite, with wonderful grounds adjacent to the Lake Baringo Club. The site is teeming with birds and is a favoured nocturnal haunt of hippo. Firewood is available. A shop at the entrance sells cold sodas and a fair variety of canned and frozen foodstuffs. There are a few bandas which can be booked by writing to PO Box 1051, Nakuru. The only problem with Robert's is the price: camping for two costs more than a cheap hotel room in most towns, and the bandas, which are not even self-contained, are priced in the tourist-class bracket.

I can't see any point in visiting a place as beautiful as Baringo to stay in a village as unattractive as Kampi ya Samaki, but I'm in the minority. The lodgings in Kampi ya Samaki are at best indifferent, but there is plenty of choice and rooms are a quarter the price of camping at Robert's. All things being relative, the Bahari and Lake View hotels are the best on offer.

8 WESTERN KENYA

Western Kenya is made up of densely populated and fertile highlands rising from the more sparsely vegetated Lake Victoria basin. The west sees few tourists, and facilities are spartan by Kenyan standards, but the area is rich in animal species normally associated with Uganda and West Africa, and thus of special interest to nature lovers.

The main gateways to western Kenya are the Lake Victoria port of Kisumu and the highlands town of Eldoret, both of which are linked to Nairobi by good roads and regular train services. Other important centres are Kakamega, Kitale, Kisii, Kericho, Webuye and Bungoma, though the latter two are mainly of interest if you are continuing on to Uganda.

Perhaps the most alluring spot in western Kenya is Kakamega Forest, a sizeable remnant of the rain forest which once formed a virtually continuous belt stretching to the Atlantic. Kakamega is the one place in Kenya every bird-watcher should make an effort to get to, and it also supports a good range of primates.

There are two national parks in the western highlands, both near Kitale. Saiwa Swamp National Park protects the localised sitatunga antelope and, like Kakamega, a good variety of forest birds and primates. Hiking visitors are not allowed into Mount Elgon National Park – which defeats the most likely objective for a visit, to climb Mount Elgon.

LAKE VICTORIA

Lake Victoria, the largest freshwater lake in the world, lies in an elevated basin between the two main forks of the Rift Valley. It lacks the dramatic scenery of Africa's other great lakes, Tanganyika and Malawi, so vividly implanted in the memory of anyone who has seen them. Lake Victoria is a murky, amorphous body of water, riddled with bilharzia and depleted of endemic fish since the misguided introduction of Nile perch in the 1950s. The Kenyan part of the lake offers some interesting off the beaten track diversions, and the islands offer some thrills for well-heeled game fishermen, but otherwise the area doesn't really warrant a special visit.

Kenya's third largest town, Kisumu, lies on Winan Gulf in the north-eastern corner of Lake Victoria. Other major lake ports include Mwanza, Bukoba and Musoma in Tanzania and Port Bell and Entebbe in Uganda. Kisumu aside, the only settlements of any size on the Kenyan side of the lake are Kendu and Homa Bay, both connected to Kisumu by a daily ferry service.

The Lake Victoria basin is home to the Nilotic-speaking Luo people, who make up Kenya's third largest ethnic group. The Luo migrated to the area from the Sudan in the 15th century. Originally pastoralists, they announced their arrival by making regular cattle raids on the existing residents, who either integrated into the Luo through war and intermarriage or else fled to the highlands around Kisii. Cattle herding still forms a part of traditional Luo lifestyle but the lake itself has long since become their most important source of food. For a more extensive survey of Luo history and traditions, read the booklet *People around the lake: Luo* by William Ochieng (Evans Brothers, 1979), which is readily available in good bookshops in Nairobi.

KISUMU

Telephone code: 035

Kisumu is a pleasantly unaffected town, with a languid, tropical character that is vaguely reminiscent of the less visited parts of the Tanzanian coast. It became the lakeside administration centre in 1901, when the railway line from Mombasa was completed, and despite a less than idyllic setting (bilharzia, malaria and sleeping sickness were rife) it formed a natural transport hub between the coast, Uganda and western Tanganyika. Kisumu suffered badly as a result of the breakdown of the East African Community in 1975. By the late 1980s it was looking very run down, but it seems to have undergone something of a facelift in the last few years.

How to get there

Road

A regular procession of buses and minibuses connects Kisumu to Nairobi and points in between, as well as other towns in western Kenya. Akamba runs a daily bus service to Nairobi; their booking office is on Alego Street. Hitching along the Nairobi-Kisumu road is a viable option.

Rail

The daily train service between Nairobi and Kisumu leaves both towns at 18h00 and the trip takes approximately 14 hours.

Air

Kenya Airways flies daily between Kisumu and Nairobi.

Lake

A daily ferry links Kisumu to Kendu Bay and Homa Bay, leaving Kisumu at around 9h00. The ferry services which once linked Kisumu to Port Bell in Uganda and various Tanzanian ports have long ceased to operate, though this might change with the recent revival of the East African Community.

Accommodation

Kisumu's flashiest hotel, the Imperial, Jomo Kenyatta Highway, PO Box 1866; tel: (035) 41485, has a transatlantic feel at odds with the rest of the town. The spacious self-contained rooms have air-conditioning and mosquito nets. It's surprisingly inexpensive – at the bottom of the modest range – but then there aren't too many tourists in Kisumu. The Sunset Hotel (AT&H), Jomo Kenyatta Highway, on the lake shore 1 km out of the town centre, has rather more atmosphere but it's not as well maintained and rooms are a lot more expensive.

There are a few decent cheap hotels in Kisumu. The Marine Hotel, PO Box 945; tel: (035) 40170, is the newest and its large self-contained rooms with mosquito nets and fans are unusually good value. The Hotel Inca, Jomo Kenyatta Road, PO Box 112; tel: (035) 40158, has self-contained rooms with fans and mosquito nets; it's centrally positioned and fair value, but nothing special. The Hotel Royale, Jomo Kenyatta Highway, PO Box 1690; tel: (035) 44240, is too scruffy to fit into the tourist-class category. The large verandah and rambling interior are the epitome of faded colonial elegance. Rooms are self-contained with air-conditioning and mosquito nets.

Dropping in price, but vastly superior to the average local lodging, the Western Hotel, Alego Street, PO Box 1519; tel: (035) 42586, has self-contained rooms with mosquito nets and a communal balcony from where you can watch the town go by. Razbi's Guesthouse, Oginga Odinga Street, is one of the best local lodgings in Kenya: dirt cheap but dirt free. The basic self-contained rooms at the Talk of the Town Otuma Street, are good value and popular with travellers, as is the attached restaurant. Committed hostellers may want to try the YMCA or YWCA on Nairobi Road opposite the bus station.

If you have a tent, you can camp at Dunga Refreshments on the lake shore about 2 km out of town. To get there follow Jomo Kenyatta Highway southwards past the Sunset Hotel. Facilities include a shower and a restaurant.

Restaurants and bars

The verandah of the Hotel Royale is a popular meeting point for aid workers, with its relaxed atmosphere and cheap, filling grills. On the more enclosed verandah of the Imperial Hotel excellent kebabs and chicken tikka are served.

Most other restaurants in Kisumu specialise in fish or Indian dishes. The Talk of the Town and adjacent Expresso Coffee House on Otuma Street both have extensive and inexpensive menus, featuring fruit juices, curries and Western dishes such as steak and hamburgers. Neither serves alcohol. For fish dishes, try Bodega's, around the corner from the Octopus Club. And if you're feeling homesick for a hamburger, there's a Wimpy on the corner of Jomo Kenyatta Highway and Angawa Avenue.

The improbably-named Octopus Bottoms Up Day and Night Club on Ogada Street consists of a tacky ground-floor disco and restaurant, and a quieter rooftop bar. There are several less salubrious clubs dotted around the town centre.

Away from the town centre, Dunga Refreshments (see accommodation) serves Indian and Western dishes and cold beers. The all-you-can-eat Sunday lunch here is highly rated, as is the similar but more expensive Sunday buffet at the Sunset Hotel.

Around town

What Kisumu lacks in tourist attractions it makes up for by having plenty of character – follow your nose. If aimless strolling doesn't appeal, a worthwhile destination is the Kisumu Museum, a short walk out of town on the Nairobi road, which, in addition to the predictable collection of stuffed animals, boasts interesting displays on the people of western Kenya and a good collection of traditional musical instruments.

To explore the lake shore, walk south of town for about 1 km past the Sunset Hotel to Hippo Point where there's a chance, fairly remote, of seeing hippo. A further 500 m down the road you can grab a cold drink or meal at Dunga Refreshments.

A 10-minute taxi ride north of the town centre takes you to the Kisumu Fisheries Department and golf course, where papyrus beds hold localised birds such as blueheaded coucal, swamp flycatcher, papyrus gonalek and slenderbilled weaver.

KENDU BAY

Kendu Bay makes for an excellent day trip or overnight excursion from Kisumu. The ferry ride there gets you out onto Lake Victoria and it arrives early enough in the day to allow for further exploration.

A short walk out of Kendu Bay, Simbi Crater Lake is steeped in legend. Local people refuse to swim in Simbi, or to take a boat onto it; they say that it was formed when an angry old lady brought down a massive flood to swamp a village and kill its residents; it is immeasurably deep (the only attempt made to measure its depth resulted in the boat capsizing and its occupants drowning – or so I'm told); and its green waters are devoid of vertebrate life. On the firmer ground of the shore, there is some interesting birdlife around: flamingos can be seen all year and in summer the lake is lined with migrant waders and wagtails.

At the nearby village of Oriang, a UN-funded centre specialises in making pottery and bead necklaces. Also at Oriang is the turn-off to Otok Bird Sanctuary, which protects a large variety of waterbirds and large mammals including hippo and waterbuck.

Kendu Bay itself sprawls untidily between the ferry jetty and the Kisumu road. About the only attractions in town are the papyrus beds around the jetty (teeming with birds) and the mosque halfway between the jetty and the road (someone's bound to invite you up to the roof, from where there's a view over the lake). If you're attracted to the idea of going out on Lake Victoria on a local boat, it should be possible to negotiate a price with the fishermen near the ferry jetty. The nearby Hippo Point would make an attractive destination.

How to get there

The best way to do a round trip from Kisumu is to catch a ferry there and return by road. The ferry leaves Kisumu daily at 9h00 and arrives at Kendu Bay at 11h00. In the opposite direction, a ferry leaves Kendu

Bay at 14h00 and arrives in Kisumu at 16h00. A good tar road connects Kisumu to Kendu Bay and minibuses and matatus leave between the towns every hour or so.

To reach Simbi from Kendu Bay, follow the Homa Bay road for about 2 km. Immediately after the first bridge, turn right into a sideroad and follow this for 1 km or so. The beautiful, and noisy, blackheaded gonalek is likely to be seen along the way.

Oriang is 5 km from Kendu Bay and any Homa Bay-bound matatu will drop you there. The owner of the Big Five Restaurant will sometimes hire out his pick-up truck for a negotiable fee – worth thinking about if you want to visit Otok Bird Sanctuary.

Accommodation

There are a few local lodgings on the main street and acceptable meals and cold drinks at the Big Five Bar and Restaurant.

HOMA BAY AND RUMA NATIONAL PARK

Homa Bay lies on the Lake Victoria shore some 40 km south of Kendu Bay. Aside from being the southernmost of the daily ferry stops on the lake shore, the town holds little of interest. If you're stuck here for an afternoon, your best bet is to hike to the top of Got Asego, the volcanic plug overlooking the town, from where there's a panoramic view of the lake and surrounding plains; the round trip only takes a couple of hours.

Ruma National Park, 25 km southwest of Homa Bay, has been set aside to protect localised mammal species such as roan antelope, oribi, Jackson's hartebeest and Rothschild's giraffe. Cheetah and leopard are also present. Not least among Ruma's attractions is that it sees very few visitors: if you do visit, you're likely to have it to yourself.

How to get there

The lake ferry leaves Kisumu daily at 9h00 and arrives at Homa Bay at 14h30 before continuing on to Asembo Bay on the opposite side of Winan Gulf. In the opposite direction, the ferry from Asembo Bay stops at Homa Bay daily at 11h00 and arrives in Kisumu at 16h00. Ferries in both directions stop at Kendu Bay.

Regular matatus connect Homa Bay to Kisumu, Kendu Bay and Kisii. Access to Ruma National Park is via Nyatoto Gate, which lies 10 km off the Homa Bay-Mbito road. Ruma is difficult to reach without your own transport.

Accommodation

Rather surprisingly, there is a tourist-class hotel in Homa Bay. The Homa Bay Hotel is situated on the lake shore; prices are modest and bookings can be made through Msafiri Inns, but there's not much danger of it being full. Best of the local lodgings is the Masawa Hotel, an ex-colonial establishment with attractive grounds and dirt cheap rates.

There is no accommodation in Ruma National Park, nor is there a designated campsite. Camping is permitted, but you must be self-sufficient in food and water.

RUSINGA AND MFANGANO ISLANDS

These two large islands in Lake Victoria are popular with fishermen due to the fly-in fishing safaris to the exclusive Rusinga and Mfangano Island Camps. It's perfectly possible, however, to visit the islands under your own steam. In addition to fishing, both islands offer good bird-watching and a good chance of seeing hippo, monitor lizards and the spotted-necked otter.

Rusinga is the easier of the two islands to reach as it is connected to Mbita on the mainland by a man-made causeway. The island is the birthplace of Tom Mboya, Jomo Kenyatta's right-hand man and potential presidential successor who was gunned down in Nairobi in 1969, sparking off a succession of riots and the effective end of multi-party politics in Kenya. Mboya is buried on the island near Kasawanga. Rusinga is also notable for being rich in fossils: it was here that Mary Leakey discovered the *Proconsul africanus* skull now housed in the Nairobi Museum.

Mfangano is more remote. There are no motor vehicles on the island and most of its inhabitants scrape a living from fishing. Wildlife aside, Mfangano's main attraction is the schematic rock paintings on the wall of a cave near Ukulu. The paintings were done by earlier inhabitants of the island, probably San-like hunter-gatherers. The largest settlement on Mfangano is Sena, where ferries dock.

How to get there

A ferry service connects Homa Bay to Mbita and Sena, leaving Homa Bay at 7h00 on Wednesday and Friday, and arriving at Mbita at 10h30 and Sena at 15h00. The return service leaves Sena at 10h00 on Thursday and Saturday and arrives at Mbita at 14h00 and Homa Bay at 17h30 In addition, there are infrequent matatus between Homa Bay and Mbita and there is a daily lake taxi between Mbita and Sena.

Mfangano and Rusinga Island Camps are visited as part of a fly-in package.

Accommodation

The luxury Mfangano Island Camp, PO Box 48217, Nairobi; tel: (02 331871; and Rusinga Island Camp (Lonrho Hotels) are similar, with an emphasis on fishing for Nile perch. Both have good lakeshore settings Fly-in packages leave from Nairobi or, more usually, Masai Mara.

Formal options for budget travellers are limited to a few local lodgings in Mbita and a Government Rest House in Sena, but it's also possible to camp in undesignated areas or rent a room in a private home or Mfangano.

KISII

This rather frenetic small town in the highlands east of Lake Victoria is noted for its soapstone and the fertility of the surrounding country side. Kisii soapstone carvings are sold at curio stalls throughout Kenya but they can be bought far more cheaply at their source, which is the Kisii Soapstone Carvers Co-op near Tabaka, about 25 km from Kisii Few tourists visit this place – carvings are generally sold directly to Nairobi wholesalers – so looking around to buy carvings is informal and without pressure.

How to get there

Kisii is connected to Kisumu and Nakuru (via Kericho) by good tar roads. There is regular public transport in all directions. Tabaka lies 5 km off the Kisii-Morogi road, and is signposted. There are a few matatus daily between Kisii and Tabaka.

Accommodation

The nicest place to stay, and firmly in the cheap hotel category, is the Kisii Hotel, PO Box 26; tel: (0381) 20954, 500 m out of town on the Kisumu road. It's seen better days, but is nevertheless charming, with overgrown gardens, a popular bar and a fair restaurant. There are several more basic lodgings in the town centre, of which the Safe Lodge and Capital Hotel are central and reliable.

KERICHO

Kericho lies in the heart of Africa's most important tea-growing region. The surrounding countryside is very pretty: orderly tea plantations stretching over rolling hills are interspersed by forested valleys, all enhanced by occasional glimpses across the Rift Valley. Kericho was founded to service the tea estates, and tea is still the lifeblood of its economy. The Kiptariet River, a few hundred metres south of the town centre, is fringed by riparian forest and offers trout fishing. Equipment can be hired from the Tea Hotel.

Chagaik Arboretum, 8 km out of town, consists of a variety of endemic and exotic trees sloping down to a small dam on the Kiptariet River. The lush indigenous forest on the opposite bank is a good spot to see forest birds such as Hartlaub's turaco, cinnamonchested bee-eater, black-and-white casqued hornbill and purplethroated cuckoo-shrike. It's the only place in Kenya where I've seen black duck. A troop of black-and-white colobus monkeys reputedly lives in the forest. There is no entrance fee.

How to get there

Kericho is connected to Nakuru, Kisii and Kisumu by good tar roads and there is plenty of public transport in all directions. To visit the arboretum, ask any vehicle heading to Nakuru to drop you at Chagaik Tea Estate; the entrance is 500 m, and signposted, from the main road.

Accommodation

The modestly priced Kericho Tea Hotel, 500 m out of town on the Nakuru road, PO Box 75; tel: (0361) 20280, the only tourist-class option in Kericho, was built by Brooke Bond in the 1950s and is presently run by Msafiri Inns (rumour is it will change hands soon). It is one of the

most attractive hotels in western Kenya, with a gracious interior, lo₃
fire in the lounge and beautiful wooded grounds. The food is good an₍
cheap: recommended even if you are sleeping elsewhere.

In the cheap hotel bracket, Kericho Lodge and Fishing Resort, P₍
Box 25; tel: (0361) 20035, 2 km out of town and signposted, has self
contained bandas and a restaurant and bar. It is next to the Kiptarie
River, making it attractive to anglers and bird-watchers. Closer to town
the Midwest Hotel, Moi Highway, PO Box 1175; tel: (0361) 20611, i
a little bland, but it's very comfortable, and you'd be pushed to fin₍
better value anywhere in Kenya.

Local lodgings in the town centre are uniformly dire. Your best be
is the Mwalimu Hotel, which has self-contained rooms and a ground
floor bar and restaurant. Tas Lodge, next to the Tea Hotel, is only ₐ
little more savoury, with pleasant grounds, a TV lounge and adequat₍
self-contained rooms. About 3 km out of town, the New Tas Hotel i₅
similarly priced to the Tas and much better value, with self-containe₍
cottages and a campsite in attractive grounds.

ELDORET

Eldoret is the largest town in the western highlands. It is unique among
Kenyan towns in that it was founded by Afrikaners, but otherwise it'₅
an unremarkable sort of place and if you arrive early enough in th₍
day there's little reason to explore beyond the bus station. On the othe₁
hand, if you've been in the sticks for a few days or want to stock u₊
for a few days' hiking or camping, Eldoret has all the facilities of ₐ
large town and a likeable enough atmosphere.

How to get there

Road

Eldoret is a major route focal point, with good roads connecting it t₍
Kisumu, Kitale, Malaba and Nakuru. There's plenty of transport in al
directions, though if you're heading to Kakamega you may need to tak₍
a matatu as far as Webuye and change vehicles there.

Approaching Eldoret from Nakuru or elsewhere in the east, the leas₁
obvious route – via the Kerio Valley – is also the most dramatic. A
steady stream of minibuses and matatus run along this route, thougŀ
you'll normally have to break the trip into stages, changing vehicles a₁
Marigat and Kabernet (see chapter seven).

Rail

Trains to Malaba leave Nairobi at 15h00 on Tuesday, Friday and Saturday and arrive in Eldoret at 3h00 the next morning. In the opposite direction, trains leave Malaba at 16h00 on Wednesday, Saturday and Sunday, pass through Eldoret at 21h00 and arrive in Nairobi at 9h00 the next morning.

Accommodation

The modestly priced Sirikwa Hotel (AT&H), Elgoyo Road, is the only tourist-class accommodation. The restaurant serves the best food in town.

The Wagon Wheel Hotel, Elgoyo Road, PO Box 551; tel: (0321) 32271, opposite the Sirikwa, is a typical cheap hotel. Much cheaper and a lot more central, the New Lincoln Hotel, Oloo Road, PO Box 551; tel: (0321) 22093, is a pleasant, crumbling colonial establishment with a busy bar and restaurant. It could be noisy at night, but it's a good place to meet people and the comfortable self-contained rooms are reasonably priced.

There are dozens of local lodgings scattered around Eldoret. Two of the better ones are Kabathayu Lodging, cnr Arap Moi and Tagore and Eldoret Valley Hotel, Uganda Road, around the corner from each other, about 10 minutes' walk west of the bus station.

An attractive out of town option, popular with overland trucks, is the Naiberi River Campsite, 20 km from Eldoret on the Kaptagat Road. In addition to camping, there are cheap bandas and self-contained cottages on the site. The area offers good rambling and nearby forests hold several unusual birds and monkeys, including black-and-white colobus monkeys. Facilities include a restaurant and bar. To get a lift there, contact the owner; tel: (0321) 31069 in Eldoret.

An interesting overnight stop between Eldoret and Kitale is the Soy Country Club, where you can camp or rent a room at cheap hotel rates. This is good value. There's a bar and restaurant at the club. The surrounding hills are green and grassy, and there are some interesting marshes along the road back to Eldoret. A remnant herd of Rothschild's giraffe roam the area. Any vehicle heading between Eldoret and Kitale can drop you at the blink-and-you'll-miss-it village of Soy.

KAKAMEGA

Although it's the main urban centre of Kenya's second-largest ethnic group, the Bantu-speaking Luhya, Kakamega would barely warrant a mention were it not for its proximity to the Kakamega Forest. If you're stuck here for an afternoon, the busy market is worth a look, or you could swim and eat a reasonable meal at the Golf Hotel, but that's about it.

How to get there

Kakamega lies on the busy Kisumu-Kitale road. There is plenty of transport from Eldoret, but you'll have to change vehicles at Webuye.

Accommodation

In the tourist class, the modest Golf Hotel, Msafiri Inns; tel: (0331) 20460, is pleasantly low-key, with friendly staff, a large lawn, a swimming pool, spacious self-contained rooms and a good restaurant. Hotel residents gain automatic membership of the adjacent golf course and sports club. The hotel manager can organise guided day trips to the forest. For budget travellers, the Banks View Hotel (opposite Kenya Commercial Bank!) and the Kakamega Wayside Hotel alongside it are acceptable local lodgings.

KAKAMEGA FOREST

The Kakamega Forest is one of Kenya's most alluring destinations for anyone with more than a passing interest in natural history. Little known to the general public, the forest is renowned by naturalists for supporting a myriad of typically West African species in isolation from other similar forests. And although the accommodation in the forest is rudimentary when compared to the lodges in the more famous game reserves, it has a low-key charm in keeping with the intimacy of its setting, and it's very cheap.

The most visible large mammals are monkeys. Baboon, black-and-white colobus monkeys, redtailed monkey and blue monkey are common throughout the forest, and De Brazza's monkey was recently discovered to be resident in the part of the forest protected by Kisere Nature Reserve (currently closed to the public).

Most other Kakamega specials are nocturnal and unlikely to be seen without some effort. The foremost attraction is the potto, a large sloth-like creature that is loosely related to the lemurs of Madagascar. Potto are quite easy to pick up at night if you drive slowly along forest roads with a large flashlight attached to your vehicle. A powerful torch should do the trick if you're on foot. Bushbaby, tree pangolin, leopard and several types of squirrel are also present. The forest is potentially big enough to harbour a population of elephant and buffalo, but none are present – presumably they have been hunted out.

Over 320 bird species have been recorded in and around the forest, 16 of which are found nowhere else in Kenya. A complete checklist, with details of abundance and favoured habitat, was compiled by Udo Savali in 1989 and is sometimes available at Bunyunga. Reasonably competent first-time visitors can expect to see between 70 and 100 species over a few days, perhaps half of which will be new to them.

Kakamega is also known for its reptiles and butterflies. You're unlikely to see many of the former (other than the odd lizard), but butterflies of all hues can be seen in abundance, especially near water.

Kakamega Forest can be visited from two sides. Isecheno Rest House and Rondo Retreat both lie 15-20 km southeast of Kakamega town, while Bunyunga's bandas and campsite lie 20 km northeast of town. Both sides of the forest are accessible with public transport, and there are knowledgable guides at Bunyunga and Isecheno who will lead guided nature walks for a small fee.

How to get there

Organised safari and self-drive

Few organised safaris include Kakamega in their itinerary; you would need to make private arrangements with a tour company, which could be costly. You could get to Kakamega town under your own steam more affordably, and arrange with the Golf Hotel to be taken to the forest. Best of all, hire a vehicle in Nairobi and drive up from there. Bunyunga can be visited in a saloon car, but you may need a 4x4 to reach Rondo or Isecheno after rains.

Getting to Bunyunga

Bunyunga lies 2 km from the main Kakamega-Webuye road. Ask a matatu driver to drop you at Kimbiri turn-off 17 km north of Kakamega town. There are two side roads, 50 m apart, running east from the main road here. Take the one signposted for Kakamega National Reserve Headquarters. It's a 20-minute walk from the main road to the headquarters, where you must check in before being taken to the campsite.

Getting to Isecheno and Rondo

Both of these places lie along the dirt road connecting Kakamega town to Kapsabet via Shinyalu. Isecheno lies about 1 km off the road; the turn-off is roughly 5 km southeast of Shinyalu. Rondo is about 8 km southeast of Shinyalu. If you don't have a vehicle, the early morning Eldoret-Kisumu bus which runs daily in each direction along this road can drop you where you want to be. Alternatively, if you don't mind walking the last stretch, there are regular matatus between Kakamega town and Shinyalu.

Accommodation

The delightful forest-fringed Bunyunga campsite, run by Kenya Wildlife Services near the reserve headquarters, is relatively little known and there's a good chance you'll have it to yourself. Accommodation consists of several lockable African-style huts with beds and mattresses but no bedding. Facilities include a communal cooking area, free firewood, longdrop toilets and an open-topped wooden enclosure where you can wash. Water for washing and drinking must be carried from the nearby stream. A limited selection of foodstuffs can be bought from the village on the main Kakamega-Webuye road 1 km north of the Bunyunga turn-off, but it's best to bring all you need with you. Camping is permitted.

Isecheno Rest House, PO Box 88, Kakamega, is the established place to stay in the forest, and arguably the best. The Rest House consists of four self-contained double bedrooms and a balcony on a raised platform with parking space underneath. You can also camp. As with Bunyunga, it's best to bring food with you; the duka at the forestry station has a few essentials and will normally prepare basic meals (chapati and sak-umawiki in all probability), but don't rely on this. If you don't have a tent, booking is advisable though not always necessary.

Rondo Retreat, PO Box 2153, Kakamega, a religious centre that has only recently opened to the public, fills a long-standing need for tourist-class accommodation in the heart of the forest. The main building is a 1928 farmhouse; accommodation is in furnished self-contained log cabins. There is a restaurant but no alcohol is served. Prices are modest and include full board.

Exploring around Bunyunga

A network of roads and footpaths branch from the campsite. Two good round trips, both about 5 km long, start at the path marked "Hiking Trail" (near the toilet). Follow this for about 1 km until you reach a signposted fork. The right fork leads to a waterfall, the left to a quarry and viewpoint.

Heading towards the waterfall the footpath passes through light forest interspersed with open grassland, before emerging at a clearing marked "Car Park". From here it descends through riparian forest (look out for Ross's turaco, the white phase of paradise flycatcher and various wattle-eyes and migrant warblers) to a stream where mountain wagtail are resident. No more than 200 m upstream is the waterfall – or more accurately rapids. Instead of returning the way you came, follow the dirt road back from the car park. This passes through a heath-like area where flowering plants attract a good variety of sunbirds, finches and seedeaters.

The path to the viewpoint passes through more developed forest. Both redtailed and colobus monkeys seem to be common in this area. You can return to the campsite by road, with views deep into the forest.

The campsite is a good place to familiarise yourself with the more common birds. It's reasonably open and you can normally get a few looks at any bird you see. Among the more interesting birds which I saw regularly were Luhder's bush shrike, snowyheaded robin chat, blue flycatcher, yellow white-eye, great blue turaco, greyheaded barbet, black-and-white casqued hornbill, joyful greenbul, Klaas's cuckoo, black cuckooshrike, whiteheaded woodhoopoe and (summer only) blackcap warbler. Redtailed and colobus monkeys are regular visitors to the site, as, more ominously, are baboons.

The forest itself is best explored from footpaths leading from the road back to the main Kakamega-Webuye road. You really need a guide to explore these paths: without one there's a real danger of getting lost, and experienced eyes are invaluable in the dense forest.

Exploring around Isecheno and Rondo

The rest house at Isecheno faces a dense stand of forest known as the Zimmerman Plot after Dale Zimmerman, the ornithologist who undertook the first detailed study of the area's avifauna. Great blue turaco are common in the area, and a troop of colobus monkeys come swinging past the rest house most evenings. The Zimmerman Plot is crisscrossed by a labyrinth of footpaths. There's a real risk of becoming lost if you explore these without a guide; the chief guide at Isecheno is good company, anyway, and he is knowledgable enough about birds to identify virtually any call.

Although there are no formal trails near Isecheno, the road towards Rondo passes through patches of dense forest and offers excellent bird and monkey viewing. Continue past Rondo for about 4 km and you come to a stream where there are butterflies in profusion. The riverine forest here is rated in *Where to watch birds in Kenya* as having the widest variety of bird species anywhere in the forest. A couple of footpaths follow the stream. If possible, drive or try to get a lift from Isecheno to the stream: bird-watching along the road is distractingly good and the 6 km walk can easily take a few hours. Birds which are frequently seen near the stream include blueheaded bee-eater, yellowbill, blue-shouldered robin chat, redheaded malimbe and a variety of wattle-eyes and forest finches.

Hiking from Bunyunga to Isecheno

Kenya Wildlife Services has cut a hiking trail from Bunyunga to Isecheno, which will be open to the public once bridges have been built over the rivers. The hike will take two days and you will have the option of hiking on your own or taking a guide. If you want current details in advance, contact the Kenya Wildlife Services office in Nairobi.

KITALE

Kitale is a useful base for exploring several of the western highlands' major attractions and it is also the starting point for trips to the western shore of Lake Turkana. The fertile highlands around Kitale were heavily settled in the 1920s and 1930s, and the modern town dates back to this period, although it was founded on the older settlement of Quitale, a slave-trading centre for much of the 19th century.

Kitale's one attraction of note is the small museum on the Eldoret side of town, which houses detailed displays of the ethnic groups of northwestern Kenya. The museum's short nature trail passes through a strip of riverine forest.

How to get there

Good tar roads connect Kitale to other towns in western Kenya and there's plenty of transport in all directions.

Accommodation

The Kitale Club, 3 km out of town on the Eldoret road, PO Box 30; tel: (0325) 20030, was built in the colonial era on the site of the old slave quarters. Facilities include a swimming pool, sauna, golf course, restaurant and bar. Accommodation is in self-contained cottages; prices are moderate and include the use of sporting facilities.

Cheap hotels include the misleadingly named New Kitale on Kenyatta Street, and the Bongo Bar, PO Box 530; tel: (0325) 20593. The Bongo Bar is the more vibrant and popular, with clean self-contained rooms, a good bar and an excellent ground-floor restaurant.

There's not much to choose between the several local lodgings around the market and matatu stand. If you are on a tight budget and have a tent, a more pleasant option is to camp at Sirikwa Safaris, out of town on the Kapenguria road (see Saiwa Swamp National Park).

MOUNT ELGON NATIONAL PARK

Mount Elgon straddles the Ugandan border. The peaks, the highest of which is Wagagai (4 321 m), surround a large volcanic caldera on the Ugandan side of the border and are currently more easily climbed from that side. The national park protects the forest and moorland zones of the mountain's eastern slopes. Its best-known feature is Kitum Cave, 3 km from the entrance gate, which is regularly visited by elephants for its salt.

Forest birds and mammals are well represented. After years of intense poaching, the elephant population is on the increase. Buffalo are abundant, as are black-and-white colobus monkeys and blue monkeys. Leopards are the only large predator present. Entry to the park is forbidden without a vehicle, but there is plenty of good walking outside the park: footpaths lead all over the place, and the cultivated areas are interspersed with patches of acacia woodland and riparian forest along the many streams in the area.

Halfway between the Mount Elgon Hotel and the park entrance gate, a left turn onto a rutted side road leads to a forest-fringed stream where, in addition to monkeys, I saw an excellent variety of forest birds: cinnamonchested bee-eater, bluespotted wood dove, greythroated and yellowbilled barbet, grey and purplethroated cuckooshrike, blue flycatcher, blackcap warbler and blackcollared apalis.

Security

The Elgon region has been the scene of several cross-border and intra-Kenyan ethnic clashes over the last decade. The situation is no longer as risky as it was in the 1980s, when Ugandan "bandits" were believed to have a hideout in the mountains and there was an ongoing war between national park rangers and elephant poachers. Nevertheless, as recently as 1992, there was a major ethnic clash which resulted in several deaths. Most of the time the area is as safe as anywhere else, and the chances of a tourist being caught in the crossfire of a local outbreak of violence are minimal, but if you're nervous it might be advisable to make enquiries in advance in Kitale. Msafiri Inns, who run the Mount Elgon Hotel, should be familiar with the current situation.

How to get there

The park gate is 25 km from Kitale by road. Follow the Kapenguria road for about 10 km, then take the signposted left fork onto a graded dirt road. The route via Endebess, shown on most maps, is in a poor state of repair.

If you don't have a vehicle, a taxi from Kitale is not prohibitively expensive for a group. Bargain hard. The Mount Elgon Hotel sends a vehicle to Kitale most days and will normally give lifts to travellers; ask at the supermarket next to Barclays Bank on Kenyatta Street. If you don't mind leaving things to chance, catch a Kapenguria matatu as far as the turn-off. With an early start, you could walk the final 15 km, but with a bit of luck you'll get a lift as far as the agricultural co-op 4 km before the entrance gate.

Accommodation

The Mount Elgon Hotel (Msafiri Inns) is a converted 1930s farmhouse, about 1 km before the park entrance gate. It has plenty of atmosphere and lovely grounds with views across to the Cherangani Hills. The self-contained rooms are a bit tatty, but comfortable enough and modestly priced.

There are two campsites in the national park. Unless you have a vehicle it's more realistic to use the campsite in the grounds of the Mount Elgon Hotel.

Climbing Mount Elgon

If you arrive at Mount Elgon expecting organised climbs along the lines of those on East Africa's other large mountains, you're in for a disappointment. Climbing Mount Elgon has never really taken off. Climbing the peaks involves a border crossing of dubious legality into Uganda, walking is forbidden in the national park, the whole region lies some way from any established tourist circuit and there is a long-standing security problem.

There's nothing preventing a determined hiker from climbing the mountain though. The best starting point is Kilimili, 45 km from Kitale. The hike from here to Little Elgon peak (the highest on the Kenyan side of the border) is a three-day round trip. Few people do this hike so you need to be entirely self-sufficient; enquire about a guide in Kilimili. There are matatus to Kilimili from Kitale, and a couple of basic lodgings in Kilimili.

The first day's goal is Austrian Hut, 39 km from Kilimili. Matatus run as far as Kapsakwony, 7 km along the road, and sometimes to Kaberwa, 4 km further on, but you'll have to walk the last 28 km. From Kaberwa, follow the signpost towards the abandoned Chepkitale Forest Station, which lies 7 km before the hut. The first 7 km or so of the trail, through the forest and bamboo zones, is rough, but once you reach the moorland, conditions improve. Little Elgon is a three hour walk from Austrian Hut. Several other excursions can be made from the hut, but your options are restricted by the illegality of crossing the Ugandan border or entering the national park on foot.

If you want to reach the peaks, or prefer things to be more organised, a climb from the Ugandan side of the mountain is a more viable option. Porters, guides, food and equipment can be organised at the Wagagai Hotel in the village of Budadiri near Mbale. Prices are reasonable. Details about crossing into Uganda are in chapter 11.

The Mount Elgon guide and map by Andrew Wielochowski is an essential purchase if you plan to hike in the area. It's normally available in Nairobi bookshops; if you can't find it, you can buy a 1:125 000 map from the Survey of Kenya office in Nairobi. Many of the books listed under "Climbing" in bookshops have detailed sections on climbing Mount Elgon.

SAIWA SWAMP NATIONAL PARK

This little-visited national park, only 2 square km in area, is the best place to see one of East Africa's most habitat-specific large mammals, the sitatunga. This swamp-dwelling antelope is not dissimilar in appearance to a bushbuck, but it is darker, larger and heavier, and has elongated hooves adapted to its marshy habitat. Sit quietly at one of the rickety viewing platforms verging the swamp and you're almost certain to see one.

The swamp is fringed by forest, where the most common large mammal is the bushbuck – more likely to be seen crashing into the undergrowth than wading through the reeds like the sitatunga. A variety of monkeys are also present. Black-and-white colobus monkeys, vervet and blue monkeys are all likely to be seen, and this is the best place in Kenya to see the shy and localised De Brazza's monkey, which is easily distinguished from the blue monkey by an orange forehead and distinctive white beard. The footpaths that connect the viewing platforms and effectively ring the swamp are the best place to see forest animals.

As you might expect, the forest is a good place to see birds more normally associated with Uganda, for example Ross's turaco, eastern grey plantain eater, doubletoothed barbet and black-and-white casqued hornbill. The swamp itself holds blackcap tchagra, blueheaded coucal and crowned crane.

How to get there

Saiwa Swamp lies 5 km east of the Kitale-Kapenguria road. The turn-off is clearly signposted about 15 km from Kitale. Without a vehicle, expect to walk from the main road. In the lush, green countryside which surrounds Saiwa, this is not an unattractive prospect.

Accommodation

The national park campsite is a peaceful spot set in dense bush rustling with birds and small mammals. Facilities amount to a small cooking area. Firewood and water are available, the latter from the staff village five minutes' walk from the campsite. A small duka near the entrance gate sporadically sells sodas but that's about it; bring everything else you need with you.

Sirikwa Safaris, PO Box 332, Kitale, is a relaxed, family-run establishment, with rooms available in the family house and comfortable, furnished standing tents in the garden. Meals are served with the family or you can barbecue your own food. If you have your own vehicle, experienced guides are available to show you the birds in the nearby

Cherangani Hills or Saiwa Swamp, or further afield to Kakamega Forest and Mount Elgon. You can camp in the garden – it's cheaper than in the national park, and facilities are better, but the national park wins ten times over for atmosphere.

CHERENGANI HILLS

This extensive metamorphic range northwest of Kapenguria rises to 3 581 m and forms the western escarpment of the Rift Valley and the barrier between the lush highlands around Kitale and the arid desert of the north. The area offers a striking contrast in scenery, particularly around Marich Pass and along the dirt road towards Tot, northeast of the range.

Biologically, the Cheranganis share several features with East Africa's other large mountains. The forest zone protects typical forest birds and monkeys and is one of the few places in Kenya where the shy bongo antelope occurs. Although severely encroached upon elsewhere, the Kapkanyar Forest on the western slopes near Kapenguria remains relatively undisturbed. The moorland zone is a mix of swamp and open heath-like country dotted with giant lobelia and senacio plants.

Although no tourist industry is based around the mountains, the area is popular with adventurous hikers. Walking is unrestricted, there are no prohibitive park fees to pay, and the range is crisscrossed by a number of dirt roads – the possibilities are endless. Hiking details can be found in the books mentioned in the hiking and walking section in chapter 3.

How to get there

The surfaced Kitale-Turkana road passes through the foothills of the range between Kapenguria and Marich Pass. North of Marich Pass, a road forks eastward towards Sigor, Tot and the Kerio valley. About 4 km past Kapenguria, a fork to the right heads deeper into the range to the village of Kaibibich and the Kapkanyar Forest. This road continues to Cheptongei in the southern foothills, where it branches: the south fork goes to Eldoret while the northwest fork completes an effective ring road around the mountains via Chesoi to Tot.

Coming from Kitale, there is plenty of public transport to Kapenguria, from where a few matatus run to Ortum and Sigor daily. The daily bus between Kitale and Lodwar (near Lake Turkana) can also drop you at Ortum or the Sigor junction.

The odd private vehicle doubles as a matatu along the Sigor-Tot road, but you may well have to foot it. No great hardship: this is marvellous walking country. The road passes through alternating patches of acacia scrub and lush cultivation (yummy mangoes) with the Cheranganis towering to the south, the desert stretching to the north and the colourful and fiercely traditional Pokot people for company.

South of the range, matatus connect Eldoret to Cheptongei and Chesoi. The 25 km between Chesoi and Tot include a dramatically steep section crossing the escarpment; this should not be contemplated without a solid 4x4 – even in perfect weather. There is no public transport along this route.

Accommodation

The only formal accommodation in the area consists of local lodgings at Kapenguria and Ortum and a District Rest House in Kaibibich. In the other places I visited people were helpful about finding me a room, but you should definitely carry a tent, even if you never use it.

9 NORTH OF NAIROBI: MOUNT KENYA AND THE NORTHERN DESERT

The fertile highlands north of Nairobi are home to Kenya's most populous tribe, the Kikuyu. The region was also heavily settled by colonials; in the 1930s, it became the setting of the Happy Valley scene (of White Mischief notoriety) and, in the 1950s, the infamous Mau-Mau rebellion in which 30-odd settlers and several thousand Kikuyu were killed.

The central highlands are characterised by lush vegetation and cultivation. The scenery is dominated by the snowcapped peaks of Mount Kenya, the second highest mountain in Africa, and the Aberdares range to the west. The tourist focal point is Mount Kenya itself, a popular goal for hikers and climbers. There is plenty of accommodation scattered throughout the area, most notably the idiosyncratic and rather wonderful tree hotels of which Treetops is the most famous.

North of Mount Kenya, the moist highlands rapidly give way to the arid plains that characterise northern Kenya. The north has a markedly different ecology to the rest of East Africa, with the plains animals of the south replaced by dry country species such as reticulated giraffe, Grevy's zebra, gerenuk and Beisa oryx.

Few parts of the north are within reach of short-stay visitors to Kenya. The most popular destination is the Samburu complex of reserves, where most northern animal species can be seen with ease. Other attractions include Meru National Park, Marsabit National Reserve and Lake Turkana, the northernmost and largest of Kenya's Rift Valley lakes.

THE MOUNT KENYA RING ROAD

Mount Kenya is encircled by a tarred road, along which lie the busy but nondescript towns of Karatina, Nyeri, Naro Moru, Nanyuki, Meru, Chogoria and Embu. The ring road starts 100 km north of Nairobi, reached on a good tar road bypassing Thika. There is plenty of public transport from Nairobi to towns such as Nanyuki, Meru and Nyeri. Public transport between the various towns in the area is also good.

Karatina

The small town of Karatina is on the route but otherwise of little interest to tourists. If you need to spend a night, the Karatina Tourist Lodge, in the cheap hotel bracket, is recommended.

Nyeri

This busy, compact market town is the administrative centre of Central Province and the gateway to the Aberdares. Although it is of little intrinsic interest to tourists, Nyeri is one of the more attractive highland towns and there are pleasant short walks along the nearby Chania River. Nyeri is the final resting place of Baden-Powell, of scouting and Mafeking fame; his grave and a memorial are at the northern end of town.

The upmarket Outspan Hotel (Block Hotels), 1 km out of Nyeri, is among the most atmospheric tourist-class hotels in Kenya. It was built in 1932 and has been beautifully maintained; the landscaped grounds, which face Mount Kenya, are also lovely. The Outspan is the base for visits to Treetops: it gets a little hectic around lunchtime, but it's very peaceful once the Treetops clientele have been herded into their buses. For bird-watchers, the guided walks along the Chania River are well worth while: expect to see about 30 highland species in an hour, with sunbirds, weavers and robin chats particularly well represented.

For a cheap hotel in town, the Central, Kanisa Road; White Rhino Kenyatta Road; and Green Hills, Mumbi Road are all good. Local lodgings are clustered on Kimathi Way near the bus station; Bahati Lodging and Maru Lodging are recommended.

Naro Moru

This small village is a popular base from which to climb Mount Kenya (see Mount Kenya National Park). It is conveniently situated astride the ring road and a useful overnight stop between Samburu and the Rift Valley or Masai Mara. The only accommodation in the village is a few local lodgings, but there are several more interesting options nearby.

The modest Naro Moru River Lodge (Alliance Hotels) consists of self-contained rooms along the forested banks of the Naro Moru River. For budget travellers, there is also a dormitory and a campsite. Facilities include a pool, tennis and squash courts, snack bar and a restaurant. The large shady grounds offer exciting bird-watching, and trout fishing in the river is good. The staff has vast experience of organising Mount

Kenya climbs. The lodge lies off the main road 1 km from Naro Moru village.

Mountain Rock Hotel, PO Box 333, Nanyuki; tel: (0176) 62625, on the Naro Moru-Nanyuki road is similar to Naro Moru Lodge. There are good walks in the surrounding forest. Mountain Rock specialises in organising Mount Kenya climbs along the Sirimon route. Camping is permitted.

The traditional base for budget travellers climbing Mount Kenya, the Mount Kenya Youth Hostel, was burnt to the ground in the late 1980s; it has since been partially restored. Dormitory beds are now available and you can camp in the grounds. The hostel lies off the ring road, 9 km from Naro Moru along the dirt road which leads towards the national park entrance gate. It's hitchable if you arrive in town before mid-afternoon. The hostel is on the fringe of the forest zone and there is some good walking in the area.

Nanyuki

Just before you reach Nanyuki, a large sign ensures that you won't miss the fact you're crossing into the northern hemisphere. You can buy a carload of curios, or have it demonstrated (by a leaping man with a bucket) that water does indeed flow anticlockwise to the north of the equator and clockwise to the south. This science lesson concluded, Nanyuki is unremarkable: pleasant enough with all the facilities but hardly worth an overnight stay.

Which cannot be said about the Mount Kenya Safari Club (Lonrho Hotels), 10 km out of town. Included in British Airways' list of leading hotels in the world, the club offers the last word in tropical luxury. The main building dates to the 1930s; the club itself was founded in 1959 by the actor William Holden and the first member list included such luminaries as Winston Churchill, Bob Hope and Bing Crosby. The large grounds contain a waterhole (currently the best spot in Kenya for seeing bongo antelope, albeit they were introduced from the Aberdares) and offer good views of Mount Kenya's peaks.

In the town centre, the altogether less ostentatious Sportsman's Arms, PO Box 3; tel: (0176) 23200, is a sprawling complex of old cottages (cheap hotel rates). Camping is permitted. There are several cheaper lodgings dotted around town.

Meru

Named after the Bantu-speaking Meru who inhabit the area, Meru town sprawls along the ring road fringing the forest zone of the northeastern slopes of Mount Kenya. Though short on prescribed tourist attractions – a small museum containing ethnographic displays on Meru culture is about the sum of it – Meru is an attractive enough place and, with a smidgen of imagination, the surrounding forest and lush cultivation could yield some good walking. Meru town is the starting point for trips into Meru National Park.

If you're looking for a room, the most upmarket address is the Meru Country Hotel, PO Box 1386; tel: (0164) 20427, which has good facilities and self-contained rooms at cheap hotel rates. The similar Stansted Hotel, PO Box 1337; tel: (0164) 20360, is a little cheaper. The best of the local lodgings is the New Milimani.

Chogoria

This is the starting point of the increasingly popular Chogoria route up Mount Kenya (see Mount Kenya National Park). There are a couple of traveller-orientated cheap hotels in town, of which the Cool Inn is recommended. A more reliable option for those who want to organise a climb is the out of town Chogoria Transit Inn, about 1 km from the turn-off towards the Chogoria entrance gate.

Embu

Embu is a town you can safely (and easily) pass through, unless, perhaps, you feel like stopping for a meal or spending a night at the rather pleasant and modestly priced Izaak Walton Inn (Msafiri Inns), 2 km out of town towards Meru. The hotel has large, shady grounds and is a good base for anglers.

MOUNT KENYA NATIONAL PARK

Mount Kenya, Africa's second highest mountain, has three main peaks: Batian (5 199 m), Nelion (5 188 m) and Lenana (4 985 m). The 600 square km area above the forest line is protected as a national park. The mountain formed volcanically around three million years ago, when its cone, since eroded by intense glaciation, may have been as high as 7 000 m. Less impressive in appearance than Kilimanjaro, Mount Kenya's snowcapped peaks nevertheless dominate the skyline of the central highlands.

Mount Kenya's vegetation zones are typical of large East African mountains. Where they are not cultivated, the slopes between 2 000 m and 3 000 m support rain forest and dense stands of bamboo up to 15 m high. The forest zone is the most biologically diverse part of the mountain, but the moorland zone between 3 000 m and 4 000 m is the most remarkable botanically, a surreal landscape of giant heather, giant lobelia and giant groundsel. Above 4 500 m, the volcanic rock and snow support little vegetation other than moss and lichen.

The mountain is home to many large mammal species. In the forest zone, the most commonly seen animals are elephant, buffalo, black-and-white colobus monkey and blue monkey. Animals such as leopard, lion, black rhinoceros, giant forest hog, bushpig, Harvey's red duiker, bushbuck and the scarce bongo are most likely to be seen at lodges such as the Mount Kenya Safari Club or Mountain Lodge. The most commonly seen mammal in the moorland zone (apart from mice, which live in many of the huts) is the rock hyrax, but eland and several smaller antelope are also quite common. Birdlife in the forest zone is profuse, and the higher slopes support rarities such as scarlet-tufted malachite sunbird and raptors including auger buzzard and lammergeyer (bearded vulture). All animal life is scarce above the snow line.

For short-stay visitors to Kenya, contact with the mountain is likely to be limited to an overnight stay at a lodge on the slopes. There are, however, several other options. The highest peaks are only suitable for expert climbers but Lenana is accessible to any fit adult. It is also possible to organise a day hike, through the Naro Moru River Lodge, from Mackinder's Camp. If you've the time, there are plenty of bases from where you could explore the forest or moorland zone cheaply over a couple of days.

Climbing Mount Kenya

Mount Kenya vies with Kilimanjaro as the most popular climb in East Africa. Lenana can be reached without specialised climbing equipment by several routes, though only the Naro Moru and Chogoria routes are used regularly by tourists. Climbs can be arranged independently at the entrance gate or through most Nairobi tour operators and local hotels such as the Naro Moru River Lodge. Self-organised four or five-day hikes work out at less than US $200 inclusive of porters, guides and park and hut fees. If you use a professional operator, expect to pay around double.

The climb to Lenana is essentially an extended uphill hike, but the mountain should not be underestimated. Sudden weather changes are normal and there is a risk of getting lost in blizzard conditions or suffering from hypothermia in mist and drizzle. In fine or overcast weather, one should be alert to the intense equatorial sun. I urge hikers on a tight budget against the temptation to cut costs by not hiring guides and porters: unguided hikers run a real risk of getting lost, especially if the weather turns bad, while porters allow one to hike without being weighed down by luggage and thus enjoy the scenery. Hikers are advised to read the section on mountain health in chapter two.

Whichever route you use, it is advisable to spend three nights on the mountain before ascending Lenana. Allowing for another night on the mountain after you've reached Lenana, this means a minimum hiking period of five days. The longer you allow, the more time you have to enjoy the scenery and look for wildlife, and the greater your chances of reaching the top. A week allows a full day each to explore the forest and moorland zones from a base, and minimises the effects of altitude.

Andrew Wielochowski and Mark Savage's *Mount Kenya map and guide* includes a good 1:50 000 map and detailed information on ecology and geology as well as tips on equipment and health. It is available for a couple of dollars from most Nairobi booksellers and is highly recommended. Climbers who wish to tackle the higher peaks or to explore the peak area over a longer period of time should obtain the Mountain Club of Kenya's *Guide to Mount Kenya and Kilimanjaro*.

Naro Moru route

This route leads from Naro Moru on the main ring road. The Naro Moru River Lodge organises packaged hikes along this route, and you can hire their equipment even if you wish to make other arrangements. The Youth Hostel is the place to make independent arrangements and to meet with other hikers to form a party.

There are two main overnight stops on the Naro Moru Route. The Met station (3 050 m) has bandas, standing tents and a campsite. It is 26 km from the main road, and it's often possible to get a lift some of the way. Before reaching the Met station, it's possible to overnight at the Youth Hostel or camp at the entrance gate (2 400 m) 17 km from the ring road. If you catch a lift to the Met station and arrive early in the day, do not continue any higher on the same day as this will virtually guarantee ill-effects from the altitude.

Mackinder's Camp, six hours from the Met station, consists of a bunkhouse and several standing tents. Ideally you should spend two nights at Mackinder's – there's no shortage of good walking in the area – before taking on Lenana. The hike from Mackinder's to Lenana takes three to four hours; a 3h00 start is recommended so that you get there around sunrise for the best view, with plenty of daylight hours left. An alternative to climbing Lenana is to spend two or three days circling the peak area in an anticlockwise direction.

Chogoria route

This is the most scenic route up the mountain and it seems to have taken over from Naro Moru as the most popular with independent travellers. Guides and porters can be arranged through either the Cool Inn or Chogoria Transit Hotel in Chogoria village.

Chogoria Gate (2 950 m) is 30 km from Chogoria village, and the roadhead (3 250 m) is a further 10 km up the mountain. If you don't want to walk this, hotels in Chogoria can arrange transport to the gate or, depending on the condition of the road, to the roadhead itself. Bargain hard. If you take a lift up, don't even think about going any further without spending a night or two at the entrance gate or roadhead to acclimatise.

You can camp at the gate, at Parklands Campsite about 1,5 km further along the road or at the roadhead. Alternatively, there is attractive banda accomodation (cheap hotel rates) near the gate at Meru Mount Kenya Lodge (Let's Go Travel). The actual park boundary is at the end of the road, so you need not pay park fees when you stay near the gate. The gate is in the forest zone and the area is teeming with wildlife; elephants often visit a waterhole near the bandas.

Minto's Hut (4 200 m), six hours from the roadhead, is run-down but attractively situated near a group of mountain pools (note that the water here should be purified before you drink it). As with Mackinder's, it's advisable to spend a day acclimatising before ascending further. Lenana is three to four hours from here; again, a 3h00 start is recommended.

ABERDARES NATIONAL PARK AND THE TREE HOTELS

Aberdares National Park protects the forested slopes and moorland of the Aberdares Mountains. It supports a good variety of large mammals, including elephant, lion, rhino and the localised and extremely beautiful bongo antelope. The range is known for melanistic leopards (black panthers) and servals. Hiking is forbidden due to the number of large mammals and the roads are often impassable. Camping is permitted, however, and with a 4x4 there's nothing preventing you from exploring. Staff at any entrance gate can give current information on roads and campsites.

The main tourist attraction in the Aberdares is the two tree hotels, The Ark and Treetops, both of which are multi-storey wooden lodges that overlook a floodlit waterhole. The emphasis is on nocturnal game viewing, with the theoretical possibility of seeing secretive forest animals in their natural habitat. The similar Mountain Lodge, on the slopes of Mount Kenya, is also covered here. It's hard to imagine that any tourist who could afford it would want to visit Kenya without staying at one of the tree hotels and, as each has its advantages, it's worth discussing them in some detail.

The oldest and most famous of the tree hotels, Treetops, bases its reputation on the fact it was where Princess Elizabeth slept on the night she became Queen of England in 1953. The place has an undeniable sense of history, but it's debatable whether this compensates for the relatively poor game viewing. The logbooks in the lounge reveal that herds of 100 or more elephant were a regular sight in the 1950s, and that black rhinoceros, bongo and giant forest hog were nightly visitors. Elephant are still common – though not in the numbers of earlier years – as are waterbuck, hyena, buffalo, greater bushbaby, large-spotted genet and white-tailed mongoose. Rhino and leopard are unusual; bongo, giant forest hog and bushpig haven't been seen in years and you can forget about seeing any forest bird smaller or less cacophonic than a hornbill. The hotel management is doing its best to restore the forest (with exotic trees?), but it will be many years before this provides adequate refuge for forest animals.

The Ark is set right in the forest and it offers far better game viewing than Treetops. Large herds of elephant come past most nights; lion, rhino, buffalo, bushbuck and leopard are regular and genet slink around the building after dark. The hotel is reached via a raised gangplank which allows you to see at eye-level into the forest canopy. If you're after forest animals, it's worth spending a quiet half hour here around dusk. I saw several unusual birds and had my first good look at a Harvey's red duiker. On the debit side, it is the only hotel that forbids flash photography, the food is well below standard – and bongo and giant forest hog were not seen at all in 1993.

One thing that I found frustrating about The Ark and Treetops is that neither hotel can be visited in a private vehicle. Visitors must check in at the Aberdare Country Club (for The Ark) or the Outspan Hotel (for Treetops), from where they are ferried to the hotel in a bus. This means that you arrive at around 15h00 and leave at 7h00 the next morning, so your daylight hours are severely restricted.

Mountain Lodge, in the forest zone of Mount Kenya, is the quietest, least publicised and by some distance the cheapest of the tree hotels. It is also in many respects the best. Rooms are large with private balconies and the food is exceptional. The setting is marvellous too. The hotel faces a large marshy pool in the heart of the forest with the peaks of Mount Kenya in the background. Game viewing is more erratic than at The Ark, but there's a far better chance of seeing forest animals. You'd be lucky to see bongo, but bushpig, bushbuck, genet and blue monkey are daily visitors; giant forest hog and Harvey's red duiker come past most nights and a family of greater canerats is resident in the swamp. Other regular visitors include elephant, buffalo, leopard and, unusually, rhino and lion. Birdlife is good and the checklist posted in the lounge is a help to identification. Mountain Lodge is less regimented than the other tree hotels: visitors can drive there themselves and they can arrive and leave when it suits them.

Which hotel you decide on depends on your interests. To sum up, The Ark has a slight edge in general game viewing but Mountain Lodge is better for forest animals. The Ark allows closer views of birds than Mountain Lodge, but the early morning departure limits bird-watching opportunities. Flash photography is forbidden at The Ark, a strong disincentive to serious photographers. Elitism and quaintness aside, Treetops falls a sorry third.

The Ark is booked through Lonrho Hotels. Treetops is booked through Block Hotels and Mountain Lodge through AT&H. All have prices in the luxury bracket, though Mountain Lodge is by far the cheapest. All can arrange transfer from Nairobi.

PRIVATE GAME RANCHES IN THE MOUNT KENYA AREA

There are several luxury lodges and tented camps on private ranches. Most of these can be added to safari itineraries from Nairobi or you can arrange transfer from Nairobi when you make a booking.

Ol Pejeta Ranch, on the plateau between Mount Kenya and the Aberdares, offers modest accommodation at Sweetwaters Tented Camp and luxury at Ol Pejeta Lodge (both Lonhro Hotels). The tents at Sweet-waters face a waterhole; elephant and reticulated giraffe are regular visitors. Both offer game drives and walks.

Lewa Downs and Ngare Niti, Wilderness Safaris, PO Box 56923, Nairobi; tel: (02) 506139, offer luxury house-stays on a private cattle ranch near Isiolo. This area is notable for spectacular northern scenery and abundant wildlife: elephant, reticulated giraffe, both types of zebra, buffalo, black rhino and similar antelope and predator species to those found in Samburu. Night drives are a major attraction; this part of Kenya is rich in small nocturnal predators. Wilderness Safaris are also agents for Segera Ranch, which offers similar facilities on a private ranch near Nanyuki.

Let's Go Travel in Nairobi has details of these and other house-stays on ranches in the area.

NYAHURURU

Kenya's highest town (2 360 m) has a cool coniferous feel belying its position virtually on the equator. Thomson's Falls, 2 km out of town, is the third highest waterfall in Kenya and a popular lunch time stop for safari minibuses on their way between the Rift Valley and Samburu.

Nyahururu is a minor route focal point and if you do pass through at some stage it's worth thinking about spending the night. The waterfall is very pretty and the forested gorge beneath it holds birds such as Hartlaub's turaco and mountain wagtail, as well as black-and-white colobus monkeys. You can descend the gorge via a path that starts in the grounds of the Thomson's Falls Lodge. More birds and a few hippo can be seen at a papyrus-fringed pool 2 km upstream; the staff at the lodge can direct you.

How to get there

From Nakuru, a scenic tarred road climbs the escarpment to Nyahururu; regular minibuses take an hour or so for the journey. There are also regular minibuses from Nyahururu to Nyeri. Transport between Nyahururu and Maralal is erratic, but you can expect something leaving every couple of hours.

If you're driving between Nyahururu and Nanyuki/Samburu, ask about the condition of the direct road: even the most cavalier tour operators appear to avoid it. A better option is to head towards Nyeri for 85 km then turn left at Siboi, where a 14 km dirt road will bring you out at Naro Moru.

Accommodation

If you fancy a whiff of Kenya's colonial past at cheap hotel rates, Thomson's Falls Lodge, PO Box 38 Nyahururu; tel: (0365) 22006, is a good reason to stay the night in Nyahururu. Built above the falls two years after the railway reached the area in 1931, its trade these days comes mainly from feeding the minibus hordes which arrive at lunchtime. The lodge itself is underpatronised but strong on atmosphere, with log fires in the public areas and the rooms, and a creaky wood-panelled lounge and dining hall. If the rooms are too expensive, there's a campsite in the lodge grounds and a choice of indifferent local lodgings near the bus station.

MARALAL

Maralal, the gateway town to the eastern shore of Lake Turkana, is the unofficial capital of the Samburu people. The town lies within Maralal Wildlife Sanctuary, but the main impetus for visiting the area seems to be the camel safaris run by Yare Safaris.

How to get there

Minibuses travelling between Nyahururu and Maralal leave every hour or two. This is a well-maintained dirt road with fair game-viewing potential: I've seen elephant 20 m from the roadside. If you have your own 4x4, Maralal can also be approached via the dirt road connecting Lake Baringo to Samburu. The condition of this road varies, so it's worth making enquiries in advance, especially after rain.

If you're interested in a camel safari, Yare Safaris can include transfer from Nairobi to Maralal in their package; discuss this with them in Nairobi.

Accommodation

About 3 km out of town towards Lake Turkana, the modest Maralal Safari Lodge, PO Box 70, Maralal; tel: (03681) 2060, is a complex of wooden chalets overlooking a waterhole. Most budget travellers end up at Yare Safaris, PO Box 63006, Nairobi; tel: (02) 725610, 3 km out of town on the Nyahururu road. This is a friendly place and the resident Samburu are very approachable. Accommodation is in self-contained bandas (cheap hotel rates). There is also a dormitory, campsite, restaurant and bar.

LAKE TURKANA

Lake Turkana is the northernmost of Kenya's Rift Valley lakes and, at 6 400 square km, the largest desert lake in the world. Also known as the Jade Sea, Turkana has long been Kenya's most talked about off the beaten track destination. I'm not sure why, but its popularity seems to have waned somewhat in the last few years.

Turkana's main attraction is the remote, primeval scenery that surrounds it; a dry, lunar landscape set off by the lake's changeable blue-green waters. Turkana is a wildlife sanctuary of sorts, supporting a staggering 22 000 crocodiles, a large hippo population and a profusion of birds, particularly migrant waders. To protect the breeding sites of crocodiles and birds, South and Central Islands have been declared national parks.

The main tourist centre on the eastern shore, Loiyangalani, was founded in the 1960s around a palm-fringed freshwater spring. The surrounding area is home to a variety of ethnic groups, most notably the Elmolo, a group of less than 500 Cushitic-speaking fishermen considered to be the oldest remaining lakeshore inhabitants and quite possibly the smallest ethnic group in the world. In recent years the Elmolo have become integrated into other local ethnic groups, mainly the Samburu. A remnant village 8 km out of town can be visited with logistical ease, though perhaps some moral discomfort: as with Uganda's famed pygmies, this sort of ethnic voyeurism tends to bring more negative results than anything else.

The only other tourist centre, Ferguson's Gulf, lies on the western shore. This is famed for its birdlife, large crocodiles and game fishing for Nile perch and tiger fish. It is the best base for visits to Central Island, an extinct volcano with three crater lakes and, in April and May, the world's largest breeding population of crocodiles. Fishing gear and trips to the island can be organised through Lake Turkana Fishing Lodge.

The remote Sibiloi National Park protects a 1 600 square km area 100 km north of Loiyangalani. This northern lake shore teems with hippos and crocodiles, and terrestrial species in the park include cheetah, Beisa oryx, Grevy's zebra and gerenuk. A more moist prehistoric climate is evidenced by the number of petrified tree trunks. Sibiloi is rich in hominid fossils, the most notable discovery being a two million year old *Homo habilis* skull unearthed by Richard Leakey at Koobi Fora in the north of the park. Sibiloi is accessible in a 4x4, though it would be wise to ask about road conditions and recent reports of banditry. You can camp in the park but you need to bring all your supplies with you. Water is available at the headquarters at Allia Bay.

How to get there

Air

The tourist-class lodges on the lake do fly-in packages.

Overland truck

Unless you have a vehicle, or infinite time, the only practical way to reach east Turkana is on one of the camping safaris which leave Nairobi every couple of weeks. A few companies run these trips and departures are coordinated so as not to clash, so you will usually end up with whatever company is heading up next. Trips are typically one to two weeks in duration. If time isn't a problem, you can safely leave making arrangements until you get to Kenya; the trucks used carry over 20 passengers and are rarely full to capacity.

Maralal to Loiyangalani by road

Loiyangalani is 216 km from Maralal along a dirt road which has become badly corrugated and potholed in parts and is sometimes impassable after rains. The drive is best attempted in a 4x4 and it is worth checking the current road condition in Maralal before you depart. As in many parts of northern Kenya, there is a spasmodic banditry problem; you may be required to travel as part of a convoy. Petrol is erratically available at Baragoi but nowhere north of that. Make sure that you fill up in Maralal and carry enough petrol in jerry cans to get you back.

There are a few possible stops en route. The largest town is Baragoi, 97 km north of Maralal, where there is a campsite 4 km north of town. A more attractive proposition perhaps is South Horr, which lies in a forested valley a further 40 km towards Loyangalani. There are a couple of basic guesthouses in town and an attractive campsite next to a stream near the Catholic mission. About 10 km north of South Horr, you can camp or rent a run-down banda at Karangu campsite. The staff here can arrange guided walks on the forested slopes of nearby Ngiro Peak (2 848 m), an area abounding with butterflies and birds, as well as large game such as elephant and buffalo.

It is possible to hitch this route, but brace yourself for disappointment. Depending on demand, the occasional matatu leaves Maralal for Baragoi and even South Horr, but they are not to be relied on. There's no public transport whatsoever beyond South Horr. Your best bet is with the occasional supply truck or private vehicles. I've also heard of people making private arrangements in Maralal with camping safaris heading to Turkana.

A rough and little-used road connects Loiyangalani to Marsabit via North Horr and the Chalbi Desert. There's virtually no chance of hitching along this route, and even with a vehicle it's risky: you're a long way from help if you break down and there's a real danger of banditry.

Kitale to Ferguson's Gulf by road

This is the more popular route with independent travellers as there is relatively reliable public transport along a surfaced road. A bus leaves Kitale for Lodwar and Kalekol every morning. There's no real reason to stop off in Lodwar, except perhaps exhaustion (seven or eight hours on a hot crowded bus can be extremely draining), but there's a fair choice of accommodation if you do: the Turkwel Hotel is about the best bet, with reasonably priced self-contained rooms with fans. Driving yourself, this is a straightforward run on a road which is far better than the one to Loiyangalani, but less scenic.

Accommodation

Loiyangalani

The upmarket Oasis Club, PO Box 24464, Nairobi; tel: (02) 750034, the focal point of the village, is set in the lush vegetation around the springs. Accommodation is in self-contained cottages; facilities include two swimming pools and the only cold beer in the village. The lodge can arrange day trips to South Island National Park and Elmolo village.

There are also two banda facilities, both of which charge cheap hotel rates. Elmolo Lodge is the more comfortable and has a swimming pool but Sunset Strip is cheaper. Both allow camping.

Ferguson's Gulf

The modest Lake Turkana Fishing Lodge, PO Box 509, Kitale; tel: (0325) 2142, is run-down and quiet since Ferguson's Gulf dried up in 1988, but it has most of the essentials: a swimming pool, fans, cold drinks and food. The lodge can rent out fishing equipment and has motorboats for trips to Central Island.

There are a couple of local lodgings in Kalekol, a small village about two hours' walk from the lake. If you want to stay closer to the lake shore, ask to camp in the Fishing Lodge grounds. Alternatively you could try to organise a room in a private house in the nearby village of Longech.

THE SAMBURU COMPLEX

The Samburu complex consists of three national reserves covering a contiguous area of 844 square km. Samburu National Reserve lies north of the Uaso Nyiro River and west of the A1 road, Buffalo Springs lies south of the river and west of the road, while Shaba lies south of the river and east of the road.

The descent from the Mount Kenya foothills to Isiolo once again illustrates Kenya's remarkable scenic diversity. Over a thrilling 10 km the landscape changes from grassy rolling hills to a skeletally-vegetated semi-desert. The Samburu reserves are typical of northern Kenya, except that the dry acacia scrub is cut through by a belt of riparian forest along the course of the perennial Uaso Nyiro River. The river is the focal point of game viewing, which, with the combination of semi-desert and lush riverine vegetation, is generally superb.

Samburu lies near the southern limit of several species' ranges, making it highly attractive to people who have already visited other East or southern African reserves. The most striking of these animals, Grevy's zebra, exists here alongside the more widespread Burchell's zebra. The two species never interbreed, but they are frequently seen together: Grevy's zebra is much larger (almost twice the body weight) and has finer stripes which make it brilliantly photogenic.

The reticulated giraffe of Samburu were once considered a distinct species, but are now more widely considered a race of the Masai giraffe because the two interbreed freely where their ranges overlap. Like Grevy's zebra, the reticulated giraffe is more photogenic than its southern counterpart. It has well-defined polygonal markings and three horns, as opposed to the jagged-edged markings and two horns of the Masai giraffe.

Samburu supports a good variety of dry country antelope. The beautiful Beisa oryx is paler than the fringe-eared race found in the drier parts of southern Kenya, and it lacks black ear tufts. Rainey's gazelle is a lighter-coloured race of Grant's gazelle with slender, straighter horns. Samburu is where the ranges of Guenther's and Kirk's dik-dik converge: Guenther's dik-dik is most common north of the Uaso Nyiro River. It is greyer than Kirk's dik-dik and has a more elongated snout.

Samburu is a good place to see gerenuk, one of East Africa's most unusual antelopes. It is a type of gazelle, similar in general shape and colour to the impala, but unique in having an exaggeratedly elongated neck. Gerenuk are exclusive browsers and are often seen standing on their hind legs with their forefeet supporting them on a low branch and their neck stretching to the highest branches of an acacia tree. Gerenuk are widespread in the drier parts of southern Kenya, but nowhere are they as common as in Samburu.

Game viewing in Samburu is not restricted to northern rarities. The riverine forest is home to buffalo, lesser kudu, impala, common waterbuck and bushbuck. Eland and warthog are both reasonably common and might be seen anywhere, while klipspringer and greater kudu are found locally in rockier parts of the reserves. The Samburu ecosystem supports some 700 elephants and groups of 20 or more are a common sight near the river, which also supports a small population of hippo and several very big crocodiles. The only primates present are olive baboon, vervet monkey and lesser bushbaby.

Cheetah and lion are common, the latter particularly so in Shaba where prides of about 20 animals have been noted. The forest along the Uaso Nyiro is one of the best places in Kenya to see leopard, though it's difficult to say how much this reputation rests on the animals which are tempted with bait to visit Samburu Lodge most nights. Early morning game drives offer a better chance than anywhere else in Kenya to see nocturnal animals such as golden and side-striped jackal, bat-eared fox, striped hyena, aardwolf, aardvark (antbear), caracal and serval. Newman's genet and lesser bushbaby are regular nocturnal visitors to Samburu Lodge. The diurnal dwarf mongoose and unstriped ground squirrel are both common along the river.

Samburu has a remarkably varied birdlife – I would rate it the best of any game reserve in Kenya – with added excitement provided by the presence of several northern species at the southern limit of their range. The vulturine guineafowl is perhaps the most attractive of the Samburu specials with its brilliant cobalt-coloured chest feathers; flocks are common in the undergrowth along the river. Other dry country birds which are likely to be seen include Somali ostrich, pygmy falcon, Somali bee-eater, whiteheaded mousebird, Von der Decken's hornbill, bare-eyed thrush, pygmy batis, eastern whitecrowned shrike, golden pipit, Fischer's, goldenbreasted and bristlecrowned starlings, Donaldson-Smith's and whitebrowed sparrowweavers and blackcapped social weaver. The river supports a good range of waterbirds, while the forested fringe holds a variety of barbets, honeyguides, flycatchers, weavers, sunbirds and finches not normally associated with such an arid habitat. Raptors are extremely well represented.

Because it isn't a national park, Samburu is still lived in by the people after whom it is named. The Samburu are closely related to the Masai and speak a dialect of the Maa language; the two groups probably diverged sometime after Maa speakers arrived in Kenya in the 17th century. The pool-side Samburu dancing on display at some of the lodges is more style than substance, but drive along the river towards the western gate and you may see spear-carrying Samburu herdsmen dressed in their characteristic red blankets bringing their livestock to drink.

How to get there

Organised safari

After Masai Mara, Samburu is the most popular reserve with Nairobi safari operators. Generally it's visited on six or seven-day itineraries combined with Masai Mara and either Lake Nakuru or one of the tree hotels of the central highlands.

Self-drive

There are good tar roads from Nairobi as far as Isiolo. This colourful town is populated by a mix of Samburu, Boran and Ethiopians, and it has a few budget hotels. If you're driving, however, the town is notable mainly for its unparalleled number of speed bumps. Having circumnavigated these, you're looking at 40 km of sheer hell across corrugations, boulders and sand drifts before you reach the well-signposted turn-off to the lodges. You don't need a 4x4 to get up to Samburu – plenty of minibuses get there – but it will help. You certainly need a vehicle with good clearance.

Public transport/hitching

There is a fair amount of transport through to Isiolo and you'll have no problem finding a room once you're up there. Beyond that, you could catch a bus towards Marsabit but this would leave you stranded at the Samburu entrance gate. It's probably more realistic to try and hitch directly to the reserve from Isiolo, but bear in mind that there's little private transport other than minibuses and the drivers are normally instructed not to give lifts. Even if you get a lift, there are the usual accommodation problems – unless you have a tent and the vehicle is heading to Samburu Lodge or the nearby campsites.

Accommodation

The upmarket Samburu Lodge (Block Hotels), the oldest lodge in Samburu, has a prime riverside site. The sandbanks below the lodge are populated by maribou storks and immense gaping crocodiles by day, and Mozambique nightjars fluttering across in the evening. Bait is used to attract nocturnal predators: leopard come past most nights. As with many Block Hotels, bird walks in the grounds can be organised; the guide is enthusiastic and knowledgeable. Accommodation is in large, comfortable cottages with private verandahs, strung attractively along the river. The only drawback, at least during peak seasons, is that the public areas get rather crowded.

Samburu Intrepids Club (Prestige Hotels) has a similar setting to Samburu Lodge, but is smaller and more luxurious. The complex is built on stilts, with wooden walkways leading between different areas. Accommodation is in covered tents. Another luxury tented camp, Larsen's (Block Hotels), has a lush setting and is designed to blend into the riverine forest. Children under 10 are not allowed.

The luxury Samburu Serena Lodge (Serena Hotels) is on the south bank of the river west of the Buffalo Springs Reserve boundary. The facility is similar to Samburu Lodge, with good game viewing from the lodge and shady grounds.

The modest Buffalo Springs Lodge (AT&H) is the only accommodation set away from the river. It's the cheapest option in the complex, and the run-down state of the bandas keeps tour groups at bay. It's a very peaceful spot and plenty of game is attracted to the surrounding swamp.

The new Sarova Shaba Lodge (Sarova Hotels) is the only accommodation in Shaba National Reserve. It is a luxury establishment built around natural springs on the palm-covered south bank of the river.

There are several campsites strung along the Uaso Nyiro River next to Samburu Lodge. The absence of facilities is compensated for by the abundant bird and animal life along the river. Campers can normally eat or have a cold beer at the neighbouring lodge, though when it's busy you might find a more encouraging reception at the quieter Buffalo Springs Lodge.

MARSABIT

North of Samburu the Trans-East African Highway continues for 250 km through the flat Kaisut Desert before reaching Marsabit town and national reserve. Marsabit lies on an isolated million year old extinct volcano which rises almost 1 km above the surrounding desert to a height of 1 707 m. Dotted with briny crater lakes, Marsabit's montane grassland and lush forest give it an oasis-like feel. Marsabit town hosts a fascinating and colourful ethnic mix: Boran, Rendille, Gabbra and Ethiopian.

Marsabit is surrounded by the 2 090 square km Marsabit National Reserve, the core of which is an extensive forest immediately south of town. The forest supports animals not normally associated with northern Kenya; in addition to some 300 elephant, renowned for their large tusks, there are black-and-white colobus monkey, blue monkey, buffalo, bushbuck, leopard and lion. Game viewing in the forest is made challenging by the dense vegetation; the crater lakes, where animals come to drink, are the best places to focus your attentions.

Cheetah, reticulated giraffe, greater kudu, Grevy's zebra and striped hyena live in the more open parts of the reserve. Unlike the forest, which may only be entered in a vehicle, these areas may be explored on foot. A worthwhile short walk is to Gof Redo Crater, 5 km north of town near the junction of the North Horr and Moyale roads.

The Marsabit area has a rich avifauna, with more than 400 species recorded. Typical dry country birds and a wide range of raptors are supplemented by a variety of forest and water-associated birds. The rare lammergeyer reputedly breeds on the cliffs of Gof Bongole Crater.

How to get there

Organised safari

Marsabit is well off the main safari circuit. I'm not aware of any tours which visit the reserve, so you'd have to make private arrangements.

Self-drive

Marsabit town lies 273 km north of Isiolo along the horribly corrugated Trans-East Africa Highway. It's a rough drive and not one you'd want to undertake without a 4x4. There is also a risk of being held up by bandits between Isiolo and Marsabit. Vehicles now travel in convoy to counter this; enquire at the police station in Isiolo a day in advance for details of the current situation. The entrance gate is about 2 km from the town centre and the lodge 3 km into the park.

Public transport

There are a few buses between Isiolo and Marsabit every week. Once in Marsabit, you can walk to the entrance gate or catch a lift with the staff vehicle which runs between the town and the lodge at least once every day.

Accommodation

The underpatronised and modestly priced Marsabit Lodge (Msafiri Inns) lies 3 km from the entrance gate on the forested rim of Gof Sokorte Dika crater lake. It is regularly visited by elephants and other large mammals.

The Marsabit Highway Hotel, PO Box 110, Marsabit; tel: (0183) 2210 in town, has self-contained rooms at cheap hotel rates. Of the local lodgings, the Somali-run Kenya Lodge is recommended.

Camping is permitted in the staff compound at the entrance gate to the national reserve. If you have a vehicle, there is an unequipped but wonderfully situated campsite deeper in the reserve at Lake Paradise (Gof Sokarte Guda).

MERU NATIONAL PARK

This lushly vegetated national park, fed by a succession of fast-flowing streams, doesn't really feel like a northern reserve; in pure geographical terms, it lies more east than north of the Mount Kenya massif. Nevertheless, it hosts several species associated with northern Kenya, and has a wild solitary quality far removed from the reserves of southern Kenya.

Meru is no less accessible than Samburu, but it has never featured as strongly as it might on Kenya's main safari circuit. If anything, it has waned in popularity in the last decade. Through much of the 1970s and 1980s, a reasonably high profile was guaranteed by the association with the Adamson name (of *Born Free* fame). During George Adamson's tenure as park warden of Meru, several animals hand-reared by Joy Adamson (the lioness Elsa and cheetah Pippa among them) were released into the park. After his wife was murdered in 1980, George Adamson continued to work in the adjoining Kora National Reserve. During this period, Meru's popularity was boosted by having Kenya's only white rhinoceros population, a herd introduced from South Africa.

In the late 1980s, however, poaching caused the park to become a virtual no-go area: the white rhino were killed in 1988, along with a ranger guarding them, and two tourists were slain when they drove into a poacher's den. Events were brought to a head by the murder of the 83-year old George Adamson in 1989. Concerted efforts by the government, aided by the moratorium on ivory sales, ensured the end of the poachers' tenure. It's been perfectly safe to visit since 1990.

Meru's continued absence from the safari schedules may be a hang-over from this period; more likely, it has something to do with the park's reputation for poor game viewing. The northern and most developed part of the park consists of tall grass dotted with acacias and baobabs; dhoum palms and tangled riverine forest grow along the streams. The ample water means that animals are dispersed and they are difficult to see in the thick cover.

Which is not to say that Meru isn't worth visiting. It is the most intimate of Kenya's major game reserves, with a meditative ambience enhanced by the lack of tourists and a brilliant backdrop provided by the Nyambeni Hills and Mount Kenya. While the game viewing may be less spectacular than in other reserves, there are plenty of animals. If you have a vehicle, Meru should be a high priority.

After being decimated by poachers, elephant numbers are again on the increase, with herds of more than 50 elephants recorded in recent years. Large herds seem to be a feature of the park: prides of 20 or more lion are not unusual, nor are large groups of buffalo. The open grassland and acacia stands north of the Rwojero River support small groups of Burchell's zebra, impala, Grant's gazelle, reticulated giraffe and Coke's hartebeest, while stretches of riverine forest are the haunt of lesser kudu, bushbuck and waterbuck. The drier acacia woodland south of the Rwojero holds gerenuk, Grevy's zebra and Beisa oryx. The usual range of large predators is present – cheetah, lion, leopard, spotted hyena – but difficult to see in the dense vegetation.

The roads north of the Rwojero are well maintained. If you have only a day or two in the park, you're unlikely to want to explore beyond these. If you have an extra day, it's worth exploring the less-used roads which lead to the Tana, Kenya's largest river, on the southern boundary. The riverine forest holds several types of monkey and is rewarding for bird-watchers. Elephant are common, and large numbers of hippo live in the river. Depending on the current state of the roads near the Tana River, and the availability of maps (the map of Meru is difficult to come by) you may be required to take a ranger with you.

The developed part of Meru is a good place to see ground birds: Somali ostriches, plovers, coursers, bustards, sandgrouse, larks, pipits and migrant wheatears. Mulika swamp holds a variety of bishops and widows in the breeding season, while the riverine forest, particularly along the Rwojero, is particularly good for kingfishers. Stands of palm trees may hold palm swift and the localised golden palm weaver.

How to get there

Organised safari

Unless you make special arrangements, you won't find any safaris heading to Meru.

Self-drive

The entrance gate to Meru National Park is about 90 km from Meru town on the Mount Kenya ring road. From Meru town, there's a good and very scenic tar road as far as Maua in the Nyambeni Mountains. From Maua, it's a further 30 km along a dirt road; it's not in the greatest shape, but you shouldn't have much problem, even in a saloon car, except perhaps after rain. The entrance gate is well signposted. There is no petrol available in the park; you should fill up at Maua.

Public transport/hitching

Meru is difficult to reach without a vehicle because so few people visit it. On the other hand, visitors tend to drive themselves, so they are more likely to give lifts than safari minibuses. And, with reasonably priced accommodation close to the lodge, you're less likely to end up spending a fortune than you are in some other parks.

Your first target is the town of Maua: there's a fair amount of public transport there from Meru town. The best hitching point is the junction 3 km out of Maua, signposted for Meru National Park, where there is a usefully positioned local lodging. Maua sees no tourists; surrounded by green hills covered in tea plantations and patches of forest, there are worse places you could get stuck.

The park vehicle which goes into Maua a few times a week will normally give a lift to hitching tourists – novelty value alone ensures you'll get a helpful reception. Park rangers should be able to drop you at the banda and campsite near the park headquarters.

Accommodation

The modest Meru Mulika Lodge (Msafiri Inns) is a likeable place, with a low-key atmosphere that comes as a welcome relief after the busy lodges in other reserves. It is a little run-down but very cheap and peaceful. The dam below it attracts elephant, buffalo, waterbuck and Burchell's zebra. A notice at reception informs you that jogging is forbidden outside the lodge grounds – just in case that was on your agenda.

There are equipped, self-contained bandas at cheap hotel rates at Leopard Rock Safari Lodge (Let's Go Travel). The bandas verge on a small, palm-fringed stream, home to hippo and crocodiles.

The large national parks campsite is in a patch of acacia woodland bounded by a small stream near the park headquarters. A fair amount of wildlife passes through, and there are plenty of birds. There are bandas which are cheaper than those at Leopard Rock.

10 TANZANIA

The map of Tanzania reads like a litany of Africa's most evocative place names: Kilimanjaro, Serengeti, Ngorongoro Crater, Olduvai Gorge, Gombe Stream, Zanzibar and Lakes Tanganyika, Victoria and Malawi. So it seems strange that Tanzania has never captured the popular imagination in the way that Kenya has. In fact, many people are quite surprised when they find that places like Kilimanjaro and Serengeti are not in Kenya.

This low profile can be attributed to several factors. Possibly because Tanzania saw relatively little European settlement, its tourist circuit came to be seen as an extension of Kenya's, and much of the revenue raised by tourism was gobbled up by Kenyan companies. To counter this, the Tanzanian government closed the border with Kenya and raised national park fees to prohibitive levels. The predictable result was that tourists stopped visiting Tanzania, even after the border re-opened. When I first visited Tanzania, in 1986, it was a trying place. Tourist facilities were non-existent, bureaucrats were openly hostile, civic amenities had become a shambles and the absurd exchange rate and heavy penalties for using the more realistic black market were enough to reduce anyone to paranoia.

Thankfully, things have improved greatly since then. The move away from socialism in 1986 signalled a period of rapid economic growth. Tanzania may lack Kenya's infrastructure, but there's running water more often than not, the need to use a black market is a thing of the past, park fees are in line with those in Kenya, and I've nowhere else encountered such helpful officials as I did on my last four-month visit. Tanzania enjoys a political stability that is rare elsewhere on the continent, and its natural assets compete with the best. The country is poised on the verge of a major tourist boom.

Tourism in Tanzania remains more low-key than in Kenya. Tourist-class hotels are utilitarian as opposed to luxurious, facilities are still relatively run-down, and English is rarely spoken away from the main tourist centres. But this is amply compensated for by a lack of the mass tourism which mars places like Masai Mara in Kenya. Most of Tanzania's national parks retain a strong wilderness character.

This chapter on Tanzania is not meant to be exhaustive, but to alert tourists who fly in to Nairobi to the possibilities that exist just across the border. I have concentrated on a few major attractions – Kilimanjaro, the northern safari circuit (which includes Serengeti National Park and Ngorongoro Crater) and Zanzibar – and treated them as excursions from Nairobi.

The Tanzanian towns which Nairobi-based tourists are most likely to visit are Arusha, Moshi, Mwanza and Dar es Salaam. Arusha is the centre for safari companies running trips to Serengeti and surroundings. Moshi is the main base for climbing Mount Kilimanjaro. Mwanza is the main link between Uganda and Tanzania. Dar es Salaam is the capital and the obvious place from which to cross to Zanzibar.

BORDER FORMALITIES

Coming from Nairobi you'll use the Namanga border post. This is a busy, straightforward crossing and there is a bank where you can exchange money on the Tanzanian side. All visitors are issued with a free visitor's pass on arrival. Those visitors who need visas may be able to get one on arrival, but it's safer to organise a visa in advance; the Tanzanian embassy in Nairobi normally issues visas within 24 hours. Other popular borders are the Lunga-Lunga border between Mombasa and Tanga and the border post between Taveta and Moshi.

MONEY

The unit of currency is the Tanzanian shilling. The current exchange rate is around US $1 = Tsh 450. There is a foreign exchange bureau at Namanga and at most banks in Arusha, Moshi and Dar es Salaam. Privately-run foreign exchange bureaus in these towns generally give better rates so it's worth shopping around before changing a large sum of money. There is no longer a black market worth talking about in Tanzania; anyone who approaches you to change money is likely to be a con artist.

GETTING THERE FROM NAIROBI

Many Nairobi tour operators organise safaris to northern Tanzania and Kilimanjaro climbs. If time is a factor, this is the most straightforward option. It is easily possible to get to Tanzania on public transport. There are direct buses between Nairobi and Arusha, but these tend to get bogged down at the border while all the passengers are processed. It's easier to catch a minibus to Namanga and pick up a shared taxi on the other side. Either way, the travelling time to Arusha is six to eight hours. A few con artists work the Nairobi-Namanga minibuses and will try to convince you to change money with them before you get to the border. However convincing their routine, you can safely ignore them.

It's also possible to fly into Tanzania from Nairobi. There are regular flights to Zanzibar, Dar es Salaam and Kilimanjaro International Airport (between Moshi and Arusha).

FURTHER INFORMATION

Buy whatever maps and books you need in Nairobi. Bookshops in Arusha are poorly stocked. Tanzania National Parks have produced a series of excellent booklets covering most of the major reserves. These can be bought very cheaply from the headquarters in the Arusha International Conference Centre, more expensively from bookshops in Arusha, and at inflated prices at park entry gates.

The information in this chapter will suffice for those wanting to visit the main places of interest in northern Tanzania. Those who want greater detail or who plan to explore the country more fully are referred to my *Guide to Tanzania* (Bradt Publications 1993).

PUBLIC TRANSPORT

A brief overview of public transport in Tanzania follows:

Rail

Between Moshi and Dar es Salaam, the most popular option is the overnight train which departs three times weekly in each direction. Departure from Moshi is on Monday, Wednesday and Friday at 16h00 and from Dar es Salaam on Tuesday, Thursday and Saturday at 16h00. Trains arrive at their destination at around 9h00. Although it is advisable to book a day or two in advance, especially for trains from Dar es Salaam, I've always managed to get tickets on the afternoon of departure on the Moshi side. Bookings for trains leaving Moshi can be made from the station in Arusha.

Other train services connect Moshi to Tanga, Tanga to Dar es Salaam, and Dar es Salaam to Mwanza, Kigoma in western Tanzania and Mbeya.

The Tazara line connects Dar es Salaam to Kapiri Mposhi (Zambia) via Mbeya. There are three classes on all Tanzanian trains and tickets are very cheap.

Bus

If you're travelling between Arusha or Moshi and Dar es Salaam by road, do yourself a favour and pay the extra to take an express bus. These are remarkably quick, covering 625 km in around 10 to 12 hours. Tickets should be booked a day in advance. Normal buses generally take around 14 hours and are very crowded, but booking isn't necessary.

Local buses cover most conceivable routes in Tanzania, though they are generally very crowded and slow. On tar roads, expect to cover about 40 km/h including stops, and on dirt roads around 20 km/h. Avoid using the overnight bus between Arusha and Dodoma – it's terribly slow and thieving is known to occur regularly.

Crossing between Arusha and Mwanza, daily buses via Serengeti are expensive compared to other buses due to national park fees, but they only take 14 hours and, at the right time of year, are a way of seeing Serengeti cheaply. The only other option, a slow bus via Singada, takes up to three days!

Boat

Tanzania has some excellent lake ferry services run by Tanzania Railways. The one most likely to be of use to Nairobi-based tourists is the weekly ferry between Mwanza and Port Bell (Uganda) on Lake Victoria (departs Mwanza on Sundays and Port Bell on Mondays). An alternative is the daily overnight service between Mwanza and Bukoba (from where there is road transport to Masaka in Uganda). The weekly Lake Tanganyika ferry between Kigoma and Mpulungu (Zambia) is pure magic, but unlikely to be used by Nairobi-based tourists.

On the Indian Ocean there are several boats daily between Dar es Salaam and Zanzibar. Erratic services connect Zanzibar to Pemba Island and Mombasa (Kenya), and Dar es Salaam to Mtwara in southern Tanzania.

NORTHWEST TANZANIA

Bukoba

This quiet town on the western shore of Lake Victoria is the introduction to Tanzania to anyone coming overland from Uganda. With an early start, you can get between Bukoba and Masaka in Uganda in a day, though you'll have to travel in hops using a variety of minibuses and pick-up trucks. There is a comfortable overnight ferry between Masaka and Mwanza six nights a week; the ferry terminal is about 2 km out of town.

If you're looking for somewhere to stay, there's no shortage of lodgings in the town centre. The Lake Hotel on the Lake Victoria shore between the town and the ferry terminal is a superior cheap hotel Camping is normally allowed in the grounds.

Mwanza

This large town on the southern shore of Lake Victoria is a major route focal point, connected by rail to Dar es Salaam on the coast, by ferry to Bukoba and Port Bell (Uganda), by regular buses to Kisumu (Kenya and by a daily bus service to Arusha via Serengeti.

Mwanza is a likeable town, with a lethargic, tropical atmosphere and a cosmopolitan Asian-influenced flavour. The surrounding countryside is notable for dramatic rock formations. Saa Nane Island, reached by a five minute boat ride from the town, crawls with lizards (including the water monitor) and crocodiles and offers excellent bird-watching.

Accommodation

Tourist-class accommodation can be found at the modestly priced New Mwanza Hotel, PO Box 25; tel: (068) 3202. The best of the cheap hotels are the Delux (Uhuru Road) and the Lake (opposite the railway station) both of which have good restaurants. There are dozens of local lodgings concentrated around the bus station.

KILIMANJARO AND SURROUNDINGS
Moshi

Moshi, the main base for climbing Kilimanjaro, is a humdrum town saved by having perhaps the most remarkable backdrop of any settlement between Cape Town and the equator. Access from Arusha is easy – buses run all day and take a couple of hours. There's no shortage of accommodation. Modest tourist-class accommodation can be found at the Moshi Hotel, PO Box 1819; tel: (055) 3071, in the town centre and the newer (and better) Keys Hotel, PO Box 993; tel: (055) 3071. The

central Coffee Tree Hotel and the YMCA, 500 m out of town on the
Arusha-Dar es Salaam road, are recommended cheapies. You can camp
at Keys Hotel.

Marangu

Marangu is in the foothills of Kilimanjaro, only 8 km from the national
park entrance gate. It's a pleasant little village with a vaguely Alpine
feel, easily reached by public transport from Moshi. There are two
modest tourist-class hotels: the atmospheric Kibo Hotel, PO Box 137,
Moshi, about 1 km past the village, and the more run-down Marangu
Hotel, PO Box 40, Moshi, 5 km out of town towards Moshi. Camping
is permitted in the grounds of the Kibo Hotel. If you're looking for a
cheapish room, the only option is the absurdly overpriced Babylon Bar
and Restaurant.

Mount Kilimanjaro National Park

Mount Kilimanjaro is the highest mountain in Africa and the highest
free-standing mountain in the world, rising almost 5 km above the
surrounding plains. The highest point is the 5 895 m Uhuru Peak. The
756 square km area above the 2 700 m contour was declared a national
park in 1977. Kilimanjaro is, in geological terms, a young mountain,
formed by volcanic activity about one million years ago. It is now
considered dormant.

Kilimanjaro displays similar vegetation zones to other large African
mountains, with moist forest up to about 3 000 m and moorland characterised by giant senacio and lobelia plants between 3 000 m and
4 000 m. The forest zone is rich in animal life, though of the larger
mammals, only black-and-white colobus and blue monkeys are seen
with regularity by hikers. Klipspringer are the most frequently seen
large mammals in the moorland zone.

The highest point on the continent, Uhuru Peak is an irresistible lure
for many tourists. It can be reached with comparative ease by non-
climbers, but be warned that although the ascent is little more than a
long uphill footslog, it should not be taken lightly. You're going a good
kilometre higher than you would on any other African mountain: almost all hikers feel some effects of altitude and many have to turn back
before reaching the top. Read the section on mountain health in chapter
two for further details.

The Marangu Route is the trail generally used by tourists. It starts at the park entrance gate 8 km from Marangu village. The round hike normally takes five days, with the first three nights spent at Mandera Hut (2 750 m), Horombo Hut (3 720 m) and Kibo Hut (4 703 m). On the fourth day, a 1h00 start is required to make Uhuru Peak at daybreak. After reaching the peak, most climbers spend the final night at Horombo Hut before descending to Marangu on the fifth day. There is a strong case for doing a six day climb and spending two nights acclimatising at Horombo Hut: this will reduce the probability of serious altitude sickness and, as a result, increase your chances of making it to the top.

All climbers are advised to carry a map. *The walker's guide and map to Kilimanjaro* by Mark Savage only costs a couple of dollars and is widely available in Nairobi. Buy it there: it's difficult to get hold of in Tanzania. The national parks booklet on Kilimanjaro is also useful, with good route descriptions and detailed information on geology and natural history. It's also cheap and is easily located in Arusha.

The vast majority of tourists organise climbs through a tour company in Moshi or Marangu. You can make arrangements yourself at the entrance gate but it's a lot of hassle and, as the bulk of costs are taken up by park fees, there's little saving to be made. Most safari companies in Arusha and Nairobi can organise Kilimanjaro climbs. This is definitely worth thinking about if your time is limited, but as most of these companies are simply acting as agencies for operators closer to the mountain, it is more expensive.

The Marangu and Kibo Hotels in Marangu are both highly experienced at organising Kilimanjaro climbs and can rent out reliable equipment. Expect to pay a minimum of US $400 for a five-day climb and an extra US $100 for each additional day. Climbs organised in Moshi are generally cheaper, but one should be more selective. Two companies that are highly recommended are Keys Hotel and Trans-Kibo (based in the YMCA). Keys Hotel is a good first port of call: it is held in high regard by safari·operators in Arusha and Nairobi, yet its prices undercut the other reliable companies by about 25 per cent. There are companies offering climbs for as little as US $250, but while they have many happy customers, they cannot be recommended without reservations. Realistically, the worst that can go wrong using a shoddy safari operator to visit a game reserve is you lose a few days. On Kilimanjaro, you could die.

Although Marangu is far and away the most popular route up Kilimanjaro, there are several quieter and more scenic routes. These are expensive to climb because special arrangements must be made and hut fees are substantially more than on the Marangu route. Tropical Tours in Arusha is worth speaking to if you're interested in a less-used route.

THE NORTHERN SAFARI CIRCUIT

The national parks and reserves of northern Tanzania need little introduction to wildlife enthusiasts. The vast Serengeti National Park, popularised in the 1950s by the book and film *Serengeti shall not die*, is arguably the finest reserve on the continent, home to millions of plains animals and a profusion of predators. The Ngorongoro Crater, the largest intact volcanic caldera in the world, has featured in countless TV documentaries. Lake Manyara National Park was made famous in the 1970s by the research done on its elephant population by Ian Douglas-Hamilton.

The area's less publicised national parks are also excellent: Tarangire for its dense elephant population and magnificent baobab-studded scenery, and Arusha National Park for containing Africa's fifth highest mountain, the 4 566 m-high Mount Meru. Add to this Ol Doinyo Lengai, an active volcano fringing the Ngorongoro Conservation Area, and Lake Natron, the breeding ground of East Africa's millions of flamingo, and it's difficult to argue with the assertion that northern Tanzania is the most exciting game-viewing area anywhere in Africa.

Arusha

Telephone code: 057

Arusha, the gateway to the reserves of northern Tanzania, lies in the hilly country at the base of Mount Meru. The lushness of the surrounding area gives Arusha a fertile appearance, especially attractive on a clear day when Mount Meru dominates the horizon. Tourist facilities are good: there are dozens of hotels and restaurants, and over 100 safari operators. A major landmark in town is the International Conference Centre (AICC), which houses the national parks headquarters and many of the safari companies.

Accommodation

Arusha's most prestigious hotel is the luxury Mount Meru Novatel, 2 km out of town on the Moshi road, PO Box 887; tel: (057) 2711. Far more attractive – and a lot cheaper – is Mountain Village Lodge, PO

Box 376; tel: (057) 2699, which overlooks forest-fringed Duluti Crate Lake 15 km out of town off the Moshi road.

There are several upmarket hotels in the town centre, of which the New Arusha, Sokoine Road, PO Box 88; tel: (057) 3241; and Equator PO Box 3002; tel (057) 3127, are recommended. In the modest price range, try the Golden Rose Hotel, Stadium Road, PO Box 361; tel: (057) 8860; or Pallson's, Market Road, PO Box 2485; tel (057) 7263.

The most popular cheap hotel is the Naaz on Sokoine Road. There are dozens of local lodgings, of which the best are the Safari Guesthouse, Ethiopia Street; Friends Corner, Sokoine Road and Kilimanjaro Villa, Swahili Road. The YMCA, India Road, is pleasant and a good place to meet other travellers, but it seems overpriced.

There is a choice of campsites in the area. The cheapest and most central is Kinyoro, 500 m out of town past the New Arusha Hotel. Masai Camp, 3 km out of town on the old Moshi road, is pricier but has better facilities. Further afield, you can camp at Duluti Club on the forested shore of a crater lake about 15 km from Arusha. It is 2 km from the Moshi road and signposted.

Restaurants

Among Arusha's better eating places are the Pizzaria (Italian, great desserts), the Bindaya (Indian) and the Chinese Restaurant (Indian, Chinese and Western dishes), all on Sokoine Road. The Chinese Restaurant is popular with travellers and a good place to ask around if you're looking for people to join you on a safari. The food is very reasonably priced and there's a lively bar with live Zaïrian music.

Organising a safari

Although safaris in Tanzania are similar in many respects to those in Kenya, there are also several differences, most of which are because of the relatively low volume of tourism in Tanzania when compared to Kenya.

The most obvious difference is that there is more of a sense of adventure attached to a Tanzanian safari. Except for the Ngorongoro Crater, whose small size creates a similar sense of crowding to that of Masai Mara, Tanzania's parks seem less touristy. The combined area of Serengeti National Park, Ngorongoro Conservation Area and Lake Manyara is about twenty times that of Masai Mara, yet at any given time there are probably less than one tenth of the tourists. The poorly maintained roads only add to a general feeling of wildness.

The industry in Arusha offers less in the way of fixed departure safaris, particularly at the budget end of the scale. The norm here is to round up a group of people with a similar itinerary in mind and make an individual arrangement with the safari operator of your choice. Most safari companies use Landrovers rather than the minibuses typical of Kenya, so groups tend to be smaller: four or five people as opposed to seven or eight. Smaller groups mean that camping safaris in Tanzania tend to be about 30 per cent more expensive than they are in Kenya, but they also allow for a greater sense of autonomy: the driver/guide is more likely to be responsive to the interests of a small group.

Self-drive safaris aren't really an option in Tanzania: hired vehicles tend to be in poor condition and the roads are very rough. The best option if you want total autonomy is to organise your own safari: effectively you're hiring a vehicle, driver and cook to follow the itinerary you want, but paying a price inclusive of meals, park fees and petrol. Using one of the budget companies recommended below, this will work out more cheaply than would hiring a vehicle to do a similar safari in Kenya.

The unregimented nature of the Tanzanian safari business places a greater onus on you to decide what you want. Read through the pocket descriptions below to decide which parks most interest you. Typical itineraries are a five-day safari taking in Lake Manyara, Ngorongoro Crater, Serengeti and Tarangire, and a three-day safari of all these parks except Serengeti. The assumption made by safari operators is that you will want to see the maximum number of parks in the shortest possible time. Bearing in mind the distances involved, this isn't perhaps the best approach: for a more relaxed trip I would add at least an extra day to each of the above itineraries. If you only have five days, skip either Serengeti or Tarangire (depending on the season). If you only have three days, Tarangire and Ngorongoro make a good combination. Tarangire is only two hours' drive from Arusha, so it makes a perfectly feasible day trip. And Arusha National Park can be covered adequately in a day.

These should be viewed as minimum times: any wildlife lover could happily spend a week in Serengeti alone. If time permitted, a 10 to 14 day safari would allow you to visit all the main parks as well as explore some of the more remote parts of the Ngorongoro Conservation Area and Lake Natron.

Most Nairobi operators can organise safaris to Tanzania. This will be more expensive than making your own way to Arusha (even if daily rates are comparable, driving from Nairobi adds two days to the safari), but the advantages are obvious if your time is limited. More altruistically, it does seem a little unfair on a country that is considered to be one of the poorest in Africa to visit its reserves with a Kenyan company.

Camping safaris

If time is tight, you might want to book a safari in advance. Otherwise, it's easier and cheaper to make arrangements when you arrive in Arusha. Most companies have next-day departures and this gives you the opportunity to shop around for a good price.

Be selective about the company you use: competition to keep prices low forces shoestring operators to use poorly maintained vehicles and incompetent drivers. Even with the cheapest operator your chances of a successful safari are better than even, but there is a high risk of breakdown. Some travellers want to have it both ways. If you pay a shoestring rate, you get a shoestring safari – it's unreasonable to moan or to expect a refund if things go wrong.

There are dozens of camping safari companies in the AICC and many more scattered around town. Bearing in mind the reservations expressed above, Amango Safaris, AICC, PO Box 8269; tel: (057) 8894 seem to be the best of the real shoestring operators. Two highly reputable companies in the town centre are Hoopoe Safaris, India Street, PO Box 2047; tel: (057) 7011, fax: 8226; and Roy Safaris, Sokoine Road, PO Box 50; tel: (057) 2854. Both are very reasonably priced and well-organised, with Hoopoe perhaps having the edge when it comes to more personalised arrangements. If you are interested in walking safaris in the Ngorongoro area, contact Tropical Tours, India Street, PO Box 727; tel: (057) 8353.

Lodge and luxury camping safaris

Upmarket safaris can be organised directly through the Arusha companies listed below.

Abercrombie and Kent, PO Box 427; tel: (057) 7803, fax: 7003.

Ker and Downey, PO Box 2782; tel: (057) 7755.

Kingfisher Safaris, PO Box 701; tel: (057) 3181.

State Travel Service, PO Box 1369; tel: (057) 3300, fax: 3113.

Takims Safaris, PO Box 6023; tel: (057) 3174, fax: 8211.

United Touring Company, PO Box 2211; tel (057) 7931, fax: 6475.

Wildersun Safaris, PO Box 930; tel: (057) 3880, fax: 7834.

Arusha National Park

Arusha National Park protects a remarkable diversity of habitats within a relatively small area of 137 square km. The dominant feature is 4 566 m Mount Meru, the eastern slopes and peak of which lie in the park. The Momella lake field, a group of shallow alkaline lakes which support a diverse range of birds, and the gorgeous Ngurdoto Crater, are also of interest. Habitats range from open grassland to the montane forest found on the lower slopes of Mount Meru and the Ngurdoto crater rim. Animals present include elephant, buffalo, Masai giraffe, black-and-white colobus, blue monkey, leopard and a variety of antelope. Despite its proximity to Arusha, relative accessibility and indisputable beauty, Arusha National Park sees relatively few tourists, which is all the more reason not to pass it by yourself.

A major attraction of Arusha National Park is that visitors are permitted to walk when accompanied by an armed ranger. The most popular hike is to the peak of Mount Meru, rated by many people who have climbed all three as more interesting than either Mount Kenya or Kilimanjaro. Mount Meru has similar vegetation zones to Africa's other large mountains and exciting encounters with animals are almost guaranteed, as are superb views across to Kilimanjaro. Mount Meru isn't high enough for altitude-related illness to be a cause for concern, and there are no crowds to contend with. Three-day hikes can be organised through most Arusha tour operators inclusive of park and hut fees, guides, porters, food and transfers. It's cheaper, but not significantly so, to make your own arrangements with the wardens at the gate. The national parks booklet on Arusha National Park is recommended to all visitors and climbers in particular.

How to get there

Momella Gate is 20 km from the main Arusha-Moshi road and clearly signposted from Usa River: it is an hour's drive if you have a vehicle. Otherwise the most straightforward way to see the park is to organise a day safari from Arusha. Hitching from the Moshi road to the gate is possible, though slow.

With an early start, you could walk from the main road to Momella Gate. The road to Momella passes through the park: even though walking is permitted and there are plenty of local pedestrians, be conscious of the presence of animals, especially buffalo.

Accommodation

Modest tourist-class accommodation can be found at the cosy, Alpine-looking Momella Lodge, PO Box 418, Arusha; (057) 4648, 2 km north of the entrance gate. There is also a small self-catering rest house near Momella (cheap hotel rates) which should be booked in advance at the national park headquarters in Arusha.

Camping is permitted at Momella Lodge and at three forest-fringed campsites a short walk from the gate.

Tarangire National Park

The Tarangire ecosystem stretches from the Masai steppes to Lake Natron and supports over a million plains animals, most abundantly wildebeest, zebra, buffalo, impala, eland and giraffe. The area protected by the national park is at its best in the dry season between June and November, when animals concentrate along the Tarangire River. At this time of year, game viewing in Tarangire is far better than it is in Serengeti. Tarangire is predominantly covered in dry acacia woodland and tall grassland, notable for large numbers of baobab trees. It has a particularly dense elephant population. The area forms the southernmost part of the range of gerenuk and fringe-eared oryx. Predators such as lion, leopard and cheetah are common, but difficult to see in the tall cover.

How to get there

The entrance gate to Tarangire lies off the Arusha-Dodoma road. The road is tarred and the drive takes approximately two hours. Tarangire is a regular inclusion in longer safari itineraries out of Arusha, but it could easily be visited as a self-contained one or two-day safari. Hitching would be difficult.

Accommodation

The only tourist-class accommodation is the modestly priced and attractively situated Tarangire Safari Lodge, PO Box 1182, Arusha; tel: (057) 3090. There are two national parks campsites along the Tarangire River.

Lake Manyara National Park

Lake Manyara is a shallow, alkaline lake at the base of the sheer cliff that forms the western Rift Valley escarpment. The national park protects the northwestern portion of the lake and the surrounding shore, much of which is covered in fig forest. The park was once notable for its dense elephant population, immortalised by Ian Douglas-Hamilton in the book *Amongst the elephants,* but poaching has reduced the population greatly. More certain attractions are large numbers of flamingo on the lake, hippos in the hippo pool, blue monkeys in the forest, and plains animals such as giraffe and zebra in grassier areas. Lake Manyara's lions have acquired a reputation for tree climbing, but this behaviour is rarely observed.

How to get there

To get to Lake Manyara from Arusha, follow the tarred road towards Dodoma for 75 km. Turn right onto a dirt road at the village of Mukunyuni. After about 50 km you reach the busy village of Mto Wa Mbu, with its overpriced curio stalls and shops selling cold sodas. The entrance gate is a short way past this. There is a daily bus between Arusha and Mto Wa Mbu.

Accommodation

The upmarket Lake Manyara Hotel, PO Box 3100, Arusha; tel: Mto Wa Mbu 10, is perched on the Rift Valley wall overlooking the lake. Kiriruma Tented Camp offers spartanly furnished tents at cheap hotel rates, in a patch of acacia woodland on the escarpment overlooking Lake Manyara. Kiriruma is run by Hoopoe Safaris but it's open to anyone; visit their office in Arusha for further information. Holiday Fig Resort, in Mto Wa Mbu village just outside the entrance gate, has basic rooms at cheap hotel rates and a crowded campsite. The national park campsites at the gate are much more attractive and quieter.

Ngorongoro Conservation Area

The Ngorongoro Conservation Area was part of the original Serengeti National Park, but its status was reduced in order to allow the local Masai to share it with the wildlife. The central feature of the conservation area is the magnificent 600 m-deep, 260 square km Ngorongoro Crater, the collapsed caldera of a volcano which, a couple of million years ago, was as high as Kilimanjaro is today.

The crater floor is a sanctuary within a sanctuary, the steep walls ensuring there is little animal movement in and out. Wildlife is abundant and the flat, open nature of the crater floor allows good visibility: it is quite possible to see all of the big five in a single game drive. Most typical plains animals are present, though not giraffe, as they are unable to descend the crater wall. The road circling the crater rim is also worth exploring, with wonderful views in both directions. The lush forest along the rim supports leopard, bushbuck, elephant and a variety of monkeys. Because it is open and relatively confined, many people complain that the crater floor feels slightly congested. Certainly this is the one place in Tanzania where queues of minibuses are a frequent occurrence, but in my opinion the ample game and marvellous scenery more than make up for this. And it's nowhere near as crowded as Masai Mara.

There are several off the beaten track options in the conservation area which can be explored if you have your own vehicle or are on a longer safari. North of the crater are two smaller craters, Olmoti and Empakaai, the mysterious stone ruins at Engakura, and the only active volcano in the region, Ol Doinyo Lengai. On the southern border of the conservation area, Lake Eyasi is much larger than Lake Manyara and home to the subterranean-dwelling Hadza hunter-gatherers. The national parks booklet on Ngorongoro Conservation Area contains useful details of these places.

How to get there

To get to Ngorongoro Crater from Lake Manyara, continue along the main road towards Serengeti for about 30 km. The Ngorongoro Crater Authority staff bus runs between Arusha and the crater rim on alternate days, and may be used by tourists; ask at the headquarters in Arusha for details.

Accommodation

There are several tourist-class lodges on the crater rim, all of which can be booked through Arusha tour operators. The newest and fanciest is the luxury Ngorongoro Sopa Lodge, PO Box 1823, Arusha; tel: (057) 6886. The modest Ngorongoro Crater Lodge, PO Box 751, Arusha; tel: (057) 3530; and Ngorongoro Wildlife Lodge, PO Box 3100, Arusha; tel: (057) 3842, are also well maintained and attractively positioned. There is a campsite on the crater rim, but no budget accommodation.

There's a cluster of accommodation around the village of Karatu between Lake Manyara and the crater. The upmarket Gibb's Farm is rated by many the best tourist-class accommodation in northern Tanzania, with excellent food and a rustic atmosphere. Safari Junction Campsite, 2 km out of Karatu, is a very pleasant establishment with a good restaurant and bar. The bungalows seem overpriced, but the standing tents (cheap hotel rates) and campsite are good value. There are some local lodgings in the village, used mainly by tour drivers but open to tourists.

Serengeti National Park

Serengeti is Africa's most famous national park and, of all the parks I have visited, the finest. Its grassy plains support an incredible 1 300 000 wildebeest, 200 000 zebra, 250 000 Thomson's gazelle, 70 000 impala, 50 000 topi and 30 000 Grant's gazelle, as well as significant numbers of Coke's hartebeest, eland, roan, fringe-eared oryx, giraffe, buffalo and warthog. Large predators such as lion, cheetah and spotted hyena are abundant and visible, and even leopard are regularly seen sleeping away the day in the acacias in the Seronera Valley.

Serengeti offers good game viewing at all times of the year, but you need to time your visit if you're hoping to see large herds of plains animals. The wildebeest follow an annual migration route which sees them concentrated in the developed area around the Seronera Valley between December and May, with calving occurring at the beginning of this period. In June, they gather for the 800 km migration northwards towards Kenya, dispersing into Masai Mara and northwestern Serengeti between July and October before starting southwards again in November.

How to get there

Seronera, the park headquarters, is 140 km from Ngorongoro Crater: there's only the main road and no chance of getting lost. On the way, you might want to stop off at Olduvai Gorge, where, in 1959, Mary Leakey discovered a 1,75 million year old hominid fossil that revolutionised contemporary ideas about human prehistory. There's a good site museum and guided walks through the gorge can be arranged.

Buses between Arusha and Mwanza will drop passengers at Seronera and collect them by prior arrangement. Hitching would be difficult.

Accommodation

The most developed part of the park is around Seronera village. The only tourist-class hotel here, the modest Seronera Wildlife Lodge, PO Box 3100, Arusha; tel (057) 3842, is attractively built around a small hill. Further south, the new luxury Sopa Lodge, PO Box 1823, Arusha; tel: (057) 6886, is highly rated by Arusha tour operators. In the north of the park, the modest Lobo Wildlife Lodge, PO Box 3100, Arusha; tel (057) 3842, similar to the lodge at Seronera, is the best base for game drives between July and November.

Budget accommodation is limited to a string of campsites near Seronera village. There are several more expensive special campsites scattered around the park: these are booked by one party and offer the opportunity to camp alone in Serengeti. In the extreme west of the park near Bunda on the Mwanza-Musoma road, there is comfortable accommodation at little more than cheap hotel rates at Kijireshi Tented Camp, PO Box 190, Mwanza; tel (068) 40139.

THE COAST

Zanzibar Island

The Indian Ocean island of Zanzibar lies off the Tanzanian coast opposite Dar es Salaam. Its main attractions are the old stone town in Zanzibar town and the beaches of the east coast. The stone town is similar in many ways to Lamu but much larger and more labyrinthine. It was established in its modern form by Sultan Said, who moved to the island from Muscat in 1840, and flourished during the middle to late 19th century, when it was the centre of the East African slave trade.

Several ruins dating to the reign of Said and his successor Barghash are dotted around the island. These include the Maharubi Palace, 3 km north of town, and the nearby Mtoni Palace. Dimbani Mosque on the south of the island dates to AD 1107. Also of interest is the Jozani Forest, which supports several endemics and near-endemics, such as Ader's duiker, Zanzibar red colobus and the possibly extinct Zanzibar leopard.

A popular excursion from Zanzibar town is an organised Spice Tour, which takes you to one of the island's many clove farms and usually also to one of the ruined palaces.

Zanzibar retains some of the trappings of a separate state. Travellers arriving from the Tanzanian mainland are required to go through immigration formalities. Provided you have a Tanzanian visa or else are of a nationality for whom visas are not required, formalities are all they are.

How to get there

From Nairobi or Mombasa, the most straightforward way to get to Zanzibar is by air. There are flights most days with Kenya Airways or Air Tanzania. Sometimes there are ferries from Mombasa to Zanzibar, but never more than one a week. You can also fly to Zanzibar from Arusha and Dar es Salaam in Tanzania.

The other option is to get to Dar es Salaam, Tanzania's capital, which is a twelve-hour bus trip or an overnight train ride from Moshi and Arusha. Several companies run ferries between Dar es Salaam and Zanzibar town; at least three do the crossing every day.

Accommodation

Tourist-class accommodation in Zanzibar town includes the modestly priced Hotel Ya Bwawani, PO Box 670; Emerson's House, PO Box 4044; and Spine Inn, PO Box 1029. There are many upmarket hotels on the beaches; any tour operator will be able to make a booking for you.

There are dozens of cheap guesthouses in town; as with Lamu, expect a horde of hotel touts to greet you on arrival. You won't have a problem finding a room. If you're looking to stay out on the beaches, there are guesthouses charging cheap hotel rates in Bwejuu and Jambiani. The Zanzibar Tourist Corporation (ZTC) has an office on Creek Road where you can book ZTC-run accommodation (cottages scattered around the island) and buy useful maps of the town and the island.

Dar es Salaam

Telephone code: 051

Tanzania's capital has a relaxed Swahili atmosphere. I must admit to being rather fond of Dar es Salaam, but I'm in the minority: most tourists can't wait to get out, and there's really very little in the way of sight-seeing. The only time Nairobi-based tourists would be likely to visit Dar is when on their way to or from Zanzibar.

Tourist-class hotels include the upmarket Kilimanjaro, PO Box 9574; tel: (051) 46528; the more modest New Africa, PO Box 9314; tel: (051)

46546; Motel Agip, PO Box 529; tel: (051) 46551; and Embassy, PO Box 3152; tel: (051) 30006. There are plenty of cheaper hotels, though if you arrive late in the day it can take a while to find a vacant room. A few recommendations: the YWCA, Maktaba Street, couples and women only; YMCA, Maktaba Street; the adjoining Jambo Inn and Safari Inn, both Libya Street; Hotel Continental, Nkrumah Street; and Hotel Skyway, Sokoine Drive.

If you're stuck for somewhere to stay, head out to Kunduchi Beach, 25 km north of town. The adjoining Rungwe Oceanic Hotel and Silversands have cheap hotel rooms and they are unlikely to be fully occupied. Both hotels allow camping. To get there, catch the shuttle bus which leaves from in front of the New Africa Hotel every couple of hours.

THE WESTERN RESERVES

In western Tanzania, on the forested shores of Lake Tanganyika, lie Gombe Stream and Mahale Mountains National Parks. Both parks are mainly known for their chimpanzees. Gombe Stream will forever be associated with the name of Jane Goodall, and Mahale's chimps have been studied by Japanese researchers. Neither reserve is a realistic goal for independent travellers based in Nairobi, but fly-in safaris to Mahale can be arranged through Ngare Sero Safaris, PO Box 425, Arusha; tel: (057) 3629.

THE SOUTHERN RESERVES

Tanzania's southern reserves are less well known than those in the north, and more expensive to visit, but they are nevertheless among the finest in Africa, and very much off the beaten tourist path. The jewel of the south is undoubtedly Selous Game Reserve, the largest reserve in Africa, with an elephant population estimated at 30 000 and some 200 000 buffalo. The central feature of the developed part of the park is the muddy Rufiji River, teeming with hippos and crocodiles and a bird-watcher's paradise. The main camps are along the river and they offer fly-in or drive-down packages, two to four days in duration, with game walks and boat trips an important feature. As with the western reserves, Selous is a little out of the normal orbit of Nairobi-based tourists. It's possible to arrange trips out of Arusha, but more normal to do so from Dar es Salaam: specialist companies include Impala Tours, PO Box 473; tel: (051) 25779; and Mbuyu, PO Box 1192; tel (051) 34535. Selous is essentially an upmarket destination.

11 UGANDA

Uganda is a remarkably lush country. Nobody who lives in Africa will fail to be impressed by the fact that a quarter of its surface area is made up of water, and that much of the remainder is swathed in rain forest or verdant cultivation. It is a land of intimate landscapes, strikingly different in feel to the vast open plains that make up much of Kenya and Tanzania.

Uganda shows biological affiliations to both West and East Africa. The rain forests of Zaïre extend into western Uganda, where they contain a fauna quite different to anything in Kenya. The most notable denizen of these forests is the mountain gorilla, the range of which is restricted to the Bwindi Hills in Uganda and the Virunga Range on the border of Uganda, Rwanda and Zaïre. Another typically West African ape, the common chimpanzee, is widespread in Uganda's forests. So too are several monkeys: Kibale Forest, for example, protects at least 10 primate species, more than have been recorded in the whole of southern Africa. Uganda's forests are also of great interest to bird enthusiasts: again, as an example, three hornbill species found in Uganda's Semliki Forest have been recorded nowhere else in East Africa.

Since independence, Uganda has suffered more than most African countries. One million Ugandans died under the despotic rules of Amin and Obote, and the country now faces one of the worst AIDS epidemics in the world. The tourist industry is in the process of being rebuilt after years of neglect, but it remains very low-key when compared to Kenya or even Tanzania. Package tourism barely exists; there are only a couple of dozen tourist-class hotels countrywide.

You should not let Uganda's past colour your decision to visit. The country has enjoyed remarkable stability since Museveni took power in 1986, and the economic growth rate has been positively astounding. Travellers regard Uganda to be among the friendliest countries in Africa; it is unquestionably one of the safest and most stimulating.

BORDER FORMALITIES

From Kenya, you're most likely to cross into Uganda at either Malaba or Busia. Crossing is straightforward. All visitors must have a visitor's pass, which can be issued free upon arrival. Nationals of many countries require visas, and these must be purchased in advance. The Uganda High Commission in Nairobi will issue same-day visas if you apply before 11h00. South Africans need visas, though this may well change now that South Africa is part of the Commonwealth. There is no Ugandan embassy in South Africa.

If you intend to cross the border into Zaïre in order to see mountain gorillas, a visa should be bought in advance. There are embassies in Nairobi and Kampala.

MONEY

The unit of currency is the Uganda shilling. The current exchange rate is around US $1 = Ush 1 100. Foreign currency can be exchanged at banks and, in the larger towns, at privately run bureaus. There is a foreign exchange bureau at the Malaba border post. There is no longer a black market in Uganda.

FURTHER INFORMATION

Uganda's tourist industry has picked up rapidly after years of isolation. New reserves and facilities are opening all the time, and anything written about the country now is bound to date rapidly.

The tourist office on Parliament Road in Kampala is very helpful. There's a good map office in the Department of Lands and Surveys in Entebbe. For current information on national parks, or to buy gorilla-viewing permits for Bwindi, contact the national parks at 31 Kanjoka Street, PO Box 3530, Kampala; tel: (041) 256534. The Forestry Department on Springs Road can furnish you with current information on forest reserves. The Natete Backpackers' Hostel in Kampala is the best source of practical travel information.

Tourists wishing to explore parts of Uganda that are not covered in this chapter are referred to my comprehensive *Guide to Uganda* (Bradt Publications, 1994).

Most of Uganda's tourist-class hotels are run by Uganda Hotels. Reservations and enquiries should be directed to the head office, PO Box 7173, Kampala; tel: (041) 234296.

KAMPALA

Telephone code: 041

Uganda's capital was once the showpiece of the East Africa Community, but it suffered badly during the civil war. In 1988, when I first visited the city, the buildings were pockmarked with bullet holes, the roads were potholed to the point where they looked like buffalo wallows, and water supplies and other civil amenities verged on the non-existent. Things have improved greatly of late: the smart part of town north of Kampala Road has been restored to its former state and in most respects Kampala now functions as a normal city. The area south of Kampala Road is less salubrious: a chaotic maze of potholed streets, the centrepiece of which is the most confusing minibus station in Africa.

Kampala is mainly of interest as a staging post for trips to western Uganda, but there is some worthwhile sightseeing if you have a day to spare. The National Museum is excellent, with diverting displays on aspects of pre-colonial Ugandan history and a great collection of musical instruments from all over the continent. The Kasubi Tombs, housed in a large thatched dome on the site of the capital of the Buganda kingdom, are the burial place of several Buganda kings.

Uganda's international airport is at Entebbe, on the shore of Lake Victoria and a 30-minute minibus ride from Kampala. Also at Entebbe, and well worth a visit, is the national botanical garden, established in 1902 and reputedly where the first Tarzan film was shot. At first glance, the garden appears to be an untended mix of exotic trees, indigenous forest and cultivation, but on closer inspection it seems that somebody does know what they are doing. It's one of the best places in East Africa for close-ups of black-and-white colobus monkeys, and the birds are exceptional. Great blue turaco and a variety of hornbills are common, and there's a good chance of seeing Lake Victoria specials such as marsh flycatcher, yellowthroated leaflove and slenderbilled weaver.

How to get there

A recently introduced overnight train service runs once a week between Nairobi and Kampala. There are also three trains per week between Nairobi and the Malaba border post, from where it's four hours to Kampala by minibus. Akamba run overnight buses between Nairobi and Kampala daily. However you do it, Kampala can be reached in 24 hours from Nairobi.

Kenya Airways fly four times a week between Nairobi and Entebbe. Uganda Airlines now fly once a week between Johannesburg and Entebbe.

Accommodation

The upmarket Kampala Sheraton, PO Box 7041; tel: 244590, is Uganda's only five-star hotel. The recently refurbished Lake Victoria Hotel (Uganda Hotels) in Entebbe is also recommended.

Budget accommodation in Kampala is thin on the ground. The very basic YMCA on Bombo Road is a perennial favourite with travellers, but it has recently been superseded by the new Natete Backpackers' Hostel, where there are private rooms, a dormitory and a campsite. Profits are used to fund permaculture projects in rural Uganda. The hostel is about 4 km out of town: to get there catch a minibus from the main minibus station to Natete roundabout.

There is a very attractive campsite at Entebbe Resort on the Lake Victoria shore 20 minutes' walk out of Entebbe town.

THE MOUNTAIN GORILLAS OF SOUTHWEST UGANDA

The mountain gorilla is the bulkiest of the three races of gorilla. It is also the most endangered, with approximately 650 individuals divided equally between the Bwindi Hills of Uganda and the Virunga Volcanoes on the border of Uganda, Zaïre and Rwanda. The plight of these gorillas was popularised by Dian Fossey, who studied gorilla behaviour in Rwanda until her brutal and unsolved murder at her research headquarters in 1985.

Since the release of the film *Gorillas in the mist*, mountain gorilla tracking has become the highlight of many a tourist's visit to Africa. There is some concern that the growing tourist influx may ultimately be to the gorillas' detriment. Gorillas are susceptible to many human diseases, and their increasing contact with humans makes them more vulnerable to poachers. To counter this, the number of gorilla viewing permits issued daily is limited and prices are kept high. Visitors are requested not to approach too closely or spend longer than an hour with the animals. For all the risks created by human contact, the one certainty is that tourist revenue and interest are probably the best guarantees of the gorillas' long-term survival.

Mountain gorillas are protected in four national parks. The recently opened Bwindi National Park in Uganda protects the Bwindi population. The Virunga population is divided between Mgahinga National Park (Uganda), Parc des Volcans (Rwanda) and Parc des Virungas (Zaïre). Tour operators currently favour the Zaïre gorillas due to the ongoing instability in Rwanda and the fact that the Bwindi gorillas are not yet sufficiently habituated to guarantee close sightings. Independent travellers also tend to favour the Zaïre gorillas, as the number of visitors allowed to Bwindi daily is more heavily restricted and the Rwanda border has been closed for a couple of years.

At the time of writing, the instability in Rwanda has escalated into perhaps the most bloody war Africa has ever seen. So, while the plight of a few hundred gorillas pales compared to the death of half a million people, I should point out that a question mark hangs over the Rwandan gorillas, if not the entire gorilla population of the Virungas. Whatever the fate of these animals, it seems unlikely that the Parc des Volcans, and possibly Mgahinga National Park, will be open to tourism in the foreseeable future.

How to visit the gorillas

Visits to the gorillas depend on your time, budget, and the level of comfort you expect. If you are flexible, and time isn't a factor, the cheapest way to visit is independently (see details under the individual reserves), in which case the cost of your permit, park fees and visas will work out to around US $200.

One popular option is to do an overland truck trip from Nairobi. These range in duration from two to six weeks. Shorter safaris go directly to the gorillas, while longer safaris are more circuitous, returning to Nairobi via Lake Victoria and Serengeti in northern Tanzania. Generally they take parties of 15 to 25 people and the trip will cost around US $500 per person for two weeks and US $1 000 for four to six weeks. This rate will not include your gorilla-viewing permit and any visas that you may need, so expect to add around US $200 to the figure you are quoted. Gorilla safaris are offered by many safari operators, but most only act as agencies for the handful of companies who run them. Recommended operators include Worldwide Adventure Travel, PO Box 76637, Nairobi; tel: (02) 210024; fax: (02) 332407; and Gametrackers, PO Box 62042, Nairobi; tel: (02) 338927; fax: (02) 330903.

Upmarket tours can be arranged either in Nairobi or in Kampala. The prices I've been quoted for a five-day safari indicate it would be cheaper to make your way to Kampala and do a tour from there. Recommended companies in Kampala include Nile Safaris, PO Box 8695; tel: (041) 244311; fax: 245967; and Hot Ice, PO Box 151; tel: (041) 242733; fax: 244779. Most tour operators in Nairobi can arrange gorilla safaris on request.

If you are going via South Africa to East Africa specifically to see gorillas and want to use a tour of some sort, think about booking a fly-in gorilla package through an operator there. Sites of Africa, PO Box 781329, Sandton; tel: (011) 8834345; fax: 8832556 are more upmarket. Wild Frontiers, PO Box 884, Halfway House; tel: (011) 3154838; fax: 3154850, do budget to mid-range tours.

Kabale

This town in southwestern Uganda is the base for visits to Bwindi National Park, and will also be passed through by travellers en route to the Virunga Mountains. Kabale is one of Uganda's prettiest towns, nestled amid fertile hills covered in neatly contoured cultivation. It's worth making a day trip to Lake Bunyonyi, which lies 6 km from the town centre. Any hotel will give you directions or organise a guide. The lake follows the contours of the surrounding hills and the largest of its 80 islands can be visited by dugout canoe. There are regular buses and minibuses between Kampala and Kabale. The journey takes approximately six hours.

The only tourist-class accommodation in Kabale is the modestly priced White Horse Inn (book through Uganda Hotels), attractively positioned on a hill above the town. The Highlands Hotel, on the main road towards Kisoro, is a cheap hotel, cosy and excellent value. There are several local lodgings in town. The Visitours and Skyblue hotels next to the bus station are popular with travellers and serve excellent cheap meals.

Bwindi National Park

Also known as the Impenetrable Forest, Bwindi was proclaimed a national park in 1991. It protects 320 gorillas in 15 troops. One troop has been habituated and there are plans to habituate two more. At present a maximum of six viewing permits are issued daily, three of which will be reserved for Windsor Hotel's new lodge when it opens. Permits cost over US $100 and should be booked in advance through the national parks office in Kampala. A once-off entrance fee of US $20 is charged.

Don't let the presence of gorillas induce tunnel vision. Bwindi supports a significant population of chimpanzees and as good a range of monkeys and forest birds as any Ugandan forest. You can visit the park even if you don't want to see gorillas; general nature walks can be arranged with rangers. The main road through the forest can be explored on foot: there are plenty of birds, black-and-white colobus swinging across the road, and stirring views across lush forested hills to the Virungas.

Windsor Hotel's luxury lodge at Bwindi was due to open in late 1994. Contact the Nairobi office, PO Box 74957; tel: (02) 219784. For budget travellers, there is a campsite at the park headquarters and bandas are under construction. A restaurant opposite the campsite serves cheap tasty food.

You can get to Bwindi from Kabale on public transport, but allow two days, and a day's travel between Kampala and Kabale, when you make your booking. Your first goal is Butotoga village, reached by matatu on Tuesday, Friday and Sunday. It's a further 17 km to the park headquarters and campsite at Buhoma: you could walk at a pinch, but there's a truck or two most days. If you need to overnight in Butotoga, the Travellers Lodge is an acceptable local lodging.

Kisoro

Kisoro lies near the Zaïrean border and is the closest town to the Virunga Mountains. There are a few local lodgings, and two decent cheap hotels: the Travellers Rest Inn and Mubondo Hotel. A few matatus run daily between Kabale and Kisoro.

Mgahinga National Park

Mgahinga protects the Ugandan portion of the Virunga range and is named after its highest peak (4 127 m). The status of the park's gorillas is uncertain and no gorilla viewing permits are issued at present, but organised nature walks allow one to seek rare forest animals such as the yellow-rumped duiker and golden monkey (a race of blue monkey). Organised day hikes to the volcanic peaks are also offered. There is a campsite at the entrance gate, 17 km by road from Kisoro. A once-off entrance fee of US $20 is charged and guided day hikes work out at US $15 to US $25 per person. Mgahinga was closed during the last outbreak of civil war in Rwanda and it only re-opened in late 1993. While Rwanda remains unstable, you are advised to contact the national parks headquarters in Kampala before heading this way.

Parc des Virungas (Zaïre)

There are three troops of habituated gorilla in the Zaïrean part of the Virungas. Gorilla tracking is based at Djomba Hut, 7 km from the Ugandan border. Permits are issued at the hut and cost US $120. The current popularity of this reserve means you may have to wait a day or two to go tracking, especially if your visit coincides with the arrival of a couple of overland trucks. Djomba is easy to visit independently. Matatus cover the 11 km between Kisoro and the Bunagana border post. Border formalities completed, it's a couple of hours' walk to the hut: the children who hang around the border post will guide you for a dollar or two. It's worth emphasising that you need a visa for Zaïre to visit Djomba.

KASESE AND THE RUWENZORI MOUNTAINS

Africa's third highest mountain, Margherita (5 109 m), lies in this extensive range along the Zaïrean border. The Ruwenzoris are thought to be the fabled Mountains of the Moon, which were cited by Ptolemy as the source of the Nile in AD 150. Although the peaks are out of reach of ordinary hikers and require specialised equipment, a six to seven-day loop trail through the bizarre vegetation of the moorland zone is very popular with hikers.

The base for Ruwenzori hikes is the town of Kasese, easily reached by bus from Kampala or Kabale. The experienced Ruwenzori Mountain Services, Alexandria Road, PO Box 33, Kasese; tel: (0493) 4115, organise all-inclusive hikes. They also stock maps of the mountain.

There is plenty of accommodation in Kasese. The only tourist-class hotel is the modest Margherita Hotel (Uganda Hotels), 2 km out of town. The Saad Hotel on Stanley Road has self-contained double rooms in the cheap hotel bracket, as well as dormitories. Most of the local lodgings are clustered along Speke Road.

Semliki Safaris, based in the Semliki Valley near Fort Portal, should also be doing Ruwenzori hikes by the time you read this. Bookings can be made through Natete Backpackers' Hostel in Kampala.

FORT PORTAL, KIBALE FOREST AND THE SEMLIKI VALLEY

The town of Fort Portal is the base for visits to Uganda's two most accessible rain forests: Semliki and Kibale. Like Kabale, it is a pretty town, with great views across to the Ruwenzori Mountains on a clear day. There are direct buses to Fort Portal from Kampala and Kasese.

Tourist-class accommodation in Fort Portal can be found at the modest Mountains of the Moon Hotel (Uganda Hotels). Other accommodation is clustered along the south end of Lugard Road: the Wooden Hotel is an acceptable cheap hotel while the Christian Guesthouse is the best of the local lodgings. Kabarole Tours on Lugard Road organise moderately priced day trips to local places of interest.

A tourism project based at Kanyunchi River Camp was started in Kibale Forest in 1992. There is a lovely campsite here and basic traveller-orientated lodgings in the village of Bigodi 6 km down the road. Guided walks leave Kanyunchi twice daily. There is a good chance of seeing habituated chimpanzees on these walks, as well as a variety of monkeys including L'Hoest's, blue, redtailed, red colobus, black-and-white colobus and grey-cheeked mangabey. The forest also supports Uganda's third largest elephant population, buffalo, giant forest hog and typical forest antelope. Over 300 bird species have been recorded. Walking on forest trails without a guide is forbidden, but the campsite, the main road through the forest, and the swamps around Bigodi village may be explored independently and offer excellent bird-watching and monkey viewing. A couple of matatus run between Fort Portal, Kanyunchi and Bigodi every day, taking about two hours for the trip.

The Semliki Valley west of Fort Portal is reached via a dramatic road which follows the contours of the Ruwenzori foothills. The valley contains the Ugandan extension of Zaïre's magnificent Ituri Forest, and harbours many primate species, including chimpanzee and, reputedly, eastern lowland gorillas, as well as dazzling bird life. Though undeveloped for tourism at present, this area has enormous potential and is a wildly exciting destination for travellers who are interested in natural history and are prepared to be a little flexible. Semliki Safaris have recently opened a campsite 200 m from Sempaya Hot Springs (contact Natete Hostel in Kampala for details) and there is basic accommodation in the region's largest settlement, Bundibugyo. A few matatus run daily from Fort Portal to Sempaya and Bundibugyo.

QUEEN ELIZABETH AND MURCHISON FALLS NATIONAL PARKS

Although neither of these reserves compares to the larger reserves of Kenya and Tanzania in game-viewing terms, they do crop up on the odd gorilla-viewing trip. Budget travellers will find them of special interest, as they are much easier to reach without a vehicle than any game reserve in Tanzania and Kenya.

Queen Elizabeth National Park protects the area between Lakes George and Albert. Tourist activity centres around Mweya Lodge on the Kazinga channel between the lakes. Hippos are abundant and readily seen on launch trips organised from the lodge. Elephant and a variety of antelope, including Uganda kob, are common, but predators are scarce. Look out for the reddish forest race of buffalo, which reaches the easternmost extension of its range here and interbreeds with the black plains buffalo of East Africa. Over 500 bird species have been recorded in this park.

Murchison Falls is also notable for launch trips. These follow the Nile upstream from Paraa to the base of the waterfall after which the park is named. Game viewing is good: there are more hippos than anywhere I've been in Africa (except perhaps the Rufiji River in Tanzania). Bird life is astounding. This is the best place in Africa to see the localised and indescribably bizarre shoebill. The falls are fantastic too; the mighty Nile erupts out of a 5 m wide gap in the escarpment. If you make arrangements in advance, the launch trip can include a half-hour walk to the top of the falls.

From Kasese, regular matatus pass the main entrance gate to Queen Elizabeth National Park. From there, it's an easy 6 km hitch to Mweya Lodge, where there is also a hostel with cheap rooms and a campsite. To get to Murchison Falls, catch the daily bus from Kampala or Masindi to the small village of Bulisa, where you can hire a bike and cycle the 33 km to Paraa.

APPENDIX 1: Selected reading

HISTORY AND BACKGROUND

Blixen, Karen. *Out of Africa* (Penguin)
Fox, James. *White mischief* (Penguin)
Hibbert, Christopher. *Africa explored: Europeans in the dark continent 1769-1889* (Penguin)
Marnham, Patrick. *Fantastic invasion* (Penguin)
Matthieson, Peter. *The tree where man was born* (Pan)
Maxon, Robert. *East Africa: a general history* (Heinemann Kenya)
Miller, Charles. *The lunatic express* (Westlands Sundries Kenya)
Murphy, Dervla. *The Ukimwi road* (John Murray)
Naipaul, Shiva. *North of south* (Penguin)
Ocheing, William. *A history of Kenya* (Macmillan)
Oliver and Sage. *A short history of Africa* (Penguin)
Packenham, Thomas. *The scramble for Africa* (Jonathan Ball)

FICTION

Boyd, William. *An ice-cream war* (Penguin)
Cartwright, Justin. *Masai dreaming* (Macmillan)
Mazrui, Ali. *The trial of Christopher Okhigo* (Heinemann)
Macgoye, Marjorie. *Coming to birth* (Virago)
Mwangi, Meja. *Going down river road* (Heinemann)
wa Thiongo, Ngugi. *Matigari* (Heinemann)
wa Thiongo, Ngugi. *Petals of blood* (Heinemann)

FIELD GUIDES

Haltemorth and Diller's *Guide to the mammals of Africa* (Collins) is the most comprehensive guide, but the continental scope and confusing detail on subspecies make it a little impractical for casual users. Steve Shelley's *Safari guide to the mammals of East and Central Africa* (Macmillan) has adequate line drawings and detailed local distribution maps, and is probably the more useful book for all but the most dedicated. Both books are widely available in Nairobi.

For detailed information on mammal behaviour Richard Estes' *The safari companion* (Russel Friedman) is highly recommended, though a little weighty for backpackers. Primate enthusiasts are referred to *Know your monkeys: a guide to the primates of Kenya* by RM Eley (National Museums of Kenya). There are also a few locally published guides to reptiles and fishes of the region.

The standard field guide to East African birds is John Williams' *Field guide to the birds of East Africa* (Collins, 1980), though CAW Guggisberg's two-volume *Birds of East Africa* (East Africa Sundries, 1986) is almost as useful. Both guides have severe limitations in that they only illustrate approximately half the species found in the region and they ignore European migrants altogether. Several more species are described in the text, but you can forget about identifying members of the more confusing families such as cisticolas and larks. A southern African field guide such as Roberts' or Newman's is essential to identify the more confusing raptors and all migrant birds with any degree of certainty.

MAPS

Probably the best general map of Kenya is the Nelles Verlag 1:1 100 000, which also includes northern Tanzania. The Macmillan maps of Amboseli and of Tsavo and Amboseli are the best for the parks they cover. Survey of Kenya maps are available for all other major national parks and reserves. All these maps are readily available in Nairobi bookshops, except for the rare Survey of Kenya map of Meru National Park.

Executive Wilderness Programmes, PO Box 44827, Nairobi, publish useful hikers' maps of the major mountains (Kilimanjaro, Kenya, Elgon and the Ruwenzoris) which can be obtained from most Nairobi bookshops or directly from the publishers.

Survey maps of Uganda can be bought from the map office in Entebbe. For maps of Tanzania, visit the map office on Kivukoni Front in Dar es Salaam. In both countries, maps are very cheap and buying them is straightforward. The same cannot be said for buying survey maps of Kenya. Maps are sold at the map office on Harambee Avenue in Nairobi, but you need written authorisation and this can take weeks. It's advisable to write well in advance to PO Box 30046 Nairobi.

GUIDE BOOKS

Dedicated explorers and people requiring minute detail on budget accommodation are referred to Richard Trillo's *Kenya: the rough guide* (Rough Guides). This is far and away the best of the budget-oriented guides to Kenya, and it is chock-a-block with off the beaten track ideas.

Campers and hikers will find David Else's *Camping guide to Kenya* (Bradt Publications) and *Mountain walking in Kenya* (Robertson McCarthy) very useful.

Upmarket tourists seeking further details on accommodation might want to buy the excellent *Kenya's best hotels, lodges and housestays* by Glenday, Southwick and Westley (Kenway Publications). *The Spectrum guide to Kenya* (Camerapix, Nairobi) is lavishly illustrated and strong on background information. It would complement the book you are holding perfectly.

Further afield, my *Guide to Uganda*, *Guide to Tanzania* and David Else's *Guide to Zanzibar* (all Bradt Publications) are the only comprehensive guides available to these countries.

Bird-watchers will find Ray Moore's *Where to watch birds in Kenya* (Transafrica Press, PO Box 49421 Nairobi) exceptionally useful for its detailed accounts of all recognised birding areas and off the beaten track suggestions.

APPENDIX 2: East African bird name alternatives

The names used for birds in East African field guides (such as Williams') and southern African field guides (such as Newman's) are often quite different. The following list of some of the more confusing names for the same birds should help.

Name in Williams'	*Name used in southern Africa*
African sand martin	brownthroated martin
African snipe	Ethiopian snipe (old name)
Allen's gallinule	lesser gallinule
amethyst sunbird	black sunbird
black-breasted apalis	yellowbreasted apalis
black-throated wattle-eye	wattle-eyed flycatcher
blackcap tchagra	marsh tchagra
black-faced waxbill	blackcheeked waxbill
black-headed weaver	spottedbacked weaver
black-winged bishop	firecrowned bishop
bronze-naped pigeon	Delegorgue's pigeon
brown parrot	Meyer's parrot
buff-crested bustard	redcrested korhaan
cliff chat	mocking chat
dark-backed weaver	forest weaver
fantailed widow	redshouldered widow
four-coloured bush shrike	gorgeous bush shrike
golden weaver	yellow weaver
great sparrowhawk	black sparrowhawk
green woodhoopoe	redbilled woodhoopoe
green-winged pytilia	melba finch
grey-backed cameroptera	greybacked bleating warbler
grosback weaver	thickbilled weaver
harrier hawk	gymnogene

Name in Williams'	*Name used in southern Africa*
Holub's golden weaver	golden weaver
Heuglin's courser	threebanded courser
kestrel	rock kestrel
lavender waxbill	grey waxbill
lemon dove	cinnamon dove
Levaillant's barbet	crested barbet
long-tailed cormorant	reed cormorant
magpie mannikin	pied mannikin
masked weaver	lesser masked weaver
morning warbler	collared palm thrush
mountain wagtail	longtailed wagtail
Nubian vulture	lappetfaced vulture
olive pigeon	rameron pigeon
plain-backed sunbird	bluethroated sunbird
red-backed scrub robin	whitebrowed robin
red-capped robin chat	Natal robin
Retz's helmetshrike	redbilled helmetshrike
ring-necked dove	Cape turtle dove
robin chat	Cape robin
rufous sparrow	great sparrow
rufous-crowned roller	purple roller
Senegal plover	lesser blackwinged plover
Shikra	little banded goshawk
speckled pigeon	rock pigeon
spotted stone curlew	spotted dikkop
Verrreaux's eagle	black eagle
Verreaux's eagle owl	giant eagle owl
violet-crested turaco	purplecrested lourie
violet-backed starling	plumcoloured starling
vitelline masked weaver	masked weaver
Wells' wagtail	Cape wagtail
white-browed robin chat	Heuglin's robin
white-headed plover	whitecrowned plover
yellow bishop	yellowrumped widow
yellow-crowned bishop	golden bishop
yellow-rumped seedeater	blackthroated canary
yellow-fronted canary	yelloweyed canary
yellow-mantled widowbird	yellowbacked widow

This list is by no means exhaustive – I notice new examples almost every time I bird-watch in East Africa – and it only covers species that are illustrated in Williams'. There are dozens more examples in the allied species. As a rule, the Latin binomial name is your most reliable guide – though even then there are anomalies. Finally, watch out for different species with the same names: the East African anteater chat, mountain chat and white-crowned shrike are not the same as the southern African equivalents.

INDEX

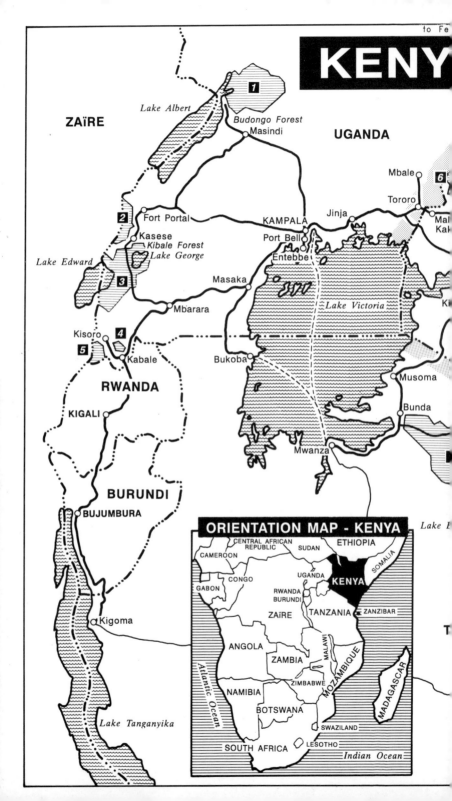